IMPERIAL DEFENCE
1868–1887

CASS SERIES: NAVAL POLICY AND HISTORY
ISSN 1366-9478

Series Editor: Holger Herwig

This series consists primarily of original manuscripts by research scholars in the general area of naval policy and history, without national or chronological limitations. It will from time to time also include collections of important articles as well as reprints of classic works.

1. *Austro-Hungarian Naval Policy, 1904–1914*
   Milan N. Vego

2. *Far-Flung Lines: Studies in Imperial Defence in Honour of Donald Mackenzie Schurman*
   Edited by Keith Neilson and Greg Kennedy

3. *Maritime Strategy and Continental Wars*
   Rear Admiral Raja Menon

4. *The Royal Navy and German Naval Disarmament 1942–1947*
   Chris Madsen

5. *Naval Strategy and Operations in Narrow Seas*
   Milan N. Vego

6. *The Pen and Ink Sailor: Charles Middleton and the King's Navy, 1778–1813*
   John E. Talbott

7. *The Italian Navy and Fascist Expansionism, 1935–40*
   Robert Mallett

8. *The Merchant Marine in International Affairs, 1850–1950*
   Edited by Greg Kennedy

9. *Naval Strategy in Northeast Asia: Geo-strategic Goals, Policies and Prospects*
   Duk-Ki Kim

10. *Naval Policy and Strategy in the Mediterranean Sea: Past, Present and Future*
    Edited by John B. Hattendorf

11. *Stalin's Ocean-going Fleet, 1935–1953: Soviet Naval Strategy and Shipbuilding Programs*
    Jürgen Rohwer and Mikhail S. Monakov

12. *Imperial Defence, 1868–1887*
    Donald Mackenzie Schurman; edited by John Beeler

IMPERIAL DEFENCE
1868–1887

Donald Mackenzie Schurman

Edited by
JOHN BEELER
Alabama University

FRANK CASS
LONDON • PORTLAND, OR

First published in 2000 in Great Britain by
FRANK CASS PUBLISHERS
Newbury House, 900 Eastern Avenue
London IG2 7HH

and in the United States of America by
FRANK CASS PUBLISHERS
c/o ISBS, 5804 N.E. Hassalo Street
Portland, Oregon 97213-3644

Website: www.frankcass.com

Copyright Text © 2000 Donald M. Schurman
Copyright Editor's Introduction © 2000 John Beeler

British Library Cataloguing in Publication Data

Schurman, Donald M. (Donald Mackenzie), 1924–
 Imperial defence, 1868–1887. – (Cass series. Naval policy
and history)
 1. Great Britain – Military policy 2. Great Britain –
Colonies – Defences 3. Great Britain – Politics and
government – 1837–1901
 I. Title II. Beeler, John
 941'.081

ISBN 0-7146-5006-4 (cloth)
ISSN 1366-9478

Library of Congress Cataloging-in-Publication Data

Schurman, D. M. (Donald M.)
 Imperial defence, 1868–1887 / by Donald Mackenzie Schurman;
edited by John Beeler.
  p. cm. – (Cass series–naval policy and history, ISSN
1399-9478; 12)
 Includes bibliographical references and index.
 ISBN 0-7146-5006-4 (cloth)
 1. Great Britain, Royal Navy–History–19th century. 2. Great
Britain–Colonies–Defenses. 3. Great Britain–Politics and
government–1837–1901. 4. Great Britain–Military policy. 5. Sea-
power–Great Britain. I. Beeler, John F. (John Francis), 1956–.
II. Title. III. Series.
VA454.S37 1999
355'.0335171'241–dc21   99-42418
                                     CIP

All rights reserved. No part of this publication may be reproduced, stored in or introduced into a retrieval system or transmitted, in any form or by any means, electronic, mechanical, photocopying, recording or otherwise, without the prior written permission of the publisher of this book.

Typeset by Vitaset, Paddock Wood, Kent
Printed in Great Britain by
MPG Books Ltd, Bodmin, Cornwall

Contents

	Series Editor's Preface	vii
	Editor's Introduction	ix
	List of Abbreviations	xviii
	Preface	xix
	Coaling Station Map	xxii
	Introduction	1
1.	Liberalism and Empire Defence	5
2.	The Beginnings of Imperial Strategy: 1868–74	22
3.	Conservative Beginnings: 1874–80	43
4.	Milne's Colonial Defence Committee: 1878–79	61
5.	The Working of the Royal Commission: 1879–82	83
6.	The Royal Commission Reports	100
7.	Aftermath of the Commission	126
8.	Experiment in Imperial Co-operation	142
	Conclusion	152
	Appendix	159
	Bibliography	169
	Index	185

Series Editor's Preface

In 1955 Donald Schurman completed a dissertation on 'Imperial Defence 1868–1887' at Cambridge University. His timing could not have been worse. The following year, Britain's bungled Suez expedition consigned 'imperial defence' to the proverbial dustbin of history. Thereafter, the historians' profession Balkanized into ever more narrow areas of investigation, many of them politically driven. In Schurman's own country, Canada, the profession ascended to the holy trinity of race, gender and ethnicity; it allowed no room for broader fields of enquiry. Thus, Schurman's 'Imperial Defence' was never published. It remained an insider's treasure trove. Happily, John Beeler of the University of Alabama, author of *British Naval Policy in the Gladstone–Disraeli Era 1866–1880* (1997), has now joined hands with Schurman to update the dissertation and to present it to a more open and receptive public. After half a century, virtue does go rewarded.

Schurman's dissertation was (and remains) the best work on the genesis of imperial defence. By analyzing the various colonial conferences and commissions, especially of the 1880s, the author first establishes the genesis of the concept of 'imperial defence', and then projects it forward to show how it helped mould the theoretical framework of the modern Commonwealth. Britain's defence, Schurman argues, was inextricably bound up with Empire defence, for the latter supplied the common theme as well as the common method of going about the treatment of imperial problems having a common interest.

On the military-strategic side, Schurman analyzes the technological revolution (RMA, or revolution in military affairs, in the current jargon) between the late 1840s and the late 1880s – iron and then steel hulls, breech-loading and rifled ordnance, gun turrets, hydraulic machinery, electricity – and its profound consequences for Britain's naval and imperial policies. Just as surely as steam freed ships from the eternal reliance on wind and tides, so surely it also tied them to docks, coal depots and colliers. Whereas sailing ships had been largely self-reliant, restricted only by wind as well as food and water for the crew, the iron-hulled, steam-propelled modern battleship was forever reliant on dry docks, graving docks, coal depots and repair yards. For the Admiralty, this translated into greater costs to keep an adequate force at sea, immense difficulties in attempting blockade, and an apparent abandoning of the offensive for the defensive in terms of maritime strategy. In effect, the modern iron-clad battlefleet was stationed close to home simply because it could not stray from its logistical bases. Put differently, battlefleet deployment was determined by technological limitations and not, as is so often argued, by the conservative mindset of Admiralty planners.

On a personal note, nothing has given me greater pleasure as series editor than this opportunity to bring Donald Schurman's seminal dissertation to light. It has inspired, and will continue to inspire, scholars of modern Britain, the Empire and maritime affairs.

Holger H. Herwig
Series Editor

Editor's Introduction

Were historical monographs published solely on grounds of scholarly merit, I would not be writing these words. Donald Schurman's PhD thesis – originally titled 'Imperial Defence 1868–1887: A Study in the Decisive Impulses Behind the Change from "Colonial" to "Imperial" Defence' – would have appeared in print very soon after it was defended, some 43 years ago. Academia may furnish fewer opportunities for the wicked to prosper than does the 'outside world' but, as elsewhere, virtue goes unrewarded all too often, as the fate of this pioneering work on the evolution of British imperial strategy in the steam age eloquently testifies.

The era on which he focused is fascinating on several counts. It was, perhaps most obviously, an era of revolutionary technological change in the weaponry of war, especially with regard to naval armaments. In the political arena, it was dominated by the great Gladstone–Disraeli rivalry, and, more generally, by an emphasis on the nineteenth-century Liberal agenda of 'peace, retrenchment, and reform'. As a consequence, both the War Office and the Admiralty underwent substantial administrative overhauls during the first Gladstone ministry (1868–74), the first courtesy of Secretary of War Edward Cardwell, the second through the efforts of First Lord of the Admiralty Hugh C. E. Childers. The principal aim in both cases was greater accountability and responsibility of the major spending departments to parliament, and by extension the electorate, but the underlying impetus was furnished by the similarly important Liberal goals of greater efficiency and economy.

The passion for economy indeed went far beyond the administrative context of Whitehall, especially with regard to the navy, which saw its operating budget drop below £10 million in four of the five fiscal years from 1869–70 to 1873–74, during a time at which the radical and rapid technological upheaval served to drive the service's *matériel* costs upwards. To provide an appropriate context for this accomplishment, the Navy estimates for 1868–69 had been £11.3 million; those of 1860–61 more than £12.5 million. In fact, the estimates of 1869–74 were lower than they had been since prior to the Crimean War, and lower than they would ever be again.

It is inappropriate, moreover, to delineate rigidly between Liberal and Conservative attitudes towards defence in general and defence spending in particular. Tories were indeed more sceptical of the pacific benefits of Free Trade economics than were Liberals such as Richard Cobden and John Bright, but the leadership of both parties strove to keep a tight rein on army and navy spending throughout the period. It was thus within this unsympathetic politico-economic framework that the imperial defence strategy detailed in the following pages evolved.

Imperial Defence is an indicator both of its author's intellectual and scholarly antecedents and of his subsequent professional development. Schurman served in the Royal Canadian Air Force during the Second World War. Following the conflict he studied at Acadia University in his native Nova Scotia, where he absorbed a curriculum which, in his own words, 'was something less than a modernist one' with regard to historiographical trends.[1] Indeed, his interest in empire and the problems of imperial federation (*Zollverein*) and defence (*Kriegsverein*) was already evident by this early date, although his attitude towards the institution, at the point that it was beginning to dissolve, was also 'something less than a modern one'. Rather than being fascinated with the centrifugal forces which were pulling the empire apart, he was more interested in the ideas, institutions and men which had bound it together. 'I liked what I saw of the British system as an Imperial system', he reflects, 'and nothing has since changed my mind.' Moreover, rather than looking at the empire from the periphery, his focus was resolutely on the hub: '[t]he work of Empire was carried out by agents of varying degrees of competence (one met them) but the stuff of Empire was manufactured within a sixty mile radius of the City of Westminster – at its centre'. Such a combination of views left little room for sympathy with the nationalist aspirations of the empire's subjects: 'I hardly ever confused the Colonial view of British incompetence with the actual experience I had of real British people. Irish, Scottish, and Welsh nationalism appeared to me as food for artists and not much else.' Indeed, Canadian parochialism furnished the impetus for Schurman's departure for Cambridge. Before leaving Acadia, however, he 'wrestled with a Masters essay on the Imperial Federation movement' which, he claims, 'added nothing to the genre' but which did prepare him for subsequent graduate work in England.

Schurman arrived at Sidney Sussex College, Cambridge in August 1950, 'with a wife, two children, a small Veteran's Grant, and no other prospects'. The choice of institutions was not accidental. During the war his aircraft was once diverted to the nearby Royal Air Force field at Lavenham (Suffolk), and he spent an evening 'wandering in and out of colleges and watching the ripples on the River Cam'.

EDITOR'S INTRODUCTION

As graduate supervisor Schurman was assigned Professor Eric Anderson Walker (1886–1976), a Fellow of St John's College and an authority on imperial history in general and South Africa in particular.[2] He recalls that Walker read his essay on imperial federation 'and asked me for my own opinion of it. I told him it was bloody awful and he immediately confirmed my judgment of my own work. He did not, however, say "go away".' Walker's then poor health, however, necessitated a change of advisers, and after half a year Schurman was assigned to Gerald Sandford Graham (1903–88), one of the foremost experts on the imperial link between Britain and Canada.[3] Simultaneously, Dr David Thomson (1912–70) of Sidney Sussex College asked Schurman to supervise undergraduates in British imperial and American history.[4] 'I was very busy' between teaching at Cambridge, attending Graham's imperial history seminars at King's College in London, conducting research (also in London), and trying to write what would become the first chapter of the present volume. Additionally, the privilege of dining at the high table at Sidney Sussex imposed its own burden of responsibilities, although it also certainly 'enhances life', as Schurman puts it.[5]

As he 'wrestled' with his topic he was confronted with adversity from several sources. First, Gerald Graham left King's College for a post at the Institute for Advanced Study at Princeton University. In addition the veteran's grant which was funding Schurman's study ran out. Finally, he realized that he stood little chance of seeing the papers of liberal imperialist politician Lord Rosebery, since these were in the keeping of Rosebery's grandson who 'spent his time moving between racetracks in a manner which I was not equipped to follow'. This juncture was, he recalls, the 'nadir' of his career, and he began to pack his bags 'to go and do something or other in Nova Scotia'.

His fortunes quickly improved, however. First, he won a Research Fellowship competition sponsored by Sidney Sussex College. Equally important, Graham turned him over to W. C. B. Tunstall (1900–70), who lectured on international relations at the London School of Economics and Political Science.[6] Of all the formative influences on Schurman's scholarship, none was more important than Brian Tunstall:

> After two interviews with him I knew that I had fallen on my feet and would soon be ready to walk on water. My judgment was sound. He knew more Imperial and Naval history than anyone, including Graham, and he was a brilliant and inspiring teacher. He made me see the relation of Empire to the Navy, dished out significant historical facts like a prepaid oracle, and had the power to make me think that I understood everything that transpired at our great sessions.[7]

In addition to the distinguished historians with whom he studied, Schurman also absorbed the views of scholars outside the field, chief among them fellow Canadians John J. Madden and James W. Dale. The former was an economics research student at Peterhouse College, the latter a chemistry graduate student at Sidney Sussex. Dale had worked for the Canadian government for several years and provided valuable insight on the interrelationships of governmental departments: 'he taught me how practical decisions were arrived at'. Madden, despite his 'acute dislike' of the British Empire, was an authority on capital investment in the imperial process. Others, too, influenced his perspective: economic historian Jack Gallagher, and economists Scott Gordon (another Nova Scotian) and Harry Johnson, the latter of whom not only introduced Schurman to numerous interesting people but could 'discuss the ideas of my thesis as if he knew all the detail and ... gave good advice'. The fruit of this interdisciplinary exposure was, Schurman believes, valuable: 'I was a bit of an outsider looking at my own craft.'

The resulting work makes abundantly clear that a viable and coherent imperial strategy for a steam-age navy was enunciated, developed and considered in systematic fashion with regard to the defence needs of Britain's colonial possession and maritime trade. Moreover, Schurman's findings leave no doubt that, so far from languishing through a 'Dark Age', as some commentators have charged, the Admiralty played an important role in the evolution of this concept of imperial defence.[8] Additionally, the study is invaluable for its masterful and balanced treatment of the larger discursive contexts within which imperial defence strategy developed. Schurman's thesis, as well as any study since Arthur Marder's *Anatomy of British Sea Power*, and better than most, places the navy and military firmly within the political and administrative context from which policy emanated.

True, the era was one of peace, a handful of colonial wars excepted, but regardless of the material consequences of 'peace dividends' and 'downsizing' – salient characteristics of British defence policy during the period – Schurman's research demonstrates conclusively that a great deal was happening at the level of theory and strategy. It also furnished a salutary reminder that 'strategy', whatever we may mean by that amorphous and elusive term, is not something invariably found in a neatly bound manual of doctrine, waiting to be read by acolytes, critics and historians. And certainly not least of all, the following pages are invaluable for illuminating the difficulties encountered in attempting to secure interdepartmental co-operation on a matter of grave concern to Admiralty, War Office, Colonial Office and Treasury. Indeed, the detailed examination given to the want of communication (to say nothing of co-operation), turf battles, and bickering which dogged consideration of imperial defence until the late 1880s, furnishes a virtual textbook example of how not to proceed in such cases. As an upshot of the lack of coordination, the department most concerned with imperial defence – the navy – had the least input in the

EDITOR'S INTRODUCTION

process of determining the strategic importance of overseas bases and the degree to which each should be defended.

So why did *Imperial Defence* fail to appear in print four decades ago? From the standpoint of contemporary interest, Schurman's study could hardly have been completed at a less serendipitous time. He wrote of imperial defence while the empire itself was in the throes of dissolution. India and Pakistan had gone their separate ways from the Mother country – not to mention each other – seven years earlier, as had the Palestinian mandate. The process of colonial divestment halted temporarily during Churchill's 1951–55 ministry, yet in the shadow of the superpower standoff Britain's importance was peripheral, as was made humiliatingly clear the following year at Suez. More to the point, Churchill's ringing declarations to the contrary notwithstanding, Britain could no longer afford empire, even had the colonized been amenable to remaining so. In such an atmosphere a work detailing the formulation of imperial defence policy at a time when the sun never set on the empire was not likely to find a receptive readership, nor even a receptive publisher. Schurman recently informed me that one distinguished publishing house expressed interest in the project were he willing to extend his coverage forward to 1939. He was not, and there the matter rested, save for the fact that if times in the second half of the 1950s were unpropitious for the reception of a work on empire, they were even less so throughout the 1960s, 1970s and 1980s, when the lingering consequences of imperialism became a convenient scapegoat for all of the woes of the ex-colonies: '[i]t has been my fate to proffer insights from the age of Empire when the results of Empire were widely (98 per cent) discredited'.[9]

From Cambridge Schurman returned to Canada, teaching for a year at the University of Alberta before moving to the Royal Military College of Canada, where he spent the following decade. This period produced *The Education of a Navy: The Development of British Naval Strategic Thought, 1867–1914* (1965), which Schurman characterizes as a manifestation of his frustration at not having graduate students at RMC: *Education* was 'a book ostensibly aimed at undergraduates, but speaking directly to the graduates I did not have'. Motives aside, *Education* further explored the themes Schurman first tackled in *Imperial Defence*. Indeed, one of the six strategic theorists and historians examined in *Education*, Sir John Charles Ready Colomb, was the pivotal public figure in Victorian and Edwardian imperial defence debates and garnered close scrutiny in the thesis.[10] Such was Colomb's influence that his pioneering 1867 pamphlet 'The Protection of Our Commerce and Distribution of our Naval Forces considered' is widely acknowledged to have been the first systematic consideration of steam-era imperial defence requirements. And just as Colomb pioneered the study of imperial defence strategy in the steam era, so did Schurman pioneer the historical examination of the men who formulated that strategy. Arthur Marder termed *The Education of a Navy* 'the first [work] of its kind – a thoroughly researched job that needed doing and that will not have to be done again in our time'.[11]

From *The Education of a Navy* to the subsequent *Sir Julian S. Corbett, 1854–1922: Historian of British Maritime Policy from Drake to Jellicoe* (1981) was a logical scholarly progression. The lengthy period between the two works was largely a consequence of Schurman's leaving the Royal Military College in 1967 for Queen's University. At the latter institution he found the graduate students for whom he had earlier yearned, producing some 30 MA and PhD students during the ten years he spent there. He found himself with other responsibilities as well; for five years he served as director of the school's Institute of Commonwealth and Comparative Studies and between 1975 and 1977 was chairman of one of the graduate divisions, overseeing the activities of no less than 22 departments. Simultaneously, he was one of the three principal investigators on Queen's ambitious Disraeli project, which aimed (and aims) at nothing less than collecting all of the statesman and author's surviving correspondence in order to publish a definitive edition. Schurman, with John Matthews and J. A. W. Gunn, produced the first two volumes of the project, which continues to this day (seven volumes have now appeared).

From Queen's Schurman went for a year to the University of Singapore, before returning to Kingston and the Royal Military College, where he served as head of the history department until his retirement in 1987. During his second stint at RMC the long-in-gestation intellectual biography of Corbett finally appeared, as did that of John Travers Lewis, first Anglican Bishop of Ontario, a work which had been commissioned in 1962 but which, like the Corbett volume, had been delayed for many years by Schurman's activities at Queen's.

The passage of time and his subsequent publications have done little to diminish the scholarly value of Schurman's PhD thesis. With the exception of an article by Bryan Ranft on the evolution of British policy for protecting seaborne trade during the final years of the nineteenth century, Donald C. Gordon's *Dominion Partnership in Imperial Defense* – which examines the topic in the context of home–colonial political relations rather than strategy – and the opening chapters of *Education of a Navy*, almost nothing has been done on the subject, let alone a book-length study, in the four-plus decades which have elapsed since it was completed. And if virtue in historical scholarship often goes unrewarded, at the very least Schurman can console himself on the good company he has kept. I am thinking especially of Theodore Ropp's masterly dissertation on late-nineteenth-century French naval policy, which languished unpublished – though hardly uncited – for even longer than *Imperial Defence* has done.

EDITOR'S INTRODUCTION

Numerous people have helped bring this project to fruition, to all of whom I extend thanks. A few deserve special mention. First and foremost I must acknowledge the generous support and assistance of Donald Schurman himself, who approached the task with enthusiasm, erudition and patience, and who bore the editor's *naiveté* with unflagging good humour. I would also like to express special thanks to his former colleagues at the Royal Military College of Canada, Dr Keith Neilson and Dr Greg Kennedy, who first approached both Schurman and myself with the idea of publishing his thesis. The task of creating a word-processing file from a photocopy of a carbon copy of the original thesis was undertaken by Ms Rebecca McIntyre and Ms Loretta Colvin, both of the University of Alabama. To the former especially I owe an immense debt of gratitude. Dr Andrew Lambert of the War Studies Department, King's College, London, graciously took time from his very busy schedule to read the manuscript and offered numerous valuable suggestions and insights. Professor Holger Herwig of the University of Calgary provided an equally valuable critique. Mr Godfrey Waller of Cambridge University Library provided crucial assistance by tracking down the original thesis to photocopy a page left out of our working copy.

My editorial efforts have been restricted to incidental points, mostly stylistic concerns and clarification. The structure of the thesis as defended has not been altered beyond a partial rearrangement of the first chapter, and splitting what was a lengthy final chapter in the original into two briefer units. Contextual information has been added in a few places to highlight Schurman's arguments. The notes and bibliography have been updated to encompass relevant works published in the past 40 years, and the original footnotes streamlined according to current practice. There are a few editorial notes regarding minor matters on which my views diverge significantly from Schurman's. He too has added a few remarks in instances where his views have changed over the years. 'The thesis', he remarked at one stage of editing, 'is worth publishing or it is not. If it is then it wants minimum words from me.' I agree wholeheartedly. Having elsewhere attempted maladroitly to summarize his groundbreaking research on imperial defence, I now feel embarrassed at having done so. As he noted in reference to Sir Julian Corbett's *Some Principles of Maritime Strategy*, 'the details that give the book strength are best read first hand and not summarized by a less expert hand than his'. The same holds for *Imperial Defence*.

John Beeler
July 1999

IMPERIAL DEFENCE 1868-87

NOTES

1. All quotations from Dr Schurman, unless otherwise noted, are drawn from personal correspondence.
2. Walker's principal works include *Lord de Villers and His Times: South Africa 1842–1914* (London: Constable, 1925); *A Modern History for South Africans* (Cape Town: Maskew Miller, 1926); *A History of South Africa* (London: Longmans, 1928); *The Great Trek* (London: A. & C. Black, 1934); *W. P. Schreiner. A South African* (London: Oxford University Press, 1937); and *The British Empire: Its Structure and Spirit* (London: Royal Institute of International Affairs, 1943). In addition, he served on the General Editorial Board of the third volume of the *Cambridge History of the British Empire: The Empire–Commonwealth, 1870–1914* (Cambridge: Cambridge University Press, 1959) and as adviser for Vol. 8, *South Africa, Rhodesia, and the Protectorates* (Cambridge: Cambridge University Press, 1936).
3. Graham's chief works include *Canada, 1774–1791: A Study in 18th Century Trade Policy* (London: Longmans, 1930); *Sea Power and British North America, 1783–1820* (1941); *Canada: A Short History* (Cambridge, MA: Harvard University Press, 1950); *Empire of the North Atlantic: The Maritime Struggle for North America* (Toronto: Toronto University Press, 1950); *The Politics of Naval Supremacy* (Cambridge: Cambridge University Press, 1965); *Great Britain in the Indian Ocean: A Study of Maritime Enterprise 1810–1850* (Oxford: Clarendon Press, 1967); and *The China Station: War and Diplomacy 1830–1860* (Oxford: Clarendon Press, 1978). In addition, he edited *The Walker Expedition to Quebec, 1711* (London: Navy Records Society, 1953); and, with R. A. Humphreys, *The Navy and South America, 1807–1823* (London: Navy Records Society, 1962) for the Navy Records Society.
4. Professor Thomson's field of expertise was western Europe. His publications include *Personality in Politics* (London: T. Nelson, 1939); *The Democratic Ideal in France and England* (Cambridge: Cambridge University Press, 1940), *Democracy in France: The Third Republic* (London: Institute of International Affairs, 1946); *The Babeuf Plot: The Making of a Republican Legend* (London: Kegan Paul, Trench, Trubner, 1947); *England in the Nineteenth Century* (Harmondsworth: Penguin, 1950); *Two Frenchmen: Pierre Laval and Charles de Gaulle* (London: Cresset Press, 1951); *World History from 1914 to 1951* (London: Oxford University Press, 1954); and *Political Ideas* (New York: Basic Books, 1966). Additionally, he edited a collection of historical documents – *France: Empire and Republic, 1850–1940* (New York: Walker, 1968) and jointly authored *The Truth About Spain*, with Harold Greaves (London: Victor Gollancz, 1938); and *Patterns of Peacemaking*, with E. Meyer and A. Briggs (London: Kegan Paul, 1945).
5. He also remembers Dr Thomson as a profoundly influential figure who advised him 'consistently, unobtrusively, and wisely' until the latter's death.
6. William Cuthbert Brian Tunstall. Tunstall's publications include *Byng and the Loss of Minorca* (London: P. Allan, 1928); *Flights of Naval Genius* (London: P. Allan, 1930); *Nelson* (London: Duckworth, 1933); *The Realities of Naval History* (London: George Allen & Unwin, 1936); *William Pitt, Earl of Chatham* (London: Hodder & Stoughton, 1938); *Ocean Power Wins* (London: Secker & Warburg, 1944); *World War at Sea* (London: Secker & Warburg, 1942); and *The Commonwealth and Regional Defence* (London: Athlone Press, 1959). Additionally, he contributed essays on imperial defence 1815–70 (Vol. 2) and 1870–97 (Vol. 3) to the *Cambridge History of the British Empire* (Cambridge:

EDITOR'S INTRODUCTION

Cambridge University Press, 1940 and 1959, respectively) and edited *The Byng Papers*, 3 vols (London: Navy Records Society, 1930–32) for the Navy Records Society.
7. Tunstall was also Sir Julian Stafford Corbett's son-in-law, although Schurman admits that the significance of this relationship 'escaped me at the time'. Tunstall kept Corbett's papers until they were placed in the National Maritime Museum.
8. The phrase was coined by Oscar Parkes and has been used by others.
9. Nor, adds Schurman, was the navy very popular at this time.
10. The remaining five were Colomb's brother Philip H. Colomb, John Knox Laughton, Alfred Thayer Mahan, Julian Stafford Corbett and Herbert W. Richmond.
11. *American Historical Review*, 71 (1966): pp. 1348–9.

Abbreviations

CO	Colonial Office
FO	Foreign Office
KP	Kimberley Papers
MLN	Milne Papers
NMM	National Maritime Museum
PRO	Public Record Office
RA	Royal Archives
RA (mil.)	Royal Artillery
RE	Royal Engineers
WO	War Office

Preface

By 1868, despite some political doubts to the contrary, it seemed fairly clear that the British Empire was likely to continue as a going concern, even though public and political interest in the concept of empire was comparatively slight. As the empire moved into the phase succeeding that of mid-Victorian pessimism, its problems of development and adjustment, social, constitutional, political and economic, became extremely diverse. In so far as the problem posed by the possession of empire was faced as a whole, however, it was faced on the basis of common defence needs. That defence should emerge as the one really empire-unifying factor in the latter part of the nineteenth century is all the more remarkable in view of a general unwillingness in so many quarters to think in broad and non-technical terms about military problems.

By 1860 the Crimea had come to be regarded as an isolated expedition of the old eighteenth-century type. The Sadowa operations (Austro-Prussian War, 1866) and the surrender of Sedan (Franco-Prussian War, 1870) had certainly perturbed the British military mind. But instead of leading to increased naval and military co-operation, these portents tended more to produce purely departmentalized defence thinking with a ditch-to-ditch defence of the Channel as its chief feature. This type of official thinking gave the army a priority over a navy that was undergoing a tremendous technical revolution. Meanwhile, the purely traditional differences between the services still persisted. Hence, several factors combined to make each service operate largely in ignorance of what the other was doing and thinking. It was the growth of an appreciation of defence as an overall imperial problem that breached this wall of indifference, and restored the idea that the security of Great Britain rested on the complementary functions of the navy and army.

This dissertation is a study of the origins of the concept that had such profound imperial and strategic consequences. Both the nature of the subject itself and the availability of sources have led to its not always being treated at the same level. Part of the story concerns government departments, and part is political; but in both cases it is highly personal. Although the study is partly one of the growth of ideas, it is on the whole more one of actual action taken, both political and military, even though such action was frequently of a very cautious, tentative and not uniformly progressive kind. As a study in the interplay between politicians on the one hand and professional soldiers, sailors, and administrators on the other, it may have some claim to be regarded as unique.

I have to acknowledge the gracious permission of Her Majesty the Queen to make use of important material from the Royal Archives, Windsor Castle.

I am indebted to the Earl of Kimberley for his kindness in making available to me the political and official correspondence of the first Earl; to the Trustees of the National Maritime Museum, Greenwich, for permission to quote from the papers of Admiral Sir Alexander Milne, and the Council of the National Trust for permission to study the papers of Benjamin Disraeli, First Earl of Beaconsfield.

These sources have been used as supplementary to War Office, Colonial Office and Admiralty records, together with the extensive collection of the political correspondence and records of the fourth Earl of Carnarvon, all preserved in the Public Record Office, London [now at the PRO's facility in Kew, London].

With two notable exceptions, little use has been made of newspaper sources.

I am grateful for the opportunity afforded me by W. C. B. Tunstall of the London School of Economics and Political Science for making available draft chapters on 'Imperial Defence' to be published shortly in the *Cambridge History of the British Empire*, Vol. 3, and for having had the stimulating experience of discussing them with him.

Finally, I am grateful to the Master and the Fellows of my College for the Research Fellowship which made it possible for me to complete this work.

D. M. Schurman
Sidney Sussex College, Cambridge University
April 1955

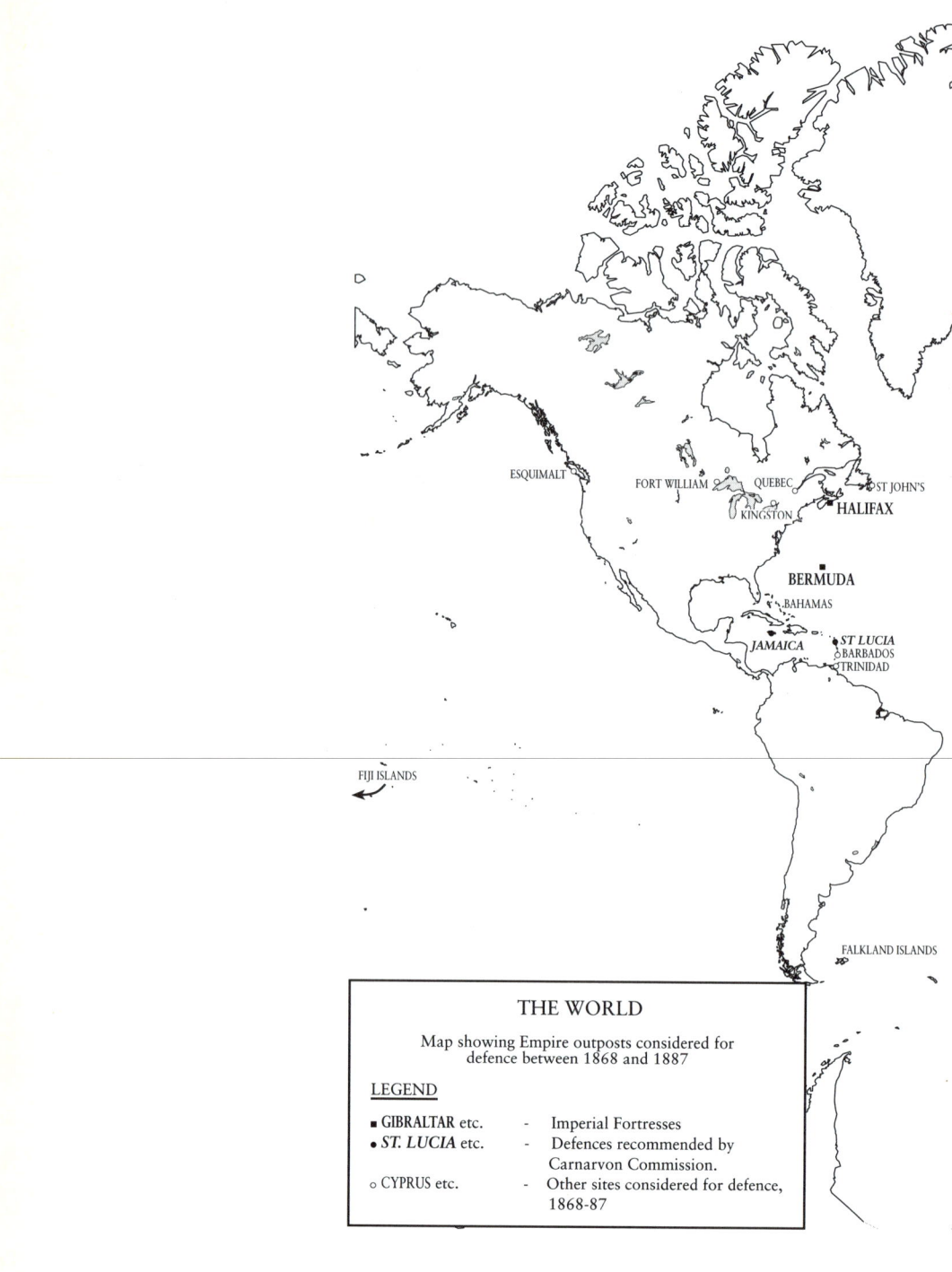

Introduction

One does not need to believe, with Lord Rosebery, that the British Empire was the greatest instrument for good ever devised by man to comprehend also that it was not the epitome of evil. What remains true is that it was an historical phenomenon difficult, under any circumstances, to explain adequately. A huge dispersion accompanied by incommensurate means and instruments of power make it fascinating. It is a paradox that many of those for whom benefits of empire were greatest nourish their present situations on tales of empire that are more amusing than revealing. The true story is more of a vast concatenation of aspirations, chances and greed than it is a record of heavy-handed repression. One has only to look at Africa and Canada since 1960 to get the point. In both cases historians wring their hands about the imperial past while their own shop is not secure. Both are threatened with fragmentation.

Across the gulf of one working lifetime the difference between an 'imperial' and an almost 'post-imperial' colonial situation may appear stark. It may well be, however, that the tyranny of a shifting terminology has not been matched by fundamental cultural changes during the 40 years or so between the 1950s and today. It may also be true that imperial changes between the late nineteenth century and today are also more surface than real. Whether these speculations are useful or not, it does seem to be true that the corpse of a once mighty empire has, since 1945, been the host of a vast army of nationalistic ghouls. Even more striking, and perhaps more surprising, has been the post-1945 attack on the empire by historians. In Britain, and in the empire–Commonwealth, these chroniclers seem to have been driven by different purposes. Viewing from the centre (London) outward, retrospective humanitarianism has spawned a generation of industrious moral judges. Overseas as well, visions of national greatness sped the idea that every advance in colonial 'progress' must be balanced by a corresponding exposure of British inefficiency or malice, or worse. These period writers have something in common. Their scenarios span the time of the two most destructive wars in human history and therefore their judgements are bound to involve military affairs. Another is that almost none of them has much familiarity with the relationship of sea-power to empire. The Royal Navy, by which, under God, the safety of all the realms mainly depended does not ordinarily exercise their minds, and is certainly not a compelling factor in their calculations. In Canada and Australia they count army corps and work out ratios between the war dead and Canadian and Australian nationality. Unfortunately the Royal Navy is often regarded, even by most of its own chroniclers, as a subject for minute rehashes of tough battles like Jutland, or of arduous campaigns like the U-boat wars. Such histories are good for patriotic memories no doubt, but they are not the stuff of empires. The vastness of the concepts and the needs of empire dwarfed the understandings of the soldier-dominated leadership in the wars and after, and such narrow thinking had an effect that was marked. The children of empire deserved a vision and have been given horse-blinkers.[1]

Yet, despite a wilful disregard of the advantages of common imperial interests, for both the British and for their nurtured allotments around the world, the residual legacy of the naval and imperial age was enough to enable them to play a significant part in the defeat of Germany by 1945. They did not 'win' the war, as the Americans did not 'win' it, but they helped the Russians win it and that was important.

Such provocative views as the above were only half-hatched in 1950, as I set out to study 'Imperial Federation'; operating from Sidney Sussex College in Cambridge University. Aside from the fact that it was wonderful to have a place in that gem of a college, I had come to England to get away from liberal historians in Canada. One of these told me that the significance of the Halifax Dockyard was its contribution to the sociology of Halifax and airily dismissed the naval significance of the facility. I did not want to study that kind of history.

In Cambridge, the Board of Research Studies assigned me to Eric Walker for supervision. Providentially this historian of South Africa forced me to look at the question of federations from both international and political theory perspectives. Swiss, Australian, South African and American sources became familiar. At that time the landscape of empire was then beginning to be shown in a new way by Jack Gallagher and Ronald Robinson. Their *Africa and the Victorians* was then in gestation, and, when published, became very influential and remained so for 20 years. Jack Gallagher was helpful to me, and the combination of Walker's international political theory and Gallagher's economic theorizing later served me well. But Jack was something of a closet romantic, and close readers of his book will see that he had difficulties with the investment economic theories and, indeed the last pages in it located the *point d'appui* of empire at some measurable but mysterious strategic distance between Cape Town and Cairo. This measurement had force, as it was used by

AUTHOR'S INTRODUCTION

Lord Salisbury and by Cecil Rhodes many years before. I was beginning to think, much to Robinson's amusement, that the place to look for origins and Victorian movements was the vast Home and Imperial Civil Service. Indeed I came to the conclusion that an expanded view of Charles Buller's 'Mr Mothercountry' held the interpretive key to imperial development, or lack of it.

My problem, and that of many imperial interpreters, was how to connect the home apparatus of empire with policy and facilitators of that policy overseas. This was in 1951; when Eric Walker took a leave of absence from supervising. By 1953 attendance at the seminars of Gerald Graham, Rhodes Professor of Imperial History at King's College, University of London, expanded my viewpoint. The seminars included Alan Pearsall, whose knowledge of navies and empires was, and is, colossal. Also, almost simultaneously, I was privileged to study under one whom I took to be *the* most knowledgeable observer of the imperial apparatus – Brian Tunstall. He taught me the history of the Royal Navy, along with its significance as a partner in empire. This was the most intensive year of study that I ever experienced. Tunstall was Lecturer in International Relations at the London School of Economics and Political Science. He had been Honorary Secretary of the Navy Records Society, and had written books on Admiral Byng and Lord Chatham. He was also then engaged in writing the history of imperial defense for *The Cambridge History of the British Empire*. I could not imagine my good luck. During this time I was elected to a research fellowship at Sidney Sussex College. It was a lively time. The pressures of research, new teaching and other college tasks were very demanding, almost overpowering, but the new environment, my family, my canny supervisor and above all the wise guidance of my great Cambridge mentor and friend, David Thomson, Senior Tutor at Sidney Sussex, saw me through an inevitable backlash and kept me productive during the last years of my fellowship.

The oceanic vision and insights that Tunstall provided were in direct opposition to the kind of narrow perceptions of imperial adjustment that any Canadian, Australian, or South African voter used at the end of the last century and that their historians still redeploy. It was really a question of making a larger whole function in the face of the fractious localism that once produced the United States of America. The power of the purse, in local assemblies, was used to force splintered 'freedom', by a refusal to pay bills. The Americans had triumphed largely because the British electorate wished them to do so. The same kinds of questions began to emerge in the residual empire in the age of Gladstone, Disraeli and Salisbury. By mid 1953 I could see that the laboratory for the future of empire, as it appeared to me, was the question of naval defence. This thesis was the result of an attempt to understand that factor.

The mechanics of the present work should be obvious to the reader and the rudiments are to be found in the Contents. In presenting a work 'warts and all' as Oliver Cromwell, a famous and ancient member of my College, used to say, it is better not to attempt to rearrange the portrait. However, the general intent of what I was trying to highlight has been perceptively outlined in a collection of essays entitled *Far-Flung Lines: Studies in Imperial Defence in Honour of Donald Mackenzie Schurman*, in the articles themselves, but particularly in the Introduction written by the editors, Keith Neilson and Greg Kennedy.[2] In this Introduction the ease with which 'imperial' history slid into its Rip Van Winkle sleep, for 30 years, is brilliantly canvassed. For me this book, quite aside from its heart-warming reference to myself, represents a return to imperial problems as I conceive them to have been 'in the round', and not just a return to 'old, unhappy, far-off things; and battles long ago'.

The present editor of this work was a contributor to that volume, and indeed sets it in the context of the historical era. His knowledge of Sir Alexander Milne makes my early study in Admiralty history seem fragmentary, and supports Hinsley's judgement mentioned in note 1. His wish to give this work to the public is welcome to me because he knows the period. It was said of me, in the spring of 1955, that I 'understood the British nineteenth-century bureaucratic mind'. Be that as it may, Beeler does broadly understand the Victorian navy as an 'instrument of policy'. I am pleased that he has seen fit to launch this piece of what is now history.

NOTES

1. Sometimes it slipped away. Habits born of army mentality fostered in the colonies (such as Canada) die hard. During my oral exam that perceptive thinker Professor Sir Harry Hinsley asked me if I had not written the first chapters with some lack of charity towards naval purposes and activities. Of course I had. I have tried to avoid such 'balance' since.
2. Published by Frank Cass, London, 1997.

1

Liberalism and Empire Defence

THE LIBERAL ATTITUDE, 1868–87

Viewing the subject of British imperial security from a late-twentieth-century perspective, there can be little doubt that the attention paid to defence problems during the years 1868–87 was hardly commensurate with the growth and population of the empire. From a military standpoint, increased responsibility should have meant a corresponding increase in security preparations. That this was not the case was the consequence of circumstances peculiar to the era. First, there existed a widely held view that colonial self-government supposed colonial self-defence.[1] Simultaneously, government costs were increasing, as was the expense of military equipment. Finally, radical and quasi-Liberal views respecting war in general, and warlike preparations in particular, exercised pronounced influence over imperial policy and strategic planning.[2]

The view that colonial self-government should beget colonial self-defence was held fairly generally by both Liberals and Conservatives at the beginning of the period, and remained broadly current until 1887. It stemmed in part from the desire, also endemic to both parties, to maintain a tight rein on governmental spending. This aim was to be accomplished in this instance by saddling self-governing colonies with the brunt of their defence costs. It correlated furthermore to the general desire – again common to both major parties but more pronounced among Liberals – to limit defence expenditures strictly. This intention, however, was confounded by the rising cost of armaments due largely to profound and rapid changes in *matériel*, especially in the navy. Fiscal problems increased with the passage of time, partly because of the steadily mounting expense of novel weaponry, and partly owing to stagnant or dwindling revenue production during much of the post-1873 era, the consequence of the Victorian Great Depression. With increasing financial difficulties came increasing authority of the Exchequer over the spending departments of government. Hence the monetary demands of large military needs confronted the jealous mistrust of Treasury officials. Economy was one of the watchwords for advocates of retrenchment, and was in particular one of the foundations of Liberal principles in political administration. The tendency to discount the possibility of war and to dislike war and war preparations likewise engaged the attention of certain Liberal politicians far more than that of Conservatives. Indeed, an extreme aversion to the idea of war and war preparations were characteristics of influential portions of the Liberal Party during these years. Hence, economical and pacifistic tendencies converged to form an integral part of Gladstonian Liberalism, and, given Gladstone's centrality to mid-Victorian politics, they require some attention.

The factors contributing to the rise of such an attitude toward military functions in Britain are diverse, but not difficult to trace. First, there was the national distrust of a standing army that had existed, in varying degrees, since 1660. In the years immediately following the Glorious Revolution the Whigs, claiming to protect and preserve the liberties of England, decried permanent military forces as potential instruments of tyranny, royal or otherwise.[3] This sentiment waned slightly during the eighteenth century, punctuated as it was by frequent wars, but reappeared after 1815, this time sponsored by radicals and Liberals.

The navy was regarded in the same light as the army.[4] By 1850 its necessity was a generally accepted fact, even by Richard Cobden, although its traditional utility was no longer correctly understood. But the navy, unlike its sister service, possessed in the Board of Admiralty an organization capable of directing warlike operations and vested with constitutional authority to do so under appropriate circumstances, two features unlikely to appeal to radicals. The national status of the army, conversely, was less assured, and it was manifestly in need of reform.[5]

A second factor contributing to the rise of these radical/Liberal views was that no war had extended the efforts and resources of Britain since the Napoleonic era. The Crimean War was an almost perfect example of 'limited war', but in this context more appropriately serves to illustrate just how defective British war planning and operations were, even in a limited context.[6] The length of time since the last major conflict also gave rise in some quarters to the idea that a general European conflagration, or at least one involving Britain, was virtually unthinkable, and that its avoidance was within the control of enlightened statesmanship.[7]

Liberal attitudes were also conditioned by the fact that, although under Gladstone's stewardship, they were the natural inheritors of the radical tradition. Gladstone was the leader, but the spiritual fathers were Richard Cobden and John Bright, and Cobden's thought struck at the very root of imperial military planning.[8] For economic reasons, he claimed, colonies were of small value.[9] Like Adam Smith he argued that overseas possessions cost more to maintain and defend than could be realized through trade with them. Equally crucially, according to Cobden and Bright's *Weltanschauung*, war was the result of mercantilist economic competition and could thus be eliminated by universal free trade.[10] Cobden and Bright joined these two ideas together to conclude that colonies, so far from being economic assets in a free-trading world, became, through their very possession, positive menaces to peace by their economic temptation to less enlightened powers.[11]

Thus Cobden irrevocably linked his economic thought and hatred of war with the possession of empire. During the heyday of the 'Manchester School' Cobden was leader of the pack, and his strain of thought, together with his hostility to social privilege in general was passed on, in a marked degree, to his successors: Gladstone and the Gladstonian Liberal Party. The feature that gives point to all of these circumstances and focuses their implications in a Liberal direction was Gladstone's ascendancy in his party. This is certainly not the place to dissect his views on defence and empire in any definitive way, and it is always dangerous to attempt to draw special conclusions by tapping the gigantic career of the great Liberal at specific junctures, but certain facts tend to link Gladstone closely with both Cobden and subsequent Liberal statesmen.

Gladstone had, first of all, no great interest in empire. Paul Knaplund claims that Gladstone laid the foundation from which the commonwealth conception later grew.[12] This speculation may be valid. It remains incontestable, however, that he did not labour to preserve the link between Britain and the self-governing colonies in the early 1870s.[13] He was not interested in extending the empire, nor was he interested in the machinery for protecting what existed. None of his great bursts of political energy was applied to imperial matters, and in private life he was not connected in an active manner with any imperial movements. What interest he displayed in defence matters was almost without exception financial.[14] Significantly, John Morley's massive, definitive, 'model' biography omits the word defence from the index.[15]

Numerous instances of his general indifference, if not outright antipathy, towards defence concerns may be adduced. Secretary for War Edward Cardwell's army reforms between 1868 and 1871 were motivated chiefly by Gladstone's demand for reduction of military expenditure. In 1874 the latter dissolved parliament because he could not agree with his colleagues on army and navy estimates. The Royal Commission on Colonial Defence appointed by Disraeli in 1879 saw its report neglected throughout much of Gladstone's second administration. In 1894 the Grand Old Man resigned from the premiership for the final time when faced with another impasse over the size of the navy estimates. He found foreign affairs uncongenial.[16] His condemnation of Turkish misrule and atrocities in Bulgaria (1876) might be considered an exception, but it is difficult to argue that the moral tone pervading his speeches regarding

Balkan atrocities was not more congenial to him than the arid traditionalism of the Foreign Office.

It therefore seems a reasonable conclusion that Gladstone had absorbed and reinterpreted in his own way much of the anti-colonial and anti-military thought current amongst the radicals by the time he first took office as prime minister. And such was his stature within the party that his views on defence policy largely informed those of the subsequent generation of Liberal leaders such as Sir Henry Campbell-Bannerman and Herbert Asquith. It was in the face of this sort of thinking that empire defence struggled for existence between 1868 and 1887.

The features and legacy of Gladstonian Liberalism are aptly illustrated by the arguments of Campbell-Bannerman in a minority report disagreeing with a proposal for the creation of a Chief-of-Staff made by the Hartington Commission on military and naval administration (1887–90).[17] The Commission's majority recommended that such an official, free from other professional and executive duties, be responsible for collecting military information and preparing war plans so that the defence requirements of the British Empire could be dealt with according to a 'definite and harmonious plan'.[18] Campbell-Bannerman's stated objection to the proposal was based more on moral than on strategic considerations, exemplifying the strong ideological current in Gladstonian Liberal thinking.[19] He pointed out, no doubt with the Franco-Prussian War in mind, that 'planning war' was a dangerous continental habit: one likely in itself to generate a conflict.[20] Since Britain had no designs on any continental power's possessions it seemed wrong to him that it should plan war against one or any of them. He admitted that Britain might become involved in small wars, but maintained that such conflicts could be planned by the officer directly responsible for the conduct of operations, and not by the War Office. 'Indian military policy', he said, 'will be settled in India itself and not in Pall Mall.'

Reasoning along these lines led Campbell-Bannerman to conclude that a Chief-of-Staff could serve only a dangerous purpose, since the proposed official would justify his existence by attempting to create a field in which to work. This meant that he might plan wars of aggression. The Liberal politician also defined exactly what, in his opinion, British 'military policy' should embrace. It should be confined, he maintained, to 'problems of army administration', including the extent of establishments, the proportion of the several arms and their organization, the conditions of service for officers and men, and the distribution of forces and their equipment. These 'humbler' activities were recommended by Campbell-Bannerman's dissenting report as the proper sphere of activity for would-be military planners.[21]

It would be neither historically useful nor academically sound to pass judgement here on the moral distinctions made by Campbell-Bannerman and other late-nineteenth-century Liberals. It is relevant, however, to consider the ramifications of their opinions. The very existence of armed forces, unless purely for deterrence, and estimates for their upkeep admits the possibility of war. It seems to follow naturally that those whose professional function is to deal with possible conflict should execute their responsibility in the most efficient manner possible. One cause of difficulty in appreciating this fact, perhaps, lies in the supposed distinction between the words offence and defence.[22] Effective defence depends largely on the intelligent use of offence. Thus, offensive operations, although they must be timed to suit fluid conditions, must be encompassed if defence is to have any security meaning whatever.[23] Campbell-Bannerman's view, however, completely divorced the former from the latter. His distinction between colonial and European wars was, furthermore, an interesting one from a moral point of view, but was valid only in so far as it could be assumed that colonial wars meant hostilities solely against 'backward' peoples.[24] Once it was admitted that such wars might lead to conflict with the colonial aspirations of other western powers it ought to have been appreciated that war with a European power might depend, as far as Britain was concerned, on whether colonial activities were being actively pursued. It was surely the duty of the responsible military authorities to plan against such a general conflict as the very possession of colonies rendered possible.

This failure to acknowledge the broader implications of colonial activity further illuminates the mentality behind Campbell-Bannerman's minority report and, by extension, the political ethos which he represented, for the Hartington Commission was a political body drawn together for the purpose of clarifying a difficult military co-operation problem and recommending solutions – including additional military machinery – for dealing with that problem. Yet the answer of a prominent Liberal Commission member was not to decide the issue on military grounds but to approach the rationale for maintaining armed forces from the standpoint of morality. Indeed, Campbell-Bannerman refused to deal with the real problem. In so doing, the underlying attitudes of Gladstonian Liberalism were again adumbrated: national defence alone was the legitimate rationale for maintaining military and naval forces; these forces were considered primarily with reference to home defence rather than imperial security; and the whole subject was framed in terms of morality

Yet, while the appeal to morality which informed the minority report may easily be ignored as being repugnant to the lessons of military experience and science, to do so is to miss a larger point. Lack of strategical insight has often been a common political lacuna; failure to address military problems on the basis of qualified moral principle simply marked more particularly the differentiation of the man and his group from the rest of the uncomprehending. In other words, pacifism was a distinctly radical/Liberal creed, but a broader lack of appreciation of imperial defence requirements was hardly confined to Campbell-Bannerman individually or the British Liberal Party as a whole during the years 1868–87. On the contrary, the want of understanding was fairly general. Mid-Victorian Conservatives, to be sure, tended to be less anti-military, less sanguine concerning the prospects of perpetual peace, and occasionally prepared to place more trust in their military advisers than were their rivals, but they shared the basic confused vision on the subject of imperial defence.[25] Moreover, Gladstone was prime minister for more than 11 of the 20 years between 1868 and 1887, and even when out of office he and his party exercised significant influence on the course of government policy in the realms of financial, foreign and imperial policy.

1868–74

Notwithstanding Gladstone's general indifference to issues of empire and imperial security, the years of his first administration (1868–74) saw the question of the future relations of Britain and its colonies directed along the path of co-operation rather than separation. It also saw the implementation of a long-approved policy of withdrawing imperial troops from the self-governing colonies. The first of these achievements, however, was largely inadvertent. Indeed, several contemporary factors militated against conceiving the empire – to say nothing of imperial security – in a global context.

First, departmental co-operation on defence problems was slight. There was some co-operation between the War and Colonial Offices and the Treasury, but Admiralty policy-making remained insular, surrounded by traditional secrecy.[26] Moreover, there was no such thing as imperial defence, if by such a term is implied a unified theory of strategic security founded on general principles, together with machinery for giving effect to those principles. Between 1868 and 1874 several events took place that were to have a bearing on subsequent attempts to create a general framework for imperial defence; they were not, however, years during which either the idea or even the hope of imperial defence, as defined above, was of political relevance. Yet it is important to understand two special aspects of these years to appreciate how the seeds of this idea began to fall on fertile ground after 1874.

One of the chief obstacles to conceiving imperial defence in terms of a unified whole was the 'separation problem'. If, as Cobden argued, colonies were military liabilities rather than economic assets, then the prudent policy would be imperial divestment, or separation of the link between mother country and colony, and, as befit Cobden's ideological heirs, the possibility of separation commanded some attention in Gladstone's first Cabinet. This fact has not escaped students of empire history, and the question of whether Gladstone was imperial or anti-imperial, separationist or non-separationist, has long been a subject of historical discussion.[27] Today it is generally agreed that a desire to force separation was never the settled policy of his government.[28] Yet if separation was not popular enough to emerge as the ministry's declared official policy, it was a constant issue throughout its life and formed a backdrop against which all colonial problems were considered, security included.

In order that some degree of perspective be maintained it should be understood that while the separation question was rarely far from the table when the Cabinet dealt with colonial affairs, those affairs themselves did not occupy a large proportion of the government's time, as a glance at the legislation accomplished during these years makes clear.[29] Nevertheless, whenever the Cabinet was confronted with a difficult problem in connection with its relations with self-governing colonies, 'separation' became an issue in the views expressed by individual ministers.

This tendency was pronounced in the case of New Zealand's requests for a British defence loan to assist in its Maori war when Gladstone's government stuck stubbornly to its policy of withdrawing the regular army forces stationed there despite the emergency. The Colonial Secretary, Lord Granville, in the first place sent a 'churlish' dispatch to the New Zealanders disclaiming responsibility for the domestic woes of the colonists, and going so far as to suggest that the original occupation of New Zealand had not and did not please the home government.[30] This was hardly the rhetoric of imperial solidarity, neither did the colonists nor British Tories interpret it as such at the time.[31] Matters were not pushed to the conclusion implied by Granville's language, and the British government did eventually guarantee a loan, but the Cabinet did not acquiesce joyfully. Lord Kimberley, then Lord Privy Seal, noted in his 'Journal' on 26 April 1870: 'We have had a Colonial question of some importance to decide. The New Zealanders are very angry at the withdrawal of the British troops. Granville proposed as a sop to them that this country should become guaranty for part of a loan they are raising. After a good deal of opposition it was agreed to.'[32] Kimberley went on for another half a page, giving expression to his view that separation should not be forced, thus implying sentiment to the contrary within the Cabinet.

In the case of the withdrawal of troops from Canada the Cabinet did not require the spur of bitter colonial protest to spawn 'a gloomy discussion' in early May 1869 'on the relations between this country and the United States'. The prospect of such an eventuality loomed as a consequence of friction over the as yet unresolved *Alabama* claims.[33] 'Nearly all the Ministers', Kimberley recorded, 'were of the opinion that it would be impossible to defend Canada successfully against the Americans, and that it is much to be desired that Canada should become independent. It would be for the interest of both England and Canada.'[34] The subject was raised again at a Cabinet meeting on 22 July 1870.[35] Again, Kimberley recorded his opinion that Canada was indefensible, yet he was not prepared to acquiesce to separation despite the fact that 'not a few influential men in our party are convinced that it would be to the advantage of England that Canada should become independent'.[36]

A third, and perhaps the most striking, example of this preoccupation with the 'separation problem' occurred in the course of negotiations over the Australian colonies' desire to regulate their own intercolonial tariffs. The Australians were eventually granted what they desired, despite a good deal of personal opposition from Gladstone and a warning from the Colonial Secretary that the result would tend to separation.[37] During these negotiations Kimberley noted: 'Gladstone, [Robert] Lowe, and [Edward] Cardwell make no secret of their opinion that we should be well rid of the Colonies, and Cardwell evidently thinks the Australian demand for power to establish an Australian inter-Colonial tariff, a good opportunity for bringing matters to a point.'[38] Kimberley himself strongly disagreed with this view and his opinion prevailed, despite Gladstone's suggestion that a definite line be established beyond which concessions could not be made without bringing about separation.[39]

That there was little active interest in imperial affairs in the Gladstone ministry did not set it apart from the governments immediately preceding it. What did set it apart was the fact that the 'separation problem' became an accepted part of Cabinet discussion when colonial matters came up, and that it was against the background of this tendency to separation that colonial defence was considered.[40] A constructive scheme for dealing with empire defence in any unified way could hardly be a practical matter, considering the political atmosphere.

Another factor hampered the elaboration of an overarching imperial security policy. When Edward Cardwell was offered the War Office by Gladstone in 1868 he accepted it on the distinct understanding that a saving in the military estimates should be effected.[41] It was in the light of the predetermined financial requirement then that the Secretary of State for War contemplated reforms in the army.[42] The withdrawal of the troops from the self-governing colonies provided the financial saving necessary to satisfy both retrenchment and political reform.[43] Spurred on by these incentives, the return of the regular army from garrison service in the self-governing colonies was largely accomplished by Gladstone's government between 1869 and 1872. In so far as it affected Canada the policy has been admirably discussed in detail by C. P. Stacey, and its operation and effect on New Zealand has been dealt with by A. J. Harrop.[44] It has, however, yet to be viewed in light of the military defence of the empire as a whole.[45]

From a domestic political standpoint it is clear that British policy had tended toward withdrawal as far back as 1850, and that only special circumstances in particular colonies had prevented earlier implementation.[46] Hence, were it not for the latent separationist tendencies apparent in the Gladstone ministry, and the fact that withdrawal was carried out despite a dangerous local military situation in two of the colonies concerned, the action could hardly be described as a radical departure in colonial policy.[47] Financial questions aside, there was much to be said, politically, for the Liberal view that self-government meant colonial self-defence and self-reliance. Certainly, the removal of the troops saw the disappearance of a constant cause of friction between the home government and the colonies and, once accomplished, its quieting effects were obvious. As Stacey observes, 'It cut the ground from under the feet of the Little Englanders.'[48]

The implementation of the troop-withdrawal policy was carried out with the co-operation of the Colonial Office. Lord Granville (Colonial Secretary 1868–70) had pronounced separationist sentiments and inclined to support Cardwell no matter what the immediate colonial situation.[49] His successor, Lord Kimberley (Colonial Secretary 1870–74), was no less determined that the troops should be withdrawn, but, as his views on the 'separation' issue suggest, he was more susceptible to colonial protests.[50] When Cardwell pressed for the withdrawal of British forces from Quebec in December 1870, in the midst of negotiations with the United States over the *Alabama* claims, Kimberley resisted him. Both Cardwell and Gladstone were angry at the delay, but Kimberley stonewalled them until July 1871.[51]

During Gladstone's first ministry there was also a change in the under-secretaryship at the Colonial Office where Lord Blachford, a convinced though passive separationist, was replaced in 1871 by Robert W. G. Herbert, who, having been one-time Chief Secretary in Queensland, had some knowledge of, and was more receptive to, colonial opinions.[52] All in all, however, both the permanent and political members of the Colonial Office supported Cardwell's policy.

Despite bitter reactions in New Zealand, some protest from Australian colonies, and reproaches from Canada, the policy was largely completed by 1872. At home, aside from the fact that the withdrawal provoked bitter resentment against the government from New Zealand sympathizers, on the grounds that such conduct toward a colony engaged in a war was thoughtless and perhaps betrayed deeper anti-empire designs, and Conservative peer Lord Carnarvon's denunciation in the Upper House of government actions toward Canada, the withdrawal policy produced little dissent in influential circles.[53]

Objections, however, came from the Queen and the Duke of Cambridge.[54] The Duke was the Queen's cousin and had been appointed

Commander-in-Chief of the army in 1856, a position he was to hold until his supersession by Lord Wolseley in 1895. During his tenure his chief preoccupation seems to have been thwarting attempts at army reform, although considering Gladstone's propensity for military reductions this was not an entirely useless occupation. While capable of carrying his conservative attitudes to the verge of absurdity where general policy was concerned, and to a point of viciousness in personal issues, his value as a defender of the military standpoint has never been adequately recognized.[55] If he had little idea of soldiering beyond formal manœuvres he did have some feeling for army welfare as opposed to army economy, and an appreciation of the fact that political interest in the service did not mean more money for it, nor increased fighting efficiency.[56] The Queen's ideas on the army were generally in sympathy with those of the Duke.

As soon as the likelihood of troop withdrawals appeared the Duke recorded his determination to safeguard imperial fortresses abroad: 'more particularly Gibraltar, Malta, Bermuda, Halifax, Quebec, Kingston (Canada), Mauritius. Those at home can be more quickly supplied in an emergency.'[57] On another occasion only the first four of those places were designated imperial fortresses.[58] As the whole question of imperial defence came to be discussed in terms of definitions, this difference is of some interest. Technically, the term imperial fortress referred only to Halifax, Malta, Gibraltar and Bermuda, since those places appeared in the army estimates on the same votes as those covering expenditure on fortifications within the United Kingdom.[59] Furthermore, in later years the term was restricted to those four.[60] In point of fact, however, imperial fortresses were not at this juncture defined as such, nor their special value explained in any official statement. Despite the omission, the strategic value of Halifax, Gibraltar, Bermuda and Malta was never directly challenged in the years that followed.

The Duke also emphasized the importance of the Cape, which he regarded, by reason of both its healthy climate and its proximity to possible eastern danger spots, as a valuable imperial supply base in the Indian Ocean and beyond.[61] These arguments based jointly on health and strategy he also applied to Canada, whence the West Indian garrisons rotated for reasons of healthy climate. In respect to Canada, however, he went even further and pleaded the sentimental and exemplary value of stationing regular troops there, declaring that the protection of Quebec was essential to the general defence of Canada.

As the government's intentions emerged the Duke expressed his misgivings at withdrawal from Canada to both the Queen and Cardwell.[62] The Queen agreed with her Commander-in-Chief that the policy was a political attempt to render the army more subservient to parliament and voiced mild objections.[63] The subject was raised by the Queen's private secretary, General George Grey, who discussed it with Cardwell and then furnished the Duke with an account of the interview. Cardwell, wrote Grey, divided the empire into two broad sections; one embraced that portion where political considerations must prevail and the other included military posts where military considerations must have precedence.[64] In the second category he mentioned Gibraltar, Malta, Bermuda and the Cape, the last being considered an important point in respect of British–Indian communications without reference to the Cape Colony proper. Here, Cardwell clearly indicated, although without full understanding, that there was such a thing as imperial as opposed to colonial defence. In his response the Duke attempted to preserve regular army presence in Canada by suggesting, though without advancing any supporting argument, that Montreal, Quebec and Kingston be maintained as imperial posts.[65] Had Cardwell been interested in paying anything more than lip-service to the idea that certain places had to be defended for imperial reasons he would have given this proposal some consideration. In rejecting the Duke's suggestion, he demonstrated no more understanding of what a point of imperial interest was than did the Duke. Of course, there was no official doctrine of imperial defence from which either man might have sought enlightenment.

Thus, not only was the general Gladstonian Liberal attitude to defence planning unfavourable during the whole period 1868–87: during the particular years 1868–74 further conditions militated against conceiving plans for imperial, or even local colonial defence. Separation was the problem that exercised the Cabinet's mind, rather than preservation, and the withdrawal of the garrisons was a manifestation of this attitude. Yet these years are important ones to this study.

On a negative level, the fact that separation was a legitimate issue, mainly within the Cabinet, at that time meant that when that particular Cabinet left office the separation problem ended as well. The death of this issue meant that military planners might take the empire out of the cupboard and place it on the defence planning table. More substantively, the withdrawal of garrisons was important in a political sense in that it removed a main point of contention that had existed between the home and colonial governments. 'Withdrawal' was moreover significant in a different sense by forcing on the colonies the idea of responsibility for their own defence. Again, the consequences were not uniformly positive: years later, when the home government asked for assistance in the execution of a general scheme of empire defence, the co-operativeness of the colonists was tempered by vivid memories of the withdrawal.

Finally, the Duke of Cambridge's and the Queen's opposition to colonial troop withdrawals forced the War Secretary to clearly distinguish between posts fortified or garrisoned for purposes of local defence only and those contributing towards the defence of the empire as a whole. This was in some respects the beginning of the differentiation in political thinking between the concepts of colonial and imperial defence. In attempting such a differentiation there was little difficulty in naming Gibraltar, Malta, Bermuda, Halifax and possibly Mauritius as having strategic value far beyond purely local defence. Not only were these posts capable of use for the launching of great naval and military expeditions outside their immediate neighbourhood, but if properly maintained their upkeep would cost more than the local inhabitants could be expected to bear. In the cases of Kingston and Quebec the basis for the differentiation was not clear. Both the Duke and Cardwell, however, saw the wider implications of the Cape's position as a part of the empire as opposed to its position as a part of South Africa.[66]

NOTES

1. C. B. Adderley, *Letter to the Rt Hon. Benjamin Disraeli, MP on the Present Relations of England with the Colonies* (London: Parker, Son & Bourn, 1861). This was an earlier opinion that found its expression in the withdrawal of troops from the self-governing colonies carried out during Gladstone's first administration.
2. William H. Dawson, *Richard Cobden and Foreign Policy* (London: George Allen & Unwin, 1926). See in particular Ch. 5.
3. It is interesting to note that Oliver Cromwell's career still cannot be dispassionately discussed in England.
4. [Ed. note: one might temper this assertion slightly. The mistrust of military institutions reappeared after 1815, albeit in a somewhat altered guise, its champions the most ardent proponents of classical liberal economic theory. Given lingering memories of the Napoleonic threat and more contemporary worries about Louis Napoleon's bellicose posturing, the necessity of military and naval forces was grudgingly admitted by all but the most pacifistic free-traders – John Bright being the principal exception. The mistrust now stemmed less from perceived threats to English civil liberties than from the armed forces' potential as agents of provocation: to drag Britain into costly and morally indefensible operations abroad. In this respect the navy, which had never engendered the degree of mistrust late Stuart Whigs held for the army, was, to nineteenth-century radicals, equally culpable.]
5. See John Fortescue, *History of the British Army* (London: Macmillan, 1930), Vol. 13, p. 555. What reform was attempted was piecemeal. 'Within twelve years seventeen Royal Commissions, eighteen Select Committees of the House of Commons, nineteen Committees of officers within the War Office and thirty-five Committees of military officers had considered sundry points of policy in the administration of the War Department; and still the clumsy machinery groaned and creaked, while the wheels, when they revolved at all, turned slowly with much friction.' Fortesque was referring specifically to 1867.
6. Julian S. Corbett, *Some Principles of Maritime Strategy* (London: Longmans, Green), p. 292. Corbett subsequently changed his mind on this point.
7. Although the Franco-Prussian War impressed the military people somewhat, and Disraeli to a degree.
8. Dawson, *Cobden and Foreign Policy*, Ch. 9.

9. John Morley, *The Life of Richard Cobden* (London: T. Fisher Unwin, 1903), Vol. 1, p. 283.
10. Ibid., Vol. 1, p. 230.
11. Ibid., Vol. 2, pp. 470–1. With particular reference to the danger of a US attack on Canada.
12. Paul Knaplund, *Gladstone and Britain's Imperial Policy* (London: George Allen & Unwin, 1927), p. 95.
13. See Ch. 1, Part 2, below.
14. John Morley, *Life of William Ewart Gladstone* (London: Macmillan, 1903), Vol. 2, p. 374. Morley notes with pride that between 1860 and 1865 Gladstone at the Exchequer reduced military, naval and civil expenditure from £38 million to £31 million. The figure rose again under Derby–Disraeli to £34.5 million but was reduced by Gladstone's first administration to £32.25 million.
15. The words defence, navy and Admiralty, are not in the index. Defence is dealt with only in connection with reducing military commitments to the colonies. It is indexed under the heading 'colonies', under which there are only six entries. Gladstone's subsequent biographer, Philip Magnus, did not himself see fit to remedy this slightness of treatment, and more recent examinations of the Liberal leader continue to slight colonial and imperial topics in favour of domestic reform and personal passions.
16. So Cabinet member Lord Kimberley concluded. In his 'Journal of Events under the Gladstone Ministry 1868–73', Kimberley stated that 'Foreign affairs are uncongenial to Gladstone who will never shine when, as now, they occupy the first place in importance.' 'Journal', Kimberley Papers. Preserved at Kimberley. Hereafter referred to as 'KP'. 25 February 1871, KP: PC/A/42. (Subsequently edited and published. See E. Drus (ed.), 'Journal of Events During the Gladstone Ministry, 1868–1874, by John, First Earl of Kimberley', *Camden Miscellany*, 3rd ser., Vol. 21, col. 90.) Also when Gladstone assumed office to find an Afghan War in progress (1880) his long and obvious hesitation as to what to do provoked Disraeli (now Lord Beaconsfield) to state that: 'Her Majesty's ministers ... go to the housetops to proclaim to every bazaar in the East that they do not know what to do in the situation in which they find themselves.' See Hansard, *Parliamentary Debates*, 3rd ser., Vol. 257 (1881), col. 18.
17. 'Further Report of Royal Commissioners appointed to enquire into the Civil and Professional Administration of the Naval and Military Departments and the relation of those departments to each other and to the Treasury' (hereafter referred to as Hartington Commission Report), *Parl. Papers*, 1890, Vol. 19, pp. 29–31. Sir Henry Campbell-Bannerman (1839–1908): Liberal politician; Financial Secretary to the War Office, 1871–74, 1880–82; Secretary to the Admiralty, 1882–84; Chief Secretary for Ireland, 1884; Secretary of State for War, 1886; member Hartington Commission, 1888–90; prime minister, 1905–8.
18. Ibid., p. 22.
19. All the more interesting because of his familiarity with army and navy administration since 1870.
20. Hartington Commission Report, *Parl. Papers*, 1890, Vol. 19, pp. 29–31.
21. J. A. Spender, *Life of Sir Henry Campbell-Bannerman* (London: Hodder & Stoughton, 1925), Vol. 1, p. 119. Of Campbell-Bannerman's views Spender says: 'Here speaks the old Liberal with his rooted dislike of continental ways and his suspicion of soldiers who "sit apart and cogitate".' Ironically, it was during Campbell-Bannerman's ministry that the army used the General Staff to undermine Britain's maritime strategy.
22. The distinction is made clear by Carl von Clausewitz, yet his nomenclature is not

universally accepted by politicians.
23. Except in the case where survival is the only object of the war, i.e., Finland in the Second World War.
24. Moral aspects aside, it was also probably more pronounced in the late 1880s than in the 1870s and early 1880s due to the impetus given to imperialism by the foundation of the Imperial Federation League (1884), General Gordon's death at Khartoum (1885) and the upsurge of imperial sentiment aroused by the festivities associated with the Queen's Golden Jubilee (1887).
25. Shown by their creation of a Royal Commission on empire defence. See Ch. 5 below.
26. W. C. B. Tunstall, 'Imperial Defence, 1815–1870', *Cambridge History of the British Empire* (Cambridge: Cambridge University Press, 1940), Vol. 2, p. 827. Such co-operation was obviously necessary to plan the withdrawal of the British troops from the self-governing colonies.
27. See C. A. Bodelsen, *Studies in Mid-Victorian Imperialism* (Copenhagen: Gyldendalske Boghandel, 1924); Knaplund, *Gladstone and Britain's Imperial Policy*; R. Schuyler, 'The Climax of Anti-Imperialism in England', *Political Science Quarterly*, 36 (December 1921). Schuyler contents himself with showing how the separation problem died. In his admirable study Bodelsen does the same in more detail. Writing later, Knaplund is constrained to show that Gladstone was never a separatist but favoured 'voluntarism'. For more recent studies, see Ronald Robinson, John Gallager and Alice Denny, *Africa and the Victorians* (New York: St Martin's Press, 1961); A. P. Thornton, *The Imperial Idea and Its Enemies: A Study in British Power* (London: Macmillan, 1959); C. C. Eldridge, *Mid-Victorian Imperialism* (London: Macmillan, 1973); *British Imperialism in the Nineteenth Century* (London: Macmillan, 1984); *England's Mission: The Imperial Idea in the Age of Gladstone and Disraeli, 1863–1880* (London: Macmillan, 1973); *Victorian Imperialism* (Atlantic Highlands, NJ: Humanities Press, 1978); and C. J. Lowe, *The Reluctant Imperialists*, 2 vols (New York: Macmillan, 1969).
28. C. P. Stacey, *Canada and the British Army 1846–71* (London: Longmans, Green, 1936), p. 251. Stacey speculates that only fear of domestic political consequences kept Gladstone's government from adopting a separatist policy.
29. It is not suggested here that Cabinet neglect of colonial questions was a trait peculiar to Gladstone's government.
30. Bodelsen, *Mid-Victorian Imperialism*, pp. 89–90. 'Churlish' was Lord Carnarvon's word for it. Granville George Leveson-Gower, 2nd Earl Granville (1815–91): Liberal politician; Vice-President of Board of Trade, 1848; Foreign Secretary 1851–52, 1870–74, 1880–85, Secretary of State for Colonies, 1868–70, 1886; KG, 1857; succeeded peerage, 1846.
31. Yet *The Times* expressed pleasure. See Bodelsen, *Mid-Victorian Imperialism*, p. 90.
32. Kimberley, 'Journal', 26 April 1870. John Wodehouse, 1st Earl of Kimberley (1886–1902): Liberal politician; Undersecretary for Foreign Affairs 1852–56, 1859–61; ambassador to Russia 1856–58; Lord Lieutenant of Ireland 1864–66; Lord Privy Seal 1868–70; Secretary for Colonies 1870–74; 1880–82; Secretary for India 1882–85, 1892–94; Foreign Secretary 1894–95.
33. The *Alabama* was a British-built Confederate commerce raider that preyed upon Northern shipping during the American Civil War. Following the war the US government claimed damages from the British government for the vessel's depredations. In 1872 Britain agreed to pay $15 million. The *Alabama*'s exploits drew attention to the trade destruction possibilities of such vessels.

34. Ibid., 8 May 1869.
35. Ibid., 22 July 1870.
36. S. C. Johnson, *British Emigration to North America* (London: George Routledge, 1913), p. 13. Certainly, contemporary military people did not interpret the troop withdrawals as intended to improve British–Colonial relations. Major-General T. Bland Strange, who served in Canada in the 1870s, wrote in 1903 that the Cardwell system tended to dissolve links between the British Army and colonial volunteers, and that officers were discouraged from serving in colonial forces.
37. Gladstone to Kimberley, 29 December 1871, KP: PC/A/8. Gladstone claimed to fear that Australian demands would conflict with Britain's existing trade commitments. This was a pretext for he admitted privately that the colonies 'maintain the closest and most affectionate relations with this country. (So does the Boa constrictor with the rabbit: but they are one-sided.) Now whatever the alleged precedents have done they have not as yet made fools of the British nation in the face of the whole world; and this is what I fear we stand in some danger of in the present case.'
38. Kimberley 'Journal', 2 March 1872. See also Schuyler, 'The Climax of Anti-Imperialism in England', p. 558. Apparently unaware of Kimberley's pronouncement, Schuyler maintains that 'anti-imperialism' died in 1870.
39. Kimberley 'Journal', 2 March 1872, and Gladstone to Kimberley, 29 December 1871, KP: PC/A/8. Gladstone informed Kimberley 'I think I am not like you if you are more or less prepared to concede everything except neutrality in war, and then to stop at that point.'
40. Only the more important quotations are given here. In almost every reference to Cabinet discussion of colonial affairs that Kimberley made in his 'Journal' he recorded the opinions for and against separation. Although he stated several times that he did not agree with separation, his preoccupation with the problem is significant.
41. Robert Biddulph, *Lord Cardwell at the War Office* (London: John Murray, 1904), p. 25. Edward, Viscount Cardwell (1813–86): Liberal politician; Secretary to Treasury 1845–46; President of Board of Trade, 1852–55; Secretary for Ireland, 1859–61; Secretary for Colonies 1864–66; Secretary of State for War 1868–74; peerage 1874.
42. See G. M. Young, *Victorian England: Portrait of an Age* (London: Oxford University Press, 1936), p. 104 and Howard D'Egville, *Imperial Defence and Closer Union* (London: P. S. King, 1913), p. 17. Young maintains that there was more than desire for army efficiency behind Cardwell's reforms. He wrote that Cardwell had attempted to hide his main work 'Behind the convenient clamour over abolition of purchase', a reference to another of the Secretary's reforms: the end to the system of purchasing officers' commissions. That Cardwell had little thought for empire defence, and was satisfied that England would be safe with fortified harbours in the British Isles and a hedgerow army was D'Egville's view. For more recent assessments of Cardwell's efforts and accomplishments, see Corelli Barnett, *Britain and her Army 1509–1970: A Military, Political and Social Survey* (London: Penguin, 1970); Brian Bond, 'The Effect of the Cardwell Reforms, 1874–1904', *Journal of the Royal United Services Institution*, 106 (1961): pp. 229–36; Arvel B. Erickson, 'Edward T. Cardwell, Peelite', *American Philosophical Society*, 49, 2 (1959): pp. 1–107; Jay Luvaas, *The Education of an Army: British Military Thought, 1815–1940* (Chicago: University of Chicago Press, 1964); and Albert Tucker, 'Army and Society in England 1870–1900: A Reassessment of the Cardwell Reforms', *Journal of British Studies*, 2 (1961): pp. 110–41.

43. Gladstone to the Queen, 19 June 1869, Royal Archives, Windsor Castle RA A38, no. 92 (hereafter referred to as RA). Gladstone hinted at the real reason for the withdrawal when he informed the Queen that some of the financial saving made possible by the troop withdrawals might be spent on improving defences at home.
44. Stacey, *Canada and the British Army*; A. J. Harrop, *England and the Maori Wars* (London: The New Zealand News, 1937).
45. A general introduction to the problem had been given by R. L Schuyler, 'The Recall of the Legions', *American Historical Review*, 26 (1920): pp. 18-36.
46. Stacey, *Canada and the British Army*, pp. 70, 72, 79.
47. Maori unrest in New Zealand and danger of a Fenian attack on Canada from the United States.
48. Stacey, *Canada and the British Army*, p. 258.
49. Bodelsen, *Studies in Mid-Victorian Imperialism*, p. 89; also Kimberley, 'Journal', 2 March 1872.
50. The office changed hands on 30 June 1870.
51. Kimberly to Gladstone (copy), 9 December 1870, and 3 July, 1871, KP: PC/A/8; Kimberley to Cardwell (copy), 2 December 1870, KP: PC/A/6.
52. A. Folsom, *The Royal Empire Society* (London: George Allen & Unwin, 1933), p. 24. Frederic Rogers, Baron Blachford (1811-89): Fellow of Oriel, 1833; barrister, Lincoln's Inn; registrar of joint stock companies, 1844; Commissioner of Lands and Emigration; Permanent Undersecretary of State for Colonies, 1860-71; GCMG, 1883; PC and peerage, 1871. Sir Robert Wyndham George Herbert (1813-1905): Fellow of All Souls 1854; DCL, 1862; Private Secretary to Gladstone, 1855; to Queensland, 1859; Premier Queensland, 1860-65; Assistant Secretary to Board of Trade 1868-70; Permanent Undersecretary at Colonial Office, 1871-92; GCB, 1902.
53. Kimberley, 'Journal', 22 July 1870. Of Carnarvon's speech Kimberley wrote: 'The motion was ingeniously framed so as to look like a mere vote of thanks to the Canadians for their gallant behaviour in the recent Fenian affair, under cover of which was slipped in a quasi censure of the Government for their policy with regard to the diminution of the garrisons, and an attempt was made to pledge us not to withdraw the troops from the colony. We exposed the artifice and the motion was withdrawn.' For general discussion of the reaction to the government's policy see Bodelsen, *Studies in Mid-Victorian Imperialism*, especially pp. 89-93.
54. George William Frederick Charles, 2nd Duke of Cambridge, Earl of Tipperary and Baron Culloden (1819-1904): born Hanover; brevet Colonel, 1837; Major-General, 1845; commanded division in Crimea with distinction; General Commander-in-Chief, 1856-95; Field-Marshal, 1862; personal aide-de-camp to the Queen, 1882.
55. Except by J. A. Spender, *Life of Sir Henry Campbell-Bannerman*, Vol. 1: Ch. 9. More recently, Brian Bond has rendered a sympathetic portrait of the Duke, whom he terms 'a soldier and a zealous administrator of the Army ...'. See Bond, 'The Late-Victorian Army', *History Today*, 11 (1961): pp. 616-24.
56. See Frederic Rogers, *Letters of Frederic Lord Blachford*, ed. George E. Marindin (London: John Murray, 1896). As evidence of the Duke's conservatism Lord Blachford recorded the fact that he determined the number of troops necessary to garrison Singapore on the basis of the number of reliefs necessary to make sentry duty tolerable for the men, rather than on the basis of the supposed requirements that Singapore's situation demanded. It serves also as striking testimony to the spirit in which he acted for the army.
57. Duke of Cambridge to General Storks, 14 September 1868, RA ADD.MSS.

58. Duke of Cambridge memorandum (private), 1868, RA ADD.MSS.
59. WO to CO 24 November 1881. PRO: CO 323/350-20577; Defence Committee memorandum, 5 June 1875, Carnarvon Papers, PRO 30/6-122. On this basis these four fortresses were withdrawn from consideration by a Royal Commission on Colonial Defence years later. When fortification of harbours both home and colonial, was considered in 1877 the fortresses were omitted from both groups.
60. WO to CO, 24 November 1881. PRO: CO 323/350-20577.
61. Duke of Cambridge, memorandum (private), 1868, RA ADD.MSS.
62. Duke of Cambridge to the Queen, 17 August 1869, RA E16, no. 91; Duke of Cambridge to Cardwell, 5 January 1869, RA ADD.MSS.
63. The Queen to Cardwell (copy), 2 March 1869, RA E58, no. 37.
64. Grey to Duke of Cambridge, 22 October 1869, RA E58, no. 59. Grey was sympathetic to Cardwell's ideas. See also Biddulph, *Lord Cardwell at the War Office*, p. 29. Cardwell had put almost the same views forward on 11 March 1869 in the House of Commons.
65. Duke of Cambridge to Grey, 28 October 1869, RA E16, no. 99.
66. It is interesting to note after the event that despite the opening of the Suez Canal the Cape maintained its position as a focal point for shipping for some time although the trade tended to become more sail-propelled than steam.

2

The Beginnings of Imperial Strategy: 1868–74

The years of the first Gladstone ministry saw the army repeatedly reel under the quick succession of shocks Cardwell administered through his reforms.[1] As a result, time that might have been devoted to empire strategic thought was fully occupied in adjusting to new forms and facts. The little general strategic vision that did exist was based on concepts embodied in the findings of the Royal Commission on the Defences of the United Kingdom (1859), and in the report of a House of Commons Select Committee on Colonial Defence (1861). The former body concluded that the navy, owing to the revolution in *matériel*, was no longer sufficient insurance against invasion, and that proper British strategy would see the army concentrated at home behind large-scale fortifications. This conclusion, which ignored the traditional role of the navy, was subsequently endorsed by the Commons Select Committee, and for many years British strategy, both at home and overseas, was based primarily on the concept of Britain as one huge well-manned fortress.[2] The 'Fortress England' mentality persisted throughout the period 1868–87 and operated parallel with, but not complementary to, other concepts that envisaged Britain's security as best ensured by a world-wide chain of defended bases for the effective deployment of the navy in the event of war.

An 1870 memorandum on army organization by General John Ayde, Director of Artillery at the War Office, did, it should be noted, point out the dangers of approaching national security questions as if the navy did not exist, explicitly stating that invasion of Britain 'without considerable previous warning' was an impossibility.[3] Ayde further maintained that elasticity of organization, not increased size, was the chief need of the army. This voice of reason, enunciating the historic strategic principles of British sea power, was not, however, heeded in 1870. Only a year earlier, the Duke of Cambridge had informed the Queen that militia and fixed defence guaranteed the security of England, and, because these alone were in good order, invasion was impossible.[4] The navy, with the exception of Ayde's lone voice, was not regarded by army planners as a vital part of either home or colonial defence.[5]

No doubt army authorities were aware of the navy's existence, and they did periodically pay lip-service to such subjects as the 'route to India' – certainly not a land route – but in the absence of any integrated strategic scheme the divergence between their views on 'Fortress England' and those on imperial defence is plain. What the army wanted, or at least what the Duke of Cambridge probably wanted, was financial backing to enlarge forces both at home and abroad. Such a development was impossible. Apart from pronounced tendencies toward retrenchment, Liberal views of the army's utility were largely based on the strategic priority of 'Fortress England', a theory for which the army was itself responsible. In such an atmosphere the need for additional troops at home, to say nothing of the situation overseas, was not admitted. The volunteers, doubtless, would make up any domestic deficit.

Nor was there any public protest against the 'Fortress England' idea by the Admiralty, although it is doubtful that senior naval officers ever seriously entertained the possibility that British command of the sea might be dangerously challenged by another power. Yet, while the army was attempting to absorb reforms in structure, the navy was undergoing a revolution in *matériel*.[6] Moreover, for a variety of reasons, not least among them the long period of general peace in Europe, imperial duties were conceived of in terms of local requirements, such as contending with Chinese piracy, African slavery, and diplomatic visiting. The attention of naval administrators tended to focus on the kinds of ship best suited to carry out such duties.

There was, for instance, between 1868 and 1875, a significant body of opinion at the Admiralty, exemplified by First Naval Lord Admiral Sir Alexander Milne which maintained that too much attention was paid to the problem of ironclads at home, and too little devoted to the type of ship that would best perform the navy's tasks overseas.[7] To such planners, adequate numbers of second- and third-class cruisers were the service's most pressing needs.[8] This was, of course, the great transitional period for the navy as regards ship design, and the launching of a ship without sails and spars, embracing in her design such innovations as screw propulsion, armour protection, iron construction, and turret guns, did not occur without considerable controversy.[9] Significantly, some of those clinging to the belief that steam would never completely supplant sail pointed to imperial duties to buttress their argument. Ships intended for distant stations should sport sails because Britain lacked adequate coal supplies abroad for the navy's operational needs in wartime. Hence in matters of both ship design and ship size navy people were conscious of imperial responsibilities.

The nature of their vision indicates, however, that they generally perceived defence in tactical or operational terms, rather than strategic ones. Hence, their views tended to be disjointed and local in nature, rather than embracing any concept of overall imperial responsibility. Yet, paradoxically, those who used imperial responsibilities as an argument to justify the continued retention of sailing cruisers unwittingly touched on the whole basis for imperial defence, theory, and practice for the next 30 years. It was not a strategic concept, but rather an economic commodity: coal.

Until the 1870s the problem of coal supply received little attention in so far as it affected the navy's imperial duties. In the early stages of the introduction of steam the Admiralty was more concerned with the ability of the new warship type to protect England from invasion, and since most of the foreign navies were still sail-propelled, this gap in naval thinking is understandable. Milne, however, while not formulating any overarching framework for the navy's imperial defence role, consistently advocated that new vessels should, as they were developed, be adaptable to the requirements of imperial, as well as home, defence. He was also concerned with the coal supply problem. In 1858, while a Junior Sea Lord at the Admiralty, and when the possibility of war with France loomed large, he at once thought of the colonial dimension of a naval war. He argued generally that the invention of the screw propeller had cut the navy's lead over France and rendered its defensive tasks more difficult. He thought, however, that perhaps the colonies might contribute to naval defence, although he did not specify how, and that the War Office take responsibility for any necessary fortifications overseas.[10] A month later he preserved an Admiralty paper suggesting that maintaining adequate coal supplies might be a difficulty in war time, especially in the colonies, and that screw colliers should be acquired to coal detached squadrons.[11]

By 1866, when it was generally accepted that steam was in the navy for good – although not that sail was *passé* – Milne's main criteria for ship construction seem to have been based on imperial requirements. Not first-class battleships, but second-class armoured cruisers were urgently needed to ensure that Britain could effectively protect her trade and commerce and fulfil her colonial responsibilities.[12] It is probable that Milne's preference for ships which would carry sailing rig was partly due to his distrust of novel naval architecture, but the fact that he founded his objections on imperial requirements is interesting, especially in view of his subsequent agitation for small vessels.[13]

Yet however interesting a study of Admiralty ship-building policy and the controversy it aroused between 1868 and 1874 might be, it would yield little to the student of empire defence.[14] In general, government policy toward the navy did not encourage *matériel* expansion. In late 1868 the *Army–Navy Gazette* looked with apprehension upon the advent of Gladstone's government, although it was not entirely convinced that the new First Lord, Hugh C. E. Childers, was bent upon a 'John Bright' type of retrenchment.[15] Nevertheless, the newspaper reminded its readers that Childers aimed to reduce the numbers of vessels in foreign squadrons, and noted his tendency to divide the Admiralty Board by making the naval lords directly and individually responsible to the First Lord, rather than to the corporate authority of the board.[16] The latter move, of course, accorded well with the Liberals' attitude toward government departments in general and the military departments in particular. In any case, large-scale naval expansion was out of the question after France's humiliating defeat in 1870, for, with the chief naval rival humbled, Gladstone firmly refused to increase the navy estimates.[17]

The policy of the government towards the navy was largely explicable, even defensible, on the grounds that these were years during which the service was divided within itself as to what direction naval architecture should take. The sinking of HMS *Captain* in 1870 seemed to vindicate opponents of technological innovation.[18] The even more radical mastless ironclad *Devastation* was only launched in 1872 and did not undergo sea trials until 1875. Until her success was assured the policy of naval planners was one of hesitation. Such hesitation, in turn, was easily exploited in political circles and 'do nothing' remained the policy of governments throughout most of the 1870s.[19] When in 1873 First Naval Lord Milne requested that a new committee be set up to report on the type and numbers of ships required by the navy, he was bluntly informed by First Lord George J. Goschen that the subject was a matter for the Cabinet, rather than the Admiralty, to decide.[20] This was an odd response from a First Lord, but characteristic from a Gladstonian one.

Coal, however, came to the brief attention of the Admiralty during the Franco-Prussian War when the consequences of British involvement were considered. At this point the Admiralty asked the Foreign Office for information regarding the length of time warships could shelter and coal in neutral ports, and in particular the frequency with which such refuge might be sought under international law.[21] Such a request clearly indicated that when the navy did consider theoretical questions of function in war, it did not think solely in terms of 'Fortress England'. The Admiralty now realized, however dimly, that one of England's greatest problems in any future war would be the availability of and security of access to coal supplies for the fleet. When the government changed in 1874 the new First Lord, George Ward Hunt, solicited reports from his board to draw attention to naval deficiencies.[22]

Outside governmental circles there were other influences ultimately directed towards a conception of imperial defence based on the supply of coal. Indeed, Gladstone's separationist tendencies became a live issue in the late 1860s and early 1870s because of revived public interest in empire. The phenomenal recent growth of the Australasian colonies and the federation of the Canadian Dominion (1867) served to focus British interest on colonial potentialities at a time when the Home economy was enduring intermittent recession.[23] This new interest was symbolized by the founding of the Royal Colonial Institute in 1868, and the unofficial colonial conference held at the Westminster Palace Hotel in 1871.[24] The latter provided a temporary platform; the Colonial Institute furnished a more permanent forum for those who did not find the idea of empire and its responsibilities repugnant. During the following years the idea that imperial trade was a vital rather than an incidental feature of Britain's economy came to be more appreciated. The fact that Disraeli flew a political kite extolling the importance of empire in his famous Crystal Palace speech (1872) testified to the symbolic power the concept continued to exert.[25] Nevertheless early ideas of a united empire were vague, and were based more on distrust of Gladstone's colonial attitude and on emigration possibilities than on awareness of imperial trade potential and defence requirements. The only apparent thing that the embryo imperialists held in common in 1870 was distrust of little Englandism: yet the beginning of something larger was apparent.

With regard to empire defence it is noteworthy that those who supported both the 1871 conference and the Royal Colonial Institute drew their strength largely from those dissatisfied with the general policy of withdrawing troops from the colonies, more particularly the government's handling of the situation in New Zealand.[26] Their objections thus remained particular and local and had little to do with general principles of empire defence. The chief concern of the conferees was encouraging emigration. Only one speaker at the Westminster Palace Hotel gathering dealt with defence as a topic about which conceptions of imperial unity might revolve.[27] The economic value of empire was no more than instinctively sensed by these pioneer imperialists, who were only dimly aware of either their common ground or their mission.

There was, however, by 1871, an available body of doctrine on the connection between empire, trade, coal and defence. It had been outlined four years earlier by Captain J. C. R. Colomb, a retired officer of the Royal Marine Artillery.[28] He stated clearly that success in war was generally a prize gained by the power that made its base of operations secure through the maintenance of undisturbed communications. In Britain's case, he emphasized, this was a naval task and he protested strongly against the 'Fortress England' mentality. In 1873 the Royal Colonial Institute provided the platform from which Colomb expounded his views on imperial defence and condemned the military policy of the government and the War Office alike.[29] This speech clearly demonstrates that Colomb was the first Englishman to understand the requirements for an effective strategy which was truly imperial. He provided the theory for subsequent empire defence planners, and it was along the lines he indicated that imperial strategy evolved for the next 59 years.

Colomb criticized the troop withdrawal policy, not because he disagreed with the withdrawals themselves, nor even because he detected Gladstonian economic motives, but because the policy seemed to be based upon the 'Fortress England' idea rather than on the idea of creating imperial strategic reserve.[30] Like Disraeli he, too, issued a challenge to the new age – the Age of Empire – but did so in reasoned terms rather than by emotional appeals. Colomb stated flatly that times had changed. The question of the commercial value of the empire was not a question for academic discussion. Rather, Britain's dependence upon empire trade was the key factor in any claim to greatness.[31] The next war in which Britain was involved would be one in which the enemy attacked India and British commerce. 'Fortress England' should have died with this speech. The results, however, were more gradual. Indeed, Colomb's views seem not to have caused much of a stir when first uttered.[32] Within a year, however, official attention was given to the problem of empire protection. Slowly, it came to be generally appreciated that war scares meant concern for imperial communications, and anxious glances at the state of the navy, not to the number of guns in English forts.

Colomb did not argue that the defence of England was unimportant. On the contrary, he maintained that the pre-1860 tendency to neglect the security of the home islands by dispersing naval resources all over the empire was just as reprehensible as the 'Fortress England' strategy.[33] Moreover, Colomb appreciated and sympathized with the political logic that led to the government's empire defence policy: the various self-governing colonies should pay for their own defence even as Britain had to pay for hers. He maintained, however, that it was unwise to treat all of the self-governing colonies as if they were alike. Not all the colonies could afford to defend themselves on the scale that their strategic location might render necessary. It would have been better, instead, had the government been guided more strongly by military considerations, and he outlined his ideas on these with greater precision.

As in 1867 he argued that the first principle of war involved the disposition of forces in such a manner that the base of operations was secured and free communication assured. This point was illustrated by reference to the Royal Commission of 1859 which reasoned that the Channel fleet could not successfully secure England against invasion because it would be scattered in order to protect empire trade.[34] Colomb's point was that Britain's seaborne trade was at its most vulnerable at its point of convergence at the mouth of the Channel: hence this was the most important, though by no means the only, point that the navy should defend. The combination of national economic requirements with strategic concepts was thus made clear.

From this point of departure he extended his reasoning to cover trade defence in areas of lesser priority but of no less important nature. Large fleets should be concentrated in the Channel and Mediterranean, and detached squadrons sent forth to cover the rest of the empire. The success of these overseas squadrons would depend on the security of the base of operations selected for each. Hence the importance of wartime availability of coal supplies which would enable distant squadrons to operate effectively and at the same time deny these coaling facilities to enemy cruisers.

Colomb argued emphatically that the defence of imperial bases should not be solely the navy's duty. Such responsibility for purely local defence would gravely detract from the fleet's capacity to protect trade at sea, its primary mission. This principle – that all naval bases should support rather than hinder fleet operations – was strictly in accordance with contemporary Admiralty policy. Colomb maintained that local defence of the bases should be an army responsibility. He furthermore enumerated those he regarded most crucial to imperial security: Halifax (Nova Scotia), Bermuda, Bahamas, Jamaica, Antigua (all in the British West Indies); Gibraltar, Malta (both in the Mediterranean); Aden (Indian Ocean); Bombay, Cape Comerin (both in India); King George Sound (Western Australia); Trincomalee (Ceylon); Singapore (Malaysia); and Hong Kong (China).[35] Suez he mentioned wistfully: the Canal had opened in 1869 but another two years would pass before Disraeli's government purchased 40 per cent interest, and another eight before Britain occupied Egypt. He tentatively added to this list Sierra Leone (West Africa); Ascension Island, St Helena (both in the South Atlantic); Simons Bay (Cape Colony); Mauritius (Indian Ocean); the Falkland Islands (South Atlantic); Sydney, (New South Wales); and Fiji (Pacific Ocean) if it was a British possession. Colomb probably regarded this second group of bases as somewhat secondary to, but hardly less essential than, the first, but he lacked the statistical information necessary to render a proper evaluation. Despite this deficiency the general strategic framework he set forth ultimately proved to be notably accurate, and his energetic plea for some reasonable base between Vancouver Island, British Columbia, and Sydney proved to be a recurrent strategic theme even after Fiji became British in 1875.[36]

Colomb posed questions as well as providing answers. To what degree should India, Australia and New Zealand contribute to this defence and where would the garrisons came from?[37] He advocated a unified command for the whole empire defence effort, but admitted that his ideas with regard to specific defence arrangements were largely impressionistic. Adequate answers could only be expected from the report of a Royal Commission set up to deal with the entire subject.[38] He strongly advocated the appointment of such a body.

While he only indicated particular paths tentatively, Colomb laid down his general principles authoritatively. These principles were eventually accepted by the government of the United Kingdom. Ironically, too, they had been part of accepted British naval doctrine in the eighteenth century. Technological circumstances had dramatically altered since then, however, and Colomb's thought was significant not simply because it brought the roles of the two armed forces into sharp focus and revived old navy trade protection formulas, for he adapted the latter so that they fitted contemporary conditions by his instinctive grasp of the fact that modern trade movement and modern trade security depended on the constant abundance and availability of coal.[39]

The coal problem had never been seriously considered before in so far as it affected imperial security, and indeed, even when coal supplies came to be generally recognized as vital requirements for naval efficiency overseas, the supply problem was never systematically investigated by a competent body. In 1869 the Admiralty did conduct investigations into the best type of coal for use in British warships.[40] They concluded that British coal was superior, and that in case of difficulty securing domestic supplies acceptable results could be obtained by mixing British and foreign coal. This conclusion accorded, not unnaturally, with naval custom. More to the point, the coal problem seems only to have interested the Admiralty to this degree. Naval administrators were concerned with using the most efficient fuel, and at moments of international tension they gave thought to coal supplies for overseas squadrons, but otherwise the strategic dimension of the issue seems not to have exercised their minds.

Yet the Admiralty was regularly forced to consider topics related to coal. In the midst of Gladstone's first administration the House of Commons was presented with the report of a select committee on domestic coal supplies.[41] This investigation followed hard upon the heels of another report, that of a Royal Commission appointed to enquire into the several matters relating to coal in the United Kingdom.[42] The Admiralty participated in both investigations by producing general statements concerning the annual naval coal consumption and its buying methods but provided no details of how coal was distributed. Declining numbers of sailing merchant vessels – which often carried coal as ballast on outbound voyages – generated delivery problems for British coal in southeast Asia. Even as early as 1868 a high proportion of the coal supplies at Hong Kong, Singapore, Mauritius and Shanghai came from New South Wales (Australia) mines.[43] Yet when one considers that non-naval coal supplies at Singapore were nearly 1,000,000 tons in 1869, and that consumption of coal in the entire Royal Navy as late as 1872 was only 2,000,000 tons, it is evident that supply was not the greatest worry.[44] It also illuminates why imperial security hinged more on defence of existing coal stocks than on ensuring the transport of continuous supplies.[45]

Individual naval administrators and officers did appreciate the centrality of coal supplies to effective empire defence. Milne, of course, had shown an ongoing interest in questions of imperial trade security when general questions of naval policy were being discussed. He also recognized that the question of coal supplies would be important in future wars. Similarly, in 1870 the Commander of the Australian Squadron, Commodore H. O. Stirling, wrote to the Admiralty pointing out that there were large stocks of undefended coal at Albany, on King George Sound (Western Australia) and requesting permission to destroy them in case of war, lest they fell into the hands of enemy raiders.[46] Stirling's letter, along with growing Admiralty realization of the intermittent nature of the availability of coal supplies in neutral ports, served to underline the importance of coal in the imperial naval problem.

Once the hampering influence of the Gladstone government was removed the Admiralty began to regard the problems of empire defence on a more coal-conscious basis, though largely via the steam–sail controversy.[47] The new First Lord, George Ward Hunt, had hardly assumed office when protagonists of various schools of thought on ship design urged that he rectify Gladstone's parsimony by adopting their particular views.[48] When he asked the advice of the naval members of the board, both sail and steam proponents leant heavily on the problem of empire responsibility in arguing their cases.[49] Beyond the opinions of the naval members of the board that of Vice-Admiral Sir Geoffrey Phipps Hornby, then commanding the Channel squadron, was also cited.[50] Phipps Hornby was the only officer to strongly urge the retention and encouragement of sailing tonnage in the navy, arguing not on grounds of strategic or tactical utility, but simply because he claimed that sail produced finer qualities in the sailor than did steam vessels. Second Naval Lord John Walter Tarleton saw the uses of a steam navy somewhat differently: heavy ironclads like *Devastation* would, he argued, be most usefully employed by serving as stationary batteries for the protection of strategic bases abroad since commerce protection would be the prime naval duty. The ships to be used for commerce protection – cruisers – must combine sail and steam because of the uncertainty of coal supplies. Hence, these cruisers should be able to patrol under sail and husband precious coal for chasing enemy commerce-raiders.[51] Lord Gilford, the Junior Naval Lord, was the most fanatical pro-sail member of the board, and buttressed his prejudice with the stock argument that sails would be essential in wartime owing to coal shortages. He even opposed the restricted use of mastless turret ships advocated by Tarleton.[52]

First Naval Lord Milne's opinions revealed a curious mixture of anti-steam and pro-Empire thought.[53] He argued that the varied duties of the navy were not adequately appreciated in ship design debates, and maintained that these duties required above all fast cruisers. The next war, he opined, would not witness the clash of large fleets in European waters.

Rather, British naval supremacy would be generally recognized and the enemy would confine its attacks to British shipping and colonial possessions. Australian waters, not the Mediterranean, would, he claimed, be the centre of a future naval war.[54] Simultaneously, however, Milne steadfastly maintained that coal shortage would force the retention of sail on vessels destined for empire protection. Hence, although his dislike for steam was discernible, he based his arguments firmly on the problem of empire security.[55] The coal problem genuinely worried him, even if he tended to avoid confronting it head-on in favour of advocating sail.

Pro-sail or not, Milne's recommendations were significant: empire needs were clearly articulated in the context of Admiralty strategic thought.[56] Nor should too much be made of more strident arguments – like Gilford's – in favour of wind traps. Three years prior to Ward Hunt's arrival at the Admiralty, the Committee on Designs had concluded (not without regret) that the combination of sails with first-class fighting efficiency was impossible, and that the navy would be better served by building heavily armoured, mastless vessels which would operate from 'centres of naval power', presumably defended bases.[57] To be sure, the committee's recommendation was too far advanced to be immediately embraced, but by the mid-1870s the Admiralty was largely committed to a steam navy, albeit one in which most ships continued to sport auxiliary sails. Gilford's and Hornby's opinions were rearguard actions: more in the nature of grumbles and protests than of substantive opposition to Admiralty design policy.

Ward Hunt had solicited his advisers' opinions in hopes of convincing Disraeli's government to embark on an ambitious shipbuilding programme, but the prime minister and the Chancellor of the Exchequer, Sir Stafford Northcote, were little more receptive to increases in the navy estimates than Gladstone had been, and the First Lord had to content himself with a much-reduced programme. Nor did his campaign result in any important developments in the field of imperial defence at the governmental level. Nevertheless, the papers by Milne and his colleagues constituted a beginning, even as the pro-empire Lord Carnarvon's appointment as Colonial Secretary brightened prospects on the Colonial Office side.

More crucially, the navy's new concern over empire defence did not fade away. By mid 1874 the Admiralty was clearly conscious of the growing maritime defence liabilities of increasing imperial population and trade.[58] In December of that year Milne circulated two additional memoranda again stressing the need for a reserve of fast cruisers for empire duties.[59] He was, furthermore, worried that the emphasis in political circles on home defence would lead to neglect of the coal question since it involved preparedness abroad. He also began to face the coal supply problem realistically, for although he still maintained that the retention of sail was necessary, he did so in a less positive manner. Coaling stations, he admitted, would be the great problem in a future war and they must be maintained and extended. Indeed, he suggested that new ones be set up at the Falkland Islands, St Helena, Cape York, King George Sound (both in Australia) and Port Said (Egypt).

Although Milne's interest in the coal station problem continued to grow with the years, the Admiralty soon ceased to be the active agent in drawing attention to the coaling station problem. The board was aware that war coaling stations would play an important part in operational efficiency in any future conflict, yet at the same time it held that the fleet's wartime obligations were to engage the enemy's main force and to protect commerce, not the responsibility of guarding its own strategic bases. The idea may have come from Sir J. C. R. Colomb, or it may have been Milne's alone. Regardless of its origin, the subject of local coaling station and overseas base defence was referred to the War Office where, in the office of the Inspector-General of Fortifications, it found a permanent home.

Specifically, the subject was turned over to Colonel Sir William Francis Drummond Jervois, RE, who had been Assistant Inspector-General of Fortifications at the War Office since 1856. In 1857 he was appointed Secretary to the Defence Committee, a permanent professional War Office deliberative body chaired by the Duke of Cambridge. In 1859 Jervois prepared plans for the committee on the defences of London. The same year he served as Secretary to the Royal Commission to inquire into the defences of the United Kingdom, and in 1862 he became Director of Works for Fortifications and Under Inspector-General of Fortifications. Having thus been much involved in the preparation and execution of defences for the security of the home islands in an invasion-conscious era, he turned to the promotion of efficient defence of the colonies, and between 1863 and 1874 he was almost constantly travelling and advising on matters of colonial defences. His knighthood was the Order of St Michael and St George and hence more in recognition of his services to Canada than to Great Britain.[60] He seems to have been able, yet with little influence to assist him on promotion's path. At one time the Queen herself barred his way to becoming Inspector-General of Fortifications, and although the Duke of Cambridge's testimonials to his ability were unreserved, commendation stopped at that point.[61] It was this man, balked in his army career and on the verge of entering the ranks of Colonial Office governors, who composed the memorandum constituting the first official statement of the problems involved in imperial defence, and who provided some connection between seemingly hitherto unrelated facts.

Jervois' memorandum resulted from the Admiralty's request for army assistance in the matter of coaling station defence.[62] He completed his survey of 'the defenceless condition of our Coaling Stations and Naval Establishments Abroad' and his proposed remedies for their defencelessness on 7 January 1875. He began by listing the bases that the Admiralty considered inadequately defended. They were not set forth in any priority: Port Royal (Jamaica); Antigua; Ascension; Simons Bay (Cape Colony); Port Louis (Mauritius); Trincomalee (Ceylon); Singapore; Hong Kong; King George Sound (Western Australia); Esquimalt (Vancouver Island); and the Falkland Islands. Of these bases King George Sound and the Falkland Islands were not recognized naval bases or official coaling stations, but were included among the places suggested by Milne in 1874 and deemed more important than St Helena, Cape York (Australia) and Port Said.[63] Certainly the list was not as adventurous as that outlined by Colomb in his 1873 lecture, although Malta, Gibraltar, Halifax and Bermuda were omitted from Jervois' list because they were considered to have been already provided for in the votes covering home defences.

Jervois blamed the undefended state of these places upon politicians: 'the policy of withdrawing troops from abroad and concentrating them in England, has fostered an opinion, felt perhaps rather than expressed, that all expenditure on places beyond the seas should be curtailed to the uttermost, and that this country need only be concerned with the defence of England.' This point of view was partially true and its emphasis was useful, yet at the same time it made insufficient allowance for the fact that the 'Fortress England' policy had been deliberately fostered by the War Office, and as such was gladly accepted by politicians for reasons of economy. Also Jervois' condemnation overlooked that fact that even Gladstone and Cardwell, when thinking in military terms, drew a distinction between imperial and colonial bases.

The security of these bases, was, Jervois stated, 'essential for Imperial interests'. 'I submit', he wrote, 'that the Imperial Government should provide for their defence', and he repeated Colomb's argument that it was no longer a question of simply maintaining sure movement of overseas trade necessary for prosperity. Rather, the disruption of that trade would mean Britain's disaster. Assuring that the flow remained uninterrupted was a prime function of the Royal Navy, which, besides fighting fleet engagements, would have to be able to deal with privateers 'such as the *Alabama*'. This function was hardly new to the navy, Jervois admitted, although its importance had grown due to increases in both population and trade. The new factor confounding imperial defence was the navy's dependence upon coal, for the steam-era fleet could not keep the sea for such lengths of time as its sail-propelled precursor, a lack of mobility and strategic reach aggravated by the frequent need of iron vessels for hull-scraping and functional repairs. Hence the great importance of coaling and repair stations situated with proper regard to fleet requirements.

According to Jervois, the need for a network of logistical bases generated two further defensive alternatives. Either the navy mounted guard over its depots or it did not. If it did, its effective striking force was reduced. If it did not, bases risked being at the mercy of a marauding enemy in wartime. If any fell to such attacks, the ships of a steam-driven navy in affected areas 'would be rendered as useless as if they had been all sunk or captured'.

Jervois then made a strong appeal for the value of fixed over floating defences, claiming that 11 coaling stations could be made secure by means of fortifications for the construction price of two first-class ironclads. Maintenance for fortifications was also cheaper, but even more important was the fact that the ships acting as stationary floating defences would diminish the seagoing resources of the fleet for its crucial strategic tasks. He thus firmly grasped the first naval principle of imperial defence, namely that 'the fleet is required for cruising, and cannot be kept in harbour to guard its own supplies'.[64]

The manpower problem involved in implementing his proposal for fixed, land-based defences was not, he claimed, pressing, since six of the bases set forth already possessed sufficient troops and Ascension and the Falkland Islands were garrisoned by Royal Marines. There were, in fact, already some 6,400 men then defending overseas bases, although Jervois pointed out that these men were 'nearly all of them useless for resisting an attack by sea; because they have not the means at their disposal for making ... resistance'. This, he charged, was a ridiculous situation. To place every one of the bases he listed in a proper state of defence would, he estimated, cost some £950,000. He urged that there be no delay in placing the overseas bases in a condition of readiness, and that the process be connected with the permanent scheme for home defences.[65]

Jervois' memorandum constituted a landmark in the history of imperial defence, yet its traceable origins, beyond the Admiralty's request for assistance, are obscure. Coming as it did, hard on the heels of the most recent airing of Colomb's views on imperial strategy, it is possible, and indeed probable, that Jervois borrowed heavily from him, though direct evidence is lacking to prove the point.[66] The memorandum may also owe something to Milne, who was in any event the driving force behind the Admiralty's request. On the other hand, Jervois, having spent long years in travel gaining experience in both defence and imperial matters, may have come to his opinions quite independently. It is most likely, however, that the memorandum was indebted to all three sources. Such an advanced and well-reasoned conception is unlikely to have been the product of one War Office official alone.

Whatever the source of inspiration, there was no immediate practical result. Jervois left the War Office and accepted the governorship of Straits' Settlements (Malaysia) in April 1875, only four months after his memorandum was completed, and hence he could not personally urge his proposals on his superiors. His conclusions and recommendations did impress Secretary of State for War Gathorne Gathorne-Hardy sufficiently that printed copies were circulated to and considered by the Cabinet.[67] No action was taken, however, and there for the moment the matter rested. Yet once Jervois was safely ensconced in Singapore, the Inspector-General of Fortifications quietly adopted his ideas and this step soon generated results.[68] Jervois' memorandum and its general acceptance at the War Office meant that a rational concept of imperial defence, based on solid strategic principles, had gained the dignity of departmental support.[69]

What was gained in the acquisition of official support was at the same time tempered by the general lack of public support, however. Had these strategic ideas been forced upon an unwilling War Office by public outcry, then imperial defence might become a political issue of some import and hence rested on a dependable popular base. What actually happened was that a reasonable idea without wide public support was early acquired by a department of state that enjoyed little confidence in either political party. Dependent for its vigour upon this suspect source, it languished until emergency called attention to its salient conclusions and recommendations. Even then it did not fully emerge from the departmental and professional shroud to which Jervois unintentionally committed it. Its value remained concealed within the pigeon-holes of Whitehall.

NOTES

1. For a general treatment of the Cardwell reforms see Robert Biddulph, *Lord Cardwell at the War Office* (London: John Murray, 1904). Biddulph's account teeters on the brink of hagiography: he was Cardwell's Private Secretary. For more recent works touching on Cardwell's work, see Corelli Barnett, *Britain and her Army 1509–1970: A Military, Political, and Social Survey* (London: Penguin, 1970); Brian Bond, 'The Effect of the Cardwell Reforms, 1874–1904', *Journal of the Royal United Services Institution*, 106 (1961): pp. 229–36; Arvel B. Erickson, 'Edward T. Cardwell, Peelite', *American Philosophical Society*, 1959: pp. 1–107; Jay Luvaas, *The Education of an Army: British Military Thought, 1815–1940* (Chicago: University of Chicago Press, 1964); and Albert Tucker, 'Army and Society in England 1870–1900: A Reassessment of the Cardwell Reforms', *Journal of British Studies*, 2 (1961): pp. 110–41.
2. W. C. B. Tunstall, 'Imperial Defence, 1815–1870', *Cambridge History of the British Empire* (Cambridge: Cambridge University Press), Vol. 2, pp. 824–9. [Ed. note: The view that Britain's traditional 'blue-water' strategy was supplanted during the Victorian era by the 'brick and mortar' school reflects the consensus of historical opinion for the past half-century. See, for instance, Arthur Marder, *The Anatomy of British Sea Power: A History of British Naval Policy in the Pre-Dreadnought Era, 1880–1905* (repr. edn, New York: Pantheon Books, 1976); Oscar Parkes, *British Battleships, 1860–1950* (London: Seeley Service, 1957); Michael Partridge, *Military Planning for the Defence of the United Kingdom, 1815–1870* (Westport, CT: Greenwood, 1989); Stanley Sandler, *The Emergence of the Modern Capital Ship* (Newark: University of Delaware Press, 1979); and Donald Schurman, *The Education of a Navy: The Evolution of British Naval Strategic Thought, 1867–1914* (London: Cassell, 1965). Some recent works, however, have begun to qualify this picture, stressing that the navy remained the

first and most vital line of British defence, notwithstanding the attention that 'brick and mortar' advocates attracted. See Andrew Lambert, 'The Shield of Empire 1815–1895', in J. R. Hill (ed.), *The Oxford Illustrated History of the Royal Navy* (New York: Oxford University Press, 1995); John Beeler, 'Steam, Strategy, and Schurman: Imperial Defence in the Post-Crimean Era', in Keith Neilson and Greg Kennedy (eds), *Far-Flung Lines: Essays in Imperial Defence in Honour of Donald Mackenzie Schurman* (London: Frank Cass, 1997); and idem, *British Naval Policy in the Gladstone–Disraeli Era* (Stanford, CA: Stanford University Press, 1997).]

3. John Ayde, 'Memorandum on Army Organization', 1870, PRO: WO 33/22. This memorandum, interestingly enough, pointed out that 'fortress England' conceptions of defence were largely based upon the Duke of Cambridge's opinions on Britain's vulnerability to invasion and remained valid only so long as another continental power showed the capacity to challenge British naval supremacy. Ayde thought especially of France, powerful in 1848 and militarily humbled in 1870.

4. Duke of Cambridge to General Grey, 2 April 1869, RA E16, 60.

5. Ayde, 'Memorandum on Army Organization'.

6. James Phinney Baxter, *The Introduction of the Ironclad Warship* (Cambridge, MA: Harvard University Press, 1933). Yet despite this admirable work, and the detailed research on warship structure in Thomas Brassey's *The Royal Navy: Its Strength, Resources, and Administration* (London: Longmans, Green, 1882), the personal story of the rearguard action of sailors who believed in sail against the new steam navy (1868–78) has never been properly recounted. [Ed. note: since Professor Schurman wrote these words, several studies dealing partly or wholly with Admiralty shipbuilding policy and technological change, 1860–80 have been published. See in particular Robert Gardiner (ed.), *Steam, Steel, and Shellfire: The Steam Warship 1815–1905* (London: Conway Maritime Press, 1992); C. I. Hamilton, *Anglo-French Naval Rivalry, 1840–1870* (London: Oxford University Press, 1994); Parkes, *British Battleships, 1860–1950*; N. A. M. Rodger, 'British Belted Cruisers', *Mariner's Mirror*, 64, no. 1 (1978): pp. 23–35; idem, 'The Design of the *Inconstant*', *Mariner's Mirror*, 61, no. 1 (1975): pp. 9–22; idem, 'The First Light Cruisers', *Mariner's Mirror*, 65, no. 3 (1975): pp. 209–30; and Sandler, *The Emergence of the Modern Capital Ship*. The innate conservatism of naval administrators during the period is questioned by Andrew Lambert, *Battleships in Transition: The Creation of the Steam Battlefleet 1815–1860* (London: Conway Maritime Press, 1984); and Beeler, 'Steam Strategy and Schurman: Imperial Defence in the Post-Crimean Era', in idem, *British Naval Policy in the Gladstone–Disraeli Era*.]

7. Alexander Milne (1806–96): Junior Lord of Admiralty 1847–59; Commander-in-Chief West Indies and North American Station, 1860–64; First Naval Lord, 1866–68; Commander-in-Chief Mediterranean, 1869–70; First Naval Lord, 1872–76; KCB, and Rear Admiral, 1858; Vice-Admiral, 1866; Baronet, 1876; chair, Colonial Office Defence Committee, 1877–78; member Carnarvon Commission, 1879–82.

8. Milne, Admiralty Board memorandum, January 1867, Milne Papers, National Maritime Museum (hereafter referred to as NMM): MLN/143/1. Also preserved clippings: *Army and Navy Gazette*, 26 December, 1868 and 2 January 1869, NMM: MLN/143/5, commenting on need for cruisers as opposed to battleships.

9. These changes were embodied in HMS *Devastation*. This vessel of revolutionary design was without sail, carried only 4–35-ton MLR (muzzle-loading rifle) guns (*Warrior*, 1860, carried 48–68-pounders) that were turret-operated; armour-

plated and screw-propelled; launched 1871. See Fred T. Jane, *The British Battle Fleet* (London: The Library Press, 1915), 1: pp. 312–15. Although completed and tried in 1873 she was not fully tested at sea until 1875. See cutting from *Pembrokeshire Advertiser*, 19 December 1874, NMM: MLN/144/6, containing speech by the designer of the *Devastation* and former Chief of Naval Construction, Edward J. Reed. This hesitation occurred despite the fact that Reed's successor at the Construction Department (and supposed rival), Nathaniel Barnaby, supported the design from the point of view of seaworthiness. See Barnaby's Confidential Paper, 10 January 1873, NMM: MLN/148/4.

10. Milne, 'Most Confidential Memorandum by Sir Alexander Milne in reply to Three Questions put by the Queen ... to the Board of Admiralty Early 1858', NMM: MLN/142/2. The Queen requested information on naval ability to deal with a war against France.

11. Opinion of the Law Officers of the Crown on the supply of Coal from Neutral Ports to Her Majesty's vessels in time of war, 10 June 1858. NMM: MLN/142/3 (3). [Ed. note: for Milne's concern about the availability of coal supplies, see especially Milne to Dundas (copy), 25 June 1859, NMM: MLN/142/3 (5). Milne's letter to the First Naval Lord is worth quoting at length for it vividly underscores the importance he attached to the subject:

> My dear Dundas,
>
> I am getting more than anxious about this very important question of Depots of Coal all over the World. I have, as you are aware, brought this subject before the Board on several occasions, and it has been submitted from the Storekeeper General of the Navy to know what supplies are to be sent to the different Foreign Stations; the large number of Ships which have been commissioned, renders it necessary that some steps should be taken; the Stores at Gibraltar and Malta have been largely increased, and so far as the present wants of the Mediterranean Fleet is [sic] concerned, there is no difficulty at these two places, but no arrangements have been made for any other Ports except Corfu. If Ships are sent to Alexandria, there is no coal Depot there, although we may obtain some moderate supply from the P. and O. Company. The movement of Ships is regulated by the Cabinet, and is entirely unknown to myself as a Member of the Board, or to the Storekeeper General; therefore it is impossible to make arrangements for coal, for such movements. Thus at Naples, Leghorn, Genoa, &c, we have no coal; the Captains of Ships must therefore purchase in the market, when they require supplies, but most likely there will be none to purchase; the only other course which the Admiralty can adopt, is for three or four Screw Colliers to be attached to the Mediterranean Fleet, to draw supplies from Malta; this ought to be done.
>
> But there is a much larger question for consideration. – Are we to prepare for War? If so, Coal Depots should be at once established all over the World, where our ships are now employed, and where they are likely to require supplies. The Members of this Board are entirely ignorant of the intentions of the Government, and therefore this becomes a Cabinet Question. – If war should be declared, our Foreign Stations will not be found ready for war operations; although we keep in store, about one year's supply for the casual wants of the Service, that small store would be found totally inefficient [sic: insufficient]. What is to be done? My own opinion on this subject should be at once submitted to the new First Lord; I therefore write to you as the Senior Naval Lord, with whom rests the Service afloat, that you may take such steps as the emergency may demand. –
>
> The expenditure of Coal by our Ships, is one tenth of the Horse Power of the Engines. This is a fair average. Thus, in the Mediterranean by the return of the 1st

June, the Horse Power of the Mediterranean Fleet was 12,830, or equal to an expenditure of 1,283 Tons per day, and say Steam is used two days in each week, the expenditure of Coal would be equal to 2,566 Tons per week; but taking it at one half of this, the monthly expenditure would be about 5,000 Tons a Month [sic] or 60,000 in the year, equal to about £100,000. –

If War should be suddenly declared, we would require large supplies at the Cape, Ascension, Trincomalee, Hong Kong, Jamaica, Barbadoes, Antigua &c. In fact, no less a sum than £250,000 would have to be <u>at once</u> laid out, in the shipment of about 100,000 Tons of Coal abroad.

The question is a momentous one, and one for the serious consideration of the Government; and it all centres in this [sic]; Is the Admiralty to keep up a supply of coal on all Foreign Stations, equal to the contingencies of a War? If not, then when War may be declared, our Fleets will be crippled for want of coals.
Pray see to this
& Believe me
Sincerely yours
[signed] A Milne

12. Milne, Admiralty memorandum, December 1866, NMM: MLN/143/2.
13. Milne, Admiralty memoranda (2), June 1867, NMM: MLN/143/2. These papers show the sail-lovers' mentality in their emphasis on the tactical value of manoeuvrability. This was a stock argument of pro-sail people, along with the claim that sail exercise produced a better breed of sailor.
14. The navy was quietly doing its world police duty but there was little talk of changed conceptions of empire defence, and no discussion of empire strategy except that dealt with herein. (This note is based on a general study of Milne's papers.) Those interested in Admiralty ship-building policy are recommended to George Ballard, *The Black Battlefleet*, ed. N. A. M. Rodger (Annapolis, MD: Naval Institute Press, 1980); Gardiner (ed.), *Steam, Steel, and Shellfire: The Steam Warship 1815–1905*; Parkes, *British Battleships*; Rodger, 'British Belted Cruisers', idem, 'HMS *Inconstant*', idem, 'The First Light Cruisers', and Sandler, *Emergence of the Modern Capital Ship*.
15. *Army and Navy Gazette*, editorial, 26 December 1868, preserved in NMM: MLN/143/5.
16. See Beeler, *British Naval Policy in the Gladstone–Disraeli Era*, pp. 34–6, 83–101. The policy of reducing overseas squadrons was begun by the preceding naval administration of Henry T. L. Corry, on impetus furnished largely by Chancellor of the Exchequer Benjamin Disraeli.
17. See Gladstone to the Queen, 23 July 1870, RA I-63, no. 63 and Ponsonby to the Queen, 26 July 1870, RA I-63, no. 171. Gladstone increased defence estimates though a Vote of Credit upon the outbreak of the Franco-German War (July 1870). This move was possibly attributable to the Queen's insistence, for on 16 July 1870 the prime minister had written that the defence measures were greater in 1870 than any time since 1815, and on 18 December 1870 wrote that the estimates were lower than in 1869 but many Liberals still thought them too high. See also RA A-40, no. 37 and A-42, no. 85.
18. The *Captain* was an experimental design combining screw-propulsion, iron construction, armour, turret-mounted ordnance, and full sailing rig. She sank off Cape Finisterre on 6 September 1870. Although the stability faults of that particular ship were explicable, anti-steam members of the Admiralty used the fate of the *Captain* as a warning against the adoption of new designs. See Jane, *The British Battle Fleet*, Vol. 1, pp. 288–91.

THE BEGINNINGS OF IMPERIAL STRATEGY: 1868–74

19. Edward Reed, ex-chief of Naval Construction wrote in 1872 that setting up a Committee on Admiralty Designs 'was on the part of the government a deliberate encouragement for a time of public mistrust in iron-clad fleet in order to secure temporary political relief postponing and complicating the final verdict regarding the loss of the *Captain*'. See E. J. Reed (ed.), *Naval Science*, Vol. 1 (1872), p. 161. [Ed. note: Reed was not invariably the most reliable of witnesses on matters relating to Admiralty design policy, since he was the Navy's Chief Constructor from 1863 to 1870, and thus took the appointment of the Committee on Designs as a personal affront. George J. Goschen, First Lord 1871–74, described the government's motives in the House of Commons as stemming from the desire to restore public confidence in the safety of the navy's vessels following the *Captain* disaster, and Reed's invective notwithstanding, it hardly appears creditable that the government would have appointed a highly qualified scientific and professional Committee and published its report, had it not been certain of a favourable outcome before the investigation commenced.]
20. Goschen to Milne, 8 May 1873, NMM: MLN/165/5.
21. FO to Admiralty, 12 July 1870, NMM: MLN/144/1. International usage laid down that neutral ports could be used once every three months by warships of a belligerent nation.
22. Remarks by Milne to George Ward Hunt, 15 April 1874, Carnarvon Papers, PRO 30/6-115 (another copy can be found in the Disraeli (Hughenden) Papers, B/XX/Hu/59). It must be emphasized that Milne's anti-*Devastation* complex was evident here. He wanted second-class cruisers for empire duty built. [Ed. note: It should also be acknowledged that regardless of how ardent a navalist Ward Hunt was, the reports of the Naval Lords were no more welcomed by Prime Minister Disraeli's Cabinet than they would have been by Gladstone's, and the First Lord, after bombastic pronouncements in Commons about the need for supplemental funding to replace the 'phantom fleet' he inherited, was forced to make do with a very modest increase in the estimates. See Beeler, *British Naval Policy in the Gladstone–Disraeli Era*, pp. 151–9.]
23. Pre-1868 and post-1873. The years 1868–73 were a period of great expansion, but the boom was hardly recognizable until 1871, for unemployment was still high. After 1873 the economy was increasingly straitened as a depression which began in agriculture gradually spread to other sectors. See W. W. Rostow, *The British Economy of the Nineteenth Century* (Oxford: Clarendon Press, 1949), pp. 23–4.
24. For a treatment of the beginnings of the Royal Colonial Institute see A. Folsom, *The Royal Empire Society* (London: George Allen & Unwin, 1933), pp. 17–56. Dislike of the Colonial Office and emigration possibilities were the central themes of the colonial conference, which did not receive the blessings of the government. See Edward Jenkins (ed.), 'Conference on Colonial Questions', in *Discussions on Colonial Questions* (London: Strahan, 1872), especially pp. 80–81.
25. No correspondence referring to the 'Crystal Palace Speech' not already published in Monypenny and Buckle can be found in Disraeli's papers. There are, however, two carefully made-up books of newspaper cuttings. One contains general London press comments on the speech delivered at Manchester on 3 April 1872; the other comments on that delivered at the Crystal Palace on 24 June 1872. Monypenny and Buckle suggest that these speeches were made to demonstrate that the Conservatives had a positive policy, but the fact that the press comments on these speeches were so carefully collected and preserved suggests that the Conservative leader was searching for a policy rather than expounding it.

26. Folsom, *Royal Empire Society*, p. 30.
27. F. P. Labilliere's paper mentioned defence, but the reference failed to stir up discussion. See Jenkins, *Discussion on Colonial Questions*, pp. 80–1.
28. John Charles Ready Colomb (1838–1909): Irish landlord; Captain, Royal Marine Artillery, retired 1869; pamphleteer and speaker on imperial defence and promoter of imperial federation; Conservative MP 1886–92; 1895–1906; KCMG 1887. Colomb's pioneering pamphlet was 'The Protection of Our Commerce and Distribution of Our Naval Forces considered' (London: Harrison, 1867). See also Howard D'Egville, *Imperial Defence and Closer Union* (London: P. S. King, 1913), p. 12. This volume is largely a description of the empire defence work of brothers Admiral P. H. and Captain J. C. R. Colomb. As the work of the Colomb brothers was pioneered in the era 1867–90, so D'Egville's work is pioneer to those wishing to understand the contribution that the Colombs made to empire strategic thought.
29. J. C. R. Colomb, 'Colonial Defence', *Proceedings of the Royal Colonial Institute*, 1873 (published separately 1877). See especially p. 7.
30. Ibid., p. 4.
31. Ibid., p. 5.
32. Folsom, *Royal Empire Society*, p. 106. Generally speaking, only when South Africa was discussed did the papers of the Royal Colonial Institute attract public attention.
33. Colomb, 'Colonial Defence', p. 7.
34. 'Report of the Royal Commission on the Defences of the United Kingdom', *Parl. Papers*, 1860, Vol. 23, pp. 439–40.
35. It will be seen that this list corresponded closely to the first Admiralty list issued the next year.
36. Colomb, 'Colonial Defence', pp. 18–19. 'I have been much struck', Colomb stated, 'by the entire want ... of any advanced position in the Pacific Ocean. We have valuable possessions on either side, as at Vancouver's Island and Sydney, but not an islet or a rock in the 7,000 miles that separated them. We have no island on which to place a coaling station, and where we could ensure fresh supplies.'
37. See India Office to CO, 1 January 1883, PRO: CO 323/355 48. Between 1873 and 1887 the protection of Indian harbours, however illogical it may appear, was investigated and dealt with by the Indian government with no reference to the empire harbour defence work being carried out in other parts of the world. The sole exception was the case of Aden, to the defence of which the Indian Government later contributed half the cost.
38. Colomb, 'Colonial Defence', p. 28.
39. Ibid., p. 19. 'Too much attention cannot be paid to the coaling stations of the Empire. They should be under our control.'
40. 'Return for six months ending 30 June 1869 showing the Description and quality of Coal consumed on board each ship of the Navy', *Parl. Papers*, 1868–69, Vol. 38, pp. 449–77. Of all non-UK coal tried, only that from New South Wales and Pennsylvania was considered good and 'fit for the service'. Nanaimo (British Columbia) coal was 'fair and fit for the service'. Often this was a commentary on the Royal Navy rather than the coal, since Pennsylvania coal could not be used in many RN ships because the boilers were not efficient enough.
41. 'Report of the Select Committee Appointed to Inquire into the Present Dearness and Scarcity of Coal, with the Proceedings, Minutes of Evidence, Appendix, and Index', *Parl. Papers*, 1873, p. 10.
42. 'Report of the Commissioners Appointed to Inquire into the Several Matters

Relating to Coal in the United Kingdom 1871; Vol. 1: – General Report, and Twenty-two Sub-reports', 1871, 18: p. 1; 'Vol. 2: – General Minutes and Proceedings of Committees A, B, C, D &c.', 1871, 18: p. 199; 'Vol. 3: – Report of Committee E, Statistics of Production, Consumption, and Export of Coal', 1871, 18: p. 815. See especially Vol. 3: – Report of Committee E.
43. Ibid., Vol. 3, p. 1067.
44. Compiled from statistics given, ibid.
45. 'Report of the Select Committee Appointed to Inquire into the Present Dearness and Scarcity of Coal, with the Proceedings, Minutes of Evidence, Appendix, and Index', *Parl. Papers*, 1873, p. 10 Minutes of Evidence of Mr Henry Johnson Cullogh, Admiralty Buyer of Coals, question no. 7000.
46. H. O. Stirling to Admiralty, 14 June 1871. See W. F. D. Jervois, 'Memorandum with Reference to the Defenceless State of our Coaling Stations and Naval Establishments Abroad', 7 January 1875, Appendix C, PRO 30/6-122.
47. Biddulph, *Cardwell at the War Office*, p. 245. Gladstone went to the country *after* he found that his two service chiefs would not agree to a reduction in the military estimates. He did not support Cardwell at this time even though he admitted that the latter was 'not an extravagant minister'.
48. George Ward Hunt (1825–77): Financial Secretary to the Treasury, 1866–68; Chancellor of Exchequer 1868; First Lord of the Admiralty 1874–77.
49. Ward Hunt to the Board of Admiralty, 3 April 1874, Carnarvon Papers, PRO 30/6-115 (another copy can be found in the Disraeli (Hughenden) Papers, B/XX/Hu/59). The Lords Commissioners of the Admiralty were (1) Ward Hunt, First Lord; (2) Alexander Milne, Senior Naval Lord; (3) John Walter Tarleton, Second Naval Lord (4); Lord Gilford, Junior Naval Lord; and (5) Sir Lopes Massey Lopes, Civil Lord.
50. Letter from Rear Admiral G. T. P. Hornby 'On What Ships to Keep in the Channel Squadron', with remarks by Milne, Tarleton, Gilford and Robert Spencer Robinson (10 April 1874?), NMM: MLN/144/2 (3).
51. Remarks of Tarleton to Ward Hunt, 15 April 1874, PRO 30/6-115 (another copy can be found in the Disraeli (Hughenden) Papers, B/XX/Hu/59).
52. Remarks of Gilford, ibid.
53. Remarks of Milne, ibid.
54. Certainly this represented a contrast to the general army preoccupation with defence of the British Isles.
55. [Ed. note: This assertion might be tempered in light of the state of contemporary technology. Milne stated bluntly that sail would be a requisite in 'any future war'. This pronouncement was, of course, wildly erroneous. It was, however, indisputable at the time he wrote, and for most of the decade which followed. Several factors – most prominently the want of a comprehensive worldwide system of coaling stations, inefficient engines and medium-pressure (50–90lbs psi) boilers plagued by continual maintenance problems – rendered a wholesale transformation of the fleet from sail to steam not merely impractical but impossible, unless the navy were to abandon its duties beyond European waters. Milne, and most of his contemporaries – Gilford was a glaring exception – were, I believe, motivated less by their antipathy towards steam than by their intimate understanding of the demands made on the service, and the imperfect tools with which they had to be answered.]
56. The application does, it must be admitted, stretch the usual meaning of the words 'strategic thought' to the limit.
57. This committee was appointed by the Admiralty in 1871 to investigate the merits of certain ship designs. It reported that the '*Devastation*-class ship represents

in its broad features the first-class fighting ship of the immediate future'. See Thomas Brassey, *The British Navy: Its Strengths, Resources, and Administration* (London: Longmans & Green, 1882), Vol. 3, p. 526.
58. A point driven home in a letter from Admiral Thomas Symonds to Ward Hunt, 1 June 1874, which was printed and distributed within the Admiralty. Copies can be found in Milne's papers, NMM: MLN/144/2 (4) and those of Geoffrey Phipps Hornby, NMM: PHI/120a/III.
59. Milne, 'Paper Relative to Unarmoured Ships, and Proposal for an Establishment', Confidential, NMM: MLN/144/3 (1); 'Position of Cruizing [sic] Ships for Protection of Trade', Confidential, NMM: MLN/144/3 (1).
60. Although his work was mainly connected with colonial fortifications, he could expect little support from colonial politicians. Only at Lord Dufferin's request did the Prime Minister of Canada, Sir John A. Macdonald, give his testimonial to support Jervois' request for the KCMG. Macdonald did not wish to be accused of meddling in Colonial Office business, although Dufferin added that the Canadian 'would not be very enthusiastic on behalf of merits from which he had no prospect of reaping further advantage'. Dufferin to Kimberley, 10 April 1873, KP: PC/A/25a.
61. Duke of Cambridge to Cardwell, 9 February 1874, RA R53, no. 52. Jervois failed to get promotion in 1869 because the Queen was annoyed that she had not been consulted in the routine fashion, and claimed that he was too junior for advancement.
62. Jervois, Memorandum with Reference to the Defenceless Condition of our Coaling Stations and Naval Establishments Abroad', PRO 30/6-122. Henceforth referred to as Jervois memorandum.
63. Ibid.
64. Although the Admiralty always firmly held that the navy's duties did not include harbour defence, it simultaneously designed and built several low-freeboard ironclad monitors explicitly intended for coast and harbour defence, and some high-ranking navy officers steadfastly maintained that even the seagoing breastwork monitors of the *Devastation* type were unsuited for any other than harbour defence. [Ed. note: it is clear from Admiralty documents that the so-called coast-defence ironclads to which Dr Schurman refers were also intended to assault enemy fortifications and harbours across the Channel or in the Baltic, thus the blurring of strategic vision was not quite as pronounced as might initially be thought. See Beeler, *British Naval Policy in the Gladstone–Disraeli Era*, pp. 214–15.]
65. The basic idea for the assertion that garrison usefulness could be measured by fortifications, probably came from a recommendation Jervois had drawn up early in 1874 respecting the defence of commercial harbours in the United Kingdom. Mentioning the large garrisons committed to this task he wrote: 'Surely it cannot be sound policy, while maintaining a force of this kind, to neglect to provide the means by which alone their services could be rendered available.' See minute of 6 January 1874, attached to Jervois memorandum, PRO 30/6-122.
66. Yet the idea is tempting on the grounds of the similarity of the interests of the two men.
67. Appended minute to Jervois memorandum by Gathorne-Hardy, 12 January 1875, PRO 30/6-122.
68. Jervois memorandum.
69. See, for confirmation, Duke of Cambridge, 'Memorandum by His Royal Highness the Field Marshal Commanding in Chief on the Defenceless Condition of Certain Coaling Stations Abroad', 12 December 1875, PRO 30/6-122.

3

Conservative Beginnings: 1874–80

THE RESULTS OF CRYSTAL PALACE

In late February 1874, following the Conservative victory in the general election, the *Daily Telegraph* addressed the prospective empire policy of the new government. The vision was rosy: the editors went so far as to suggest that imperial federation might be a future possibility. The appointment of pro-empire Lord Carnarvon as Colonial Secretary was applauded as portending an end to 'small mindedness' in dealing with the colonies. Prime Minister Benjamin Disraeli, however, was probably never as empire-conscious as the *Telegraph*'s welcome suggested.[1] His Crystal Palace speech touting the importance – not to mention the glory – of empire probably amounted more to an attempt to determine the extent to which Gladstone had misgauged public sentiment by his indifference to the colonies (and a pre-emptive strike to avoid that pitfall himself), than it did any sincere conversion to zealous imperialism.[2] The occasion seems to have been too isolated, his words too flamboyant, and the effort made too late in his life. Likewise, his actions in office seem to encourage the conclusion that his imperial thought and policy differed from Gladstone's only in so far as he was bent on fooling the nation into believing that the Conservative Party was more solicitous of the empire. Such a conclusion is unwarranted. The Conservatives may not have staked their political future on empire but they entirely lacked that distinguishing feature of many Gladstonian Liberals on imperial questions: pessimism. The difference was one of intent. Disraeli may have done little while in office to act on his implied desire to recast the whole basis of empire, outlined at Crystal Palace, but, on the other hand, there is no evidence that he or members of his ministry ever embraced the separatist hopes of some of their predecessors. In fact the second Disraeli administration, while hardly exemplifying colonial consciousness, did exhibit a pronounced pro-colonial bent.[3]

This attitude was at once evident in Disraeli's selection of Henry

Howard Molyneux Herbert, 4th Earl of Carnarvon, to fill the office of Secretary of State for the Colonies. Not only had Carnarvon's sympathy with and tact for dealing with colonial populations and politicians been amply demonstrated by successfully overseeing the delicate negotiations leading to the formation of the Dominion of Canada, he was clearly a man with faith in the future of empire, as indicated by his determined opposition to Liberal policy in the turbulent circumstances surrounding troop withdrawal in New Zealand.[4] Since he had once deserted the Conservative leader's standard – over the 1867 Reform Bill – there is some reason to suppose that Disraeli may have hesitated in making the appointment.[5] If the Conservatives wished to appear committed to a course in direct contrast to public perceptions of the previous administration's policy, Carnarvon was the obvious choice, since, aside from Crystal Palace, only he was identified in the public mind with Conservative pro-colonial, or at least anti-Gladstone, imperial views.

Disraeli also revealed some personal interest in the problem of colonial–home relationship along with his selection of Carnarvon as Colonial Secretary. This interest, and its extent, is best illustrated by Carnarvon's efforts to reverse the policy that Cardwell had just succeeded in effecting: to return the British Army to garrison duty in the self-governing colonies.[6] In the autumn of 1874 Carnarvon wrote privately to the governors of all the large self-governing colonies to sound colonial sentiment on the practicability of troop restoration.[7] He pointed out that the proposal looked to an entirely new arrangement, one distinct from 'that which Cardwell put an end to'.[8] New South Wales returned a flat negative, the proposal being declared impracticable by both the premier, Sir Henry Parkes, and the governor, Sir Hercules Robinson.[9] Canada's refusal was just as forthright as that of New South Wales as far as the politicians went, but its governor-general, the Earl of Dufferin and Ava, did not meekly bow to this decision as did Robinson in New South Wales.[10] Indeed, he suggested that Canadian objections to the reopening of a closed book might be overcome by cunning.[11] If extra troops were sent to the fortress of Halifax, he proposed, Canadians might then be persuaded to make use of them for training purposes, or for some similar reason. Once there, the need for early departure might not seem overwhelmingly urgent, and eventually some more permanent arrangement might be reached. Like another of Dufferin's schemes – that Canada be made into a viceroyalty with himself as first viceroy – this proposal never received Cabinet attention.[12]

Towards the end of November 1875, however, the Colonial Secretary received a ray of hope in the form of an enquiry from the colony of Victoria asking what shape a new troop agreement might take.[13] At once he appealed to the prime minister for advice and support.[14] Carnarvon reminded Disraeli of an earlier talk they had had on the question.

Moreover, any new arrangement involved matters of such high policy that he could not properly proceed without being assured of the prime minister's support. Disraeli replied: 'I look upon the restoration of our publicity relations with our Colonies as questions of high policy, which ought never to be absent from our thoughts. The question involves social and political, as well as military considerations, and you may rely on my earnest support of any steps, on your part, to accomplish this great end.'[15]

With this seemingly unequivocal support behind him, Carnarvon then solicited the interest and backing of the Secretary of State for War, Gathorne-Hardy.[16] To lend force to his argument he stated that the idea had been urged, in the first instance, by the prime minister, and went on to explain how the possibility had come about. Carnarvon had previously raised the subject with Hardy and probably expected support.[17] In any event, since for the moment he wanted to do little more than open tentative negotiations, he needed no more than the Secretary of State for War's agreement to explore the situation. He was disappointed. Gathorne-Hardy claimed personally to favour the troop restoration idea but there were, he felt, two insuperable objections. First, the manpower losses suffered through desertion from units stationed in the self-governing colonies were unacceptable. Second, he reminded Carnarvon that colonial self-defence was held to be a valuable principle by many Conservatives as well as Liberals.[18]

This cool reception ensured that the troop restoration idea would not be immediately followed up. Gathorne-Hardy, knowing that Carnarvon wished to settle the question without raising a large question of colonial policy in the Cabinet, wrote on 6 March 1876 to suggest that it be dropped.[19] Carnarvon, however, made one more effort to secure a private departmental acquiescence to his scheme.[20] Gathorne-Hardy replied that 'the principle of supplying troops at a cheap rate to the Colonies ... is a very poor one and might involve consequences so large that the policy of doing it at all must be settled in the first instance'.[21] When the Cabinet was eventually informed of Carnarvon's proposal it was rejected owing to Gathorne-Hardy's opposition.[22] On 13 April 1876 Carnarvon wrote him to suggest dropping the matter and 'the question of sending troops to the Australian Colonies as one open for future consideration'.[23] Hence the Colonial Secretary saved some face, but nothing of his plan. Cardwell's accomplishment was to stand.

It is not surprising that Carnarvon's scheme for troop restoration failed. By 1875 the self-governing colonies had largely recovered from the bitterness accompanying the withdrawal of the garrisons, and Carnarvon did not realize that the old wound had healed. There was no real colonial or British demand for such a reversal of policy, and Carnarvon put forward his suggestion with the intention of promoting good relations within the empire rather than on political or military considerations. Yet the fact that Carnarvon and his half-hearted chief went through the motions of offering the colonies what the War Office firmly opposed, and most of the colonies did not want, is some measure of the difference between the Conservative and Liberal approaches. Although it missed the mark, the troop restoration scheme was a definite attempt on the part of a leading member of the Conservative government to carry through an action with no other object in view but that of improving relations between home and colonial governments.

From the point of view of imperial military requirements the episode indicates both how casually politicians considered moving soldiers about without the slightest military purpose in view, and how the military realized this and resisted such plans. It is clear that Carnarvon then understood little of what imperial defence (in the Colomb–Jervois sense) entailed. Hence this troop restoration policy was not conceived in any spirit of hostility to empire, nor was it based on any sense of strategic utility or pragmatism. Carnarvon simply believed that a policy of empire friendliness was necessary. This same trait was evident in the case of the *Rosario*.

The *Rosario* was a second-class sloop stationed in New Zealand waters due to come home for refit.[24] On 18 March 1875 Carnarvon wrote First Lord George Ward Hunt, informing him that the colony had offered to purchase the ship and suggesting the possibility that an outright gift might be made of her.[25] Ward Hunt consulted the First Sea Lord, Sir Alexander Milne, who replied that such an action would be akin to giving a ship to the Orkneys and that the navy could not afford the loss. On receipt of this opinion Ward Hunt informed Carnarvon that the ship was in such poor condition that she would be both a dangerous and inadequate gift.[26] There the matter stood, but the navy's cavalier attitude apparently rankled with Carnarvon, for he aimed a brisk parting salvo at the First Lord: 'Hereafter perhaps you will be able to consider whether anything can be done for the Colony.'[27] Here again Carnarvon's cardinal object – to improve home–colonial relations – was defeated because he had not sufficiently considered the military implications of his request.

This trait was also apparent in his attitude toward colonial military appointments. The grand object of imperial friendliness came first with him. He required that all appointees be judged more on grounds of personal adaptability than on military proficiency. Consequently, the Duke of Cambridge's candidate to fill the vacant post of Commandant of the Canadian Military College at Kingston – Captain J. E. Lovell – was opposed because the Colonial Secretary felt him to be deficient in the personal qualities necessary to securing close co-operation between colonials and Britons.[28] Carnarvon's priorities, although admirable in intent, made the task of the War Office somewhat difficult and certainly did not increase the likelihood of departmental co-operation. Curiously, the War Office was less demanding. When the Colonial Secretary applied to it for an opinion on the acceptability of Sir William Jervois' appointment to investigate and advise on the defences of Australasian colonies, Gathorne-Hardy responded that since Jervois was employed by the Colonial Office, the proposal respecting his employment was not one upon which the army authorities felt required to render an opinion.[29]

It may be said then that Lord Carnarvon's arrival at the Colonial Office marked a new determination that the large self-governing colonies should be treated not only on a fair basis, but that behind that treatment there should be an intention of fostering stronger imperial ties through a more sympathetic attitude towards colonial desires, better personal relations and, where possible, the distribution of British largesse. The attempt to make judicious gifts to the colonies was not a success, and the gestures never really assisted the colonies whose gratitude Carnarvon was determined to earn, but the sympathetic approach was, from the pro-imperial perspective, sound and welcome policy, especially after Gladstone's remote disinterest and strictly correct attitude.

Although Carnarvon's approach to empire initially took little note of actual imperial military requirements, it can be seen in retrospect that after 1874 he was moving in the direction of greater awareness. He first presumed that the problem of empire unity depended almost completely on establishing mutual sympathy and understanding. In pursuing a course based on that premise, however, he also laid the foundation for whatever co-operation in military matters that the years 1878–87 were to witness.

THE WAR OFFICE AND EMPIRE STRATEGY: 1875–78

Among his reforms, Cardwell brought the War Office and House Guards under the one roof, but he did not completely merge the two staffs as far as function was concerned.[30] The War Office, overseen by the civilian Secretary of State for War, administered some aspects of the service, the Commander-in-Chief was responsible for others. Hence the *Army List* continued to show army command and administration divided between separate War Office and Horse Guards departments.[31] The Ordnance Department, under the command of the Surveyor-General of Ordnance, was subordinate to the War Office. The office of Director of Works – headed by the Inspector-General of Fortifications – was one of that department's offices.[32] The Inspector-General was assisted, apart from his general clerical staff, by two Deputy Directors of Works, one for general duties and another specifically designated Deputy Director of Works for Fortifications. In 1872 an Assistant Director of Works for Fortifications was added.[33] Contact with the Commander-in-Chief was maintained, however tenuously, by the Inspector-General of Fortifications' membership on the Defence Committee, a body presided over by the Duke of Cambridge. Since the committee's principal concern was fortifications, the Inspector General of Fortifications' participation was of considerable importance. Between 1862 and 1875 contact was rendered even closer by the fact that the Deputy Director of Works for Fortifications, Jervois, was also Secretary to the Defence Committee. It was in his capacity of Deputy Director of Works that Jervois had produced his landmark memorandum in 1875. Apart from political support, the success of his ideas within the army depended upon the degree of importance attached to them by his immediate superior, the Inspector-General of Fortifications, and by the Duke of Cambridge in his capacity as president of the Defence Committee.

In December 1875 Jervois' memorandum was again put forward by the Inspector General of Fortifications with his unreserved endorsement. Coaling station defence, he argued, was of equal importance to home harbour defence.[34] Such a verdict indicates how much Jervois' ideas had modified the 'Fortress England' concept hitherto so prevalent at the War Office. The Secretary for War then submitted the memorandum to the head of the other half of army administration, the Duke of Cambridge, who disagreed with the Inspector-General of Fortifications that coaling station defence should be placed on a priority level with home harbour defence, reaffirming the primacy of the latter in his own views.[35] Nevertheless, he was sufficiently impressed with Jervois' conclusions to state that the urgency of neither should be underestimated and that both needs be met as soon as possible – if possible, simultaneously.

There can be little doubt, however, that the Duke's small drop of cold water was sufficient encouragement for Gathorne-Hardy to continue to neglect the coaling station issue. This attitude was realized by the Inspector-General of Fortifications who reminded the Secretary of State for War of Jervois' argument that troops without guns were useless. He made particular reference to Port Royal, Jamaica, where a considerable garrison was maintained on an absolutely defenceless island. The argument evidently impressed Gathorne-Hardy enough to pass on the information to the First Lord of the Admiralty.[36]

On 30 June 1875 the Inspector-General composed a further memorandum on the coaling station problem, pointing to the *Alabama*'s depredations during the American Civil War as an example of what one lone armed merchant cruiser could do to restrict commerce, even of a superior naval power, in wartime.[37] Gathorne-Hardy remained unimpressed, but the Duke of Cambridge was now more thoughtful, having come to the conclusion that the real difficulty was lack of co-operation between the War Office and Admiralty. He acknowledged that when it came to imperial defence everybody was at 'sixes and sevens', save for the navy, which was left out altogether.[38] He suggested that a special interdepartmental Committee of Imperial Defence be set up, to consist of the Secretary of State for War, the First Lord of the Admiralty, and the Commander-in-Chief of the army, with power to add to their numbers if and when they saw fit.[39]

From Gathorne-Hardy's point of view the chief objection to such a proposal may well have been the fact that the Duke himself would serve on the committee. Nevertheless the latter had realized that want of departmental co-operation must make effective imperial defence an all but impossible undertaking, and his suggestion was, in the light of future events, extremely significant. He was, however, for the moment, swimming against the stream, a tendency to separation of duties being more in line with current thought. Only a few days later, agreement was reached between War Office and Admiralty whereby submarine defences – including the manufacture of the navy's torpedoes – which had previously been a matter for co-operation between the two departments, became the sole responsibility of the War Office. Thus even this slight token of army–navy co-operation ended.[40] With Milne's retirement in 1876, moreover, the Board of Admiralty adopted a more insular attitude, attempting to solve the problems involved in trade defence without reference to army authorities or the Colonial Office. The Director of Naval Construction publicly stated that the existence of fast armed merchant cruisers made defence by convoy impossible.[41] He even went so far as to suggest that one day the use of fast armed merchant cruisers would entirely supplant warships for purposes of trade defence. This view was never put before army authorities, however: each defence department largely went its own way.[42]

In 1877, however, the growing threat of war with Russia stimulated fresh attention to imperial defence. First, colonies expressed concerned that war with Russia might see their trade and harbours menaced by the Russian navy (such as it was). Second, the Russian war scare gave some impetus in Whitehall for consideration of Jervois' recommendations.

Australasians felt, the Governor of New Zealand reported at the time, that Disraeli's Crystal Palace speech presaged greater British concern for the empire and caused more interest there than it did at home.[43] Also many colonists, largely through the literature and influence of the Royal Colonial Institute, were aware of Colomb's ideas on empire defence and were perhaps naturally more concerned with the question of imperial unity than was public opinion at home.[44] Hence, as Russo-British relations deteriorated in early 1877, the Australasians began to take steps to provide for their own local defence, requesting the assistance of British defence experts, and soliciting an increase in the Pacific squadron's strength.[45]

These requests, in turn, fostered Carnarvon's growing awareness of the defencelessness of imperial coaling stations. During negotiations over the annexation of Fiji (1875) he had been exposed to the strategic situation in the Pacific, and probably read Jervois' memorandum.[46] He had also had reason to reflect on the strategic importance of the Cape should Suez become impassable in war.[47] From this point onwards he became actively interested in what was to be, for many years, his most important field of endeavour: imperial defence, as conceived of by Colomb and Jervois.

His first move was to send Jervois to Australasia, in answer to the request for a military fortifications adviser.[48] In May Carnarvon wrote to Ward Hunt with evident concern about coaling station defence, asking for Admiralty charts with which to study the problem more closely.[49] It was a beginning, both for Carnarvon and the members of the Colonial Office who, like their chief, had not taken much interest in strategic matters since the troop withdrawal policy was implemented.[50] Moreover, thanks to the Russian scare, public opinion had been slightly aroused as to the importance of overseas bases. On 2 March 1877 South African ship-owner Donald Currie addressed the Royal United Services Institution on the relationship of coaling stations to the preservation of trade in war.[51] He further emphasized the importance of the Cape route in case Suez should become blocked in war and the value of cable communications during hostilities. The *Daily Telegraph* paid tribute to Currie's speech, suggesting that he had evolved a new approach to the problem of maritime warfare. Such a pronouncement, of course, was a telling commentary on the slight public impact of J. C. R. Colomb's views.[52] Carnarvon, the amateur strategist, preserved this editorial even as he did another in the *Pall Mall Gazette* on 27 April 1877 which informed its readers that coaling station defences could not be suddenly improvised, nor could they be entirely provided by Britain, and that a sharing of the burden, along the lines indicated by the encouraging request for professional military advice from the Australasian Colonies, should be the mark of empire defence in the future.[53] These editorial comments, however, were mere ephemeral reactions to the Russian crisis rather than measured assessments of the problem of imperial defence as a whole. No Fleet Street newspaper editor shared Colomb's breath of vision.[54]

Russia declared war on the Ottoman empire on 24 April 1877. Just as the war scare gave imperial defence its first honourable mention in the press in the spring of 1877, so it also led to a reawakened interest in the subject at the War Office, especially as regards Jervois' memorandum. At the beginning of April Colonel C. H. Nugent, Secretary of the Duke of Cambridge's Defence Committee, prepared a memorandum on the defence of coaling stations.[55] He laid down the standards for judging the importance of coaling stations as depending on (1) proximity to passing commerce; (2) position *vis-à-vis* the nearest naval squadron; and (3) position *vis-à-vis* likely enemy attack. Using these criteria he listed the overseas stations in order of precedence: (1) Simons Bay, Cape of Good Hope; (2) Hong Kong; (3) Singapore; (4) St Lucia, Jamaica; (5) King George Sound, Western Australia; (6) Trincomalee; (7) Mauritius; (8) Esquimalt, Vancouver Island; (9) the Falkland Islands; (10) Ascension Island. Fiji and Honolulu were also adjudged desirable.[56]

By this time the Inspector General of Fortifications, General John Lintorn Simmons, was fully alive to the necessity of protecting coaling stations.[57] When asked to prepare a paper for the Secretary of State for War estimating the time the Russian army would need to invest Turkey, he inserted in it by way of conclusion a sharp warning of the inadequacy of coaling station defences.[58] This highly important, though in its immediate context, highly irrelevant, statement was no doubt a protest at Gathorne-Hardy's apparent indifference to empire defence. Simmons' stratagem was evidently successful, for shortly afterwards he was called into a Cabinet meeting for consultations concerning fortifications.[59] The interest of the Duke of Cambridge was also reawakened, and the Defence Committee began to deal with the problem with some hope that action might be taken upon recommendations that were produced.

The Defence Committee then asked Simmons to draw up plans both for temporary and permanent fortifications for undefended coaling stations.[60] Particular reference was made to Simons Bay (Cape Colony) which the Admiralty had specially requested that the army defend. Although convinced of the need for overseas coaling station defences, the Inspector General of Fortifications did not completely abandon the old concept of 'Fortress England'. Under his direction Colonel Nugent produced a memorandum assessing invasion possibilities, describing past invasions, allowing the feasibility of a present one, and quoting the Duke of Wellington's well-known opinion as evidence.[61] In the particular case of Simons Bay, Simmons displayed the same tendencies, his attitude, like that of the Duke of Cambridge, being that home defences should first be attended, those of the colonies later. The Defence Committee's recommendations listed the coaling stations in order of importance – following Nugent's standards – and estimated the cost of placing them in a reasonable state of defence at £2,297,412.[62] The Committee supported Simmons' recommendations that a loan be procured to begin the proposed works at once, that telegraphy between Britain and Cape Colony and between Halifax and Bermuda would be decided assets in the event of a maritime war, and that, pending the completion of permanent works, defences of sufficient strength to deal with unarmoured cruiser attacks should be improvised. Yet despite the flurry of activity generated by the Russo-Turkish War, no government action followed the Defence Committee recommendations on coaling stations and it is clear that once again the War Office tendency to establish priorities provided politicians with the excuse for economy once the immediate danger had passed away.

It seems incredible that proposals concerning matters with which the Admiralty was intimately concerned should be handled almost entirely by the War Office. Colomb, speaking to the Royal Colonial Institute in May, again stressed the value coal bases would have in any future war, repeating that one of the greatest obstacles to getting on with the defence of these places was lack of Admiralty–War Office co-operation.[63] As will become evident presently, the blame for this state of affairs did not rest wholly with the War Office. To understand this situation it is necessary to turn to the bases themselves, and study the method of their selection.

The first list of coaling stations, that unofficially suggested by Colomb in 1873, was too long, too indeterminate, and, besides, was not official. Colomb's paper was interesting more because of its novelty, suggestive nature, and the probable effect of its ideas on officialdom than for any significant correlation between its concrete suggestions and subsequent government actions. Jervois' list was more significant mainly because it owed its existence to an official Admiralty request for assistance. Indeed it was itself suggested by the Admiralty. Yet it is difficult to see what specific reasoning lay behind the Admiralty's selections. The most reasonable basis for the navy to request military defence of a particular place would presumably be official acknowledgement of its status and importance. A *base* might be the station headquarters of a squadron, as for instance Hong Kong was to the Pacific Squadron and Simons Town for the South African Squadron. Such a classification does not, however, account for places like Ascension Island, neither a rendezvous nor headquarters, but located in a strategically useful site in the South Atlantic, and possessing certain health advantages.[64] The fact is that the term 'naval base' did not exist in any official sense: it had not been defined, and logical criteria for designating bases did not exist. What the navy possessed were certain 'establishments' abroad: official dockyards, victualling yards and medical facilities. If an overseas station harboured any such establishments it undoubtedly interested the Admiralty, and if it had the additional importance of being a fleet or squadron rendezvous, it might be termed a base in service parlance.

Port Royal, Jamaica, Hong Kong and Simons Town, Cape of Good Hope, all possessed the necessary qualifications in every regard.[65] Antigua possessed a naval dockyard, Trincomalee a dockyard and victualling establishment, Ascension a dockyard and medical establishments. Admiralty concern for the defence of these places is clear. Such cannot, however, be said for King George Sound, Western Australia, Singapore, Mauritius and the Falkland Islands. None of these places were squadron stations nor did they possess docking, victualling or medical establishments.[66] Yet there were unquestionable strategic – as opposed to administrative, logistical, or even traditional – grounds for fortifying all of them. King George Sound lay on the main Cape–Australia trade route and was already used by steamship companies. In fact it was with reference to that place that Commodore H. O. Stirling wrote in 1870 when the undefended coal stocks there worried him. The Falkland Islands were the only possible rendezvous for a British fleet if South American ports were denied it in wartime.[67] Mauritius already possessed a garrison and was strategically valuable, lying as it did on the route to India.[68] Moreover, the threat it posed if held by a determined enemy had been demonstrated long before the days of coal.[69] Singapore, as a natural focal point for shipping and as a commercial centre in its own right, was an obviously useful point from which to control the Malacca Strait. These places, however, were surely chosen by the Admiralty because of their position with regard to coal supplies to the fleet, not because they were *official* Admiralty coaling stations, or even on the grounds of rational strategic assessment. Yet they were included from the start in Jervois' list, probably because the navy, or, more particularly, First Naval Lord Milne, was becoming more coal-conscious. In 1874 he had urged that additional coaling stations be established at Falkland Islands, King George Sound, St Helena, Cape York (Australia) and Port Said. There was Admiralty coal stored at Singapore and facilities for coal purchase at Mauritius, but the other stations he enumerated had no such supplies. The picture was confused – as confused as the Admiralty itself was when it asked the War Office for assistance in defending these places. All that can be safely concluded is that the Admiralty was worried about coal supplies generally and asked for War Office assistance for places that were, and might in the future be, strategically important as coaling stations in a full-scale maritime war.

Yet despite the want of clear strategic vision, between 1875 and 1877 the idea was completely taken over by the Fortifications Branch at the War Office and developed with a sympathy and sureness of grasp far in advance of the original Admiralty stimulus. Jervois had set out the general strategy in his memorandum, and the Duke of Cambridge attempted to place the whole scheme on a reasonable footing by advocating an interdepartmental Defence Committee involving politicians as well as specialists. When his proposal failed, the fortifications branch continued to support Jervois' ideas and, at the time of the Russian war scare crisis of 1877, attempted to deal more precisely with the problem of determining the requisite scale of fortification for each base. In his capacity as Secretary to the Defence Committee, Nugent generated the data by which the importance of the various bases could be determined and the amount and type of defensive work required for each decided.[70] Jervois had stated that the purpose of the whole system was the protection of maritime commerce; Nugent went one step further and gauged the importance of each base according to the proximity to the cruising area of any naval squadron, the annual amount of floating trade in its area, and the probability of its being attacked. Henceforth trade value became an important criterion in the determination of War Office standards of judgement as to the defence of specific places. The Admiralty, having lost the initiative, was never completely to regain it.

Nugent's list included the same ports that Jervois had suggested, with the exception that St Lucia in the Windward Islands replaced Antigua, and that Fiji was added. Taking the bases in detail, he maintained that Simons Bay, Cape of Good Hope, was most important. Not only did a seventh of all Britain's trade annually pass the Cape; if Suez were closed all eastern trade would of necessity pass that way, to say nothing of military supplies for India. Its importance, he stated unequivocally, could 'hardly be overrated'. The fact that it was headquarters of the South African Squadron was not mentioned. Nor was Hong Kong's position as the rendezvous for the Pacific Fleet given as a reason for its being ranked second in importance. Nugent referred to Britain's expanding trade with China, and stated that: 'it is absolutely necessary to support and develop this trade, and to hold a firm position from which we may interpose as our interests demand, in the event of hostile combinations between the Russians, the Chinese, and the Americans'. Furthermore, loss of face in China would probably have destabilizing consequences in India and Burma. Singapore was the centre for most of Britain's eastern trading activities. Like Hong Kong, it too helped to ensure protection for Australasia. Yet Singapore still possessed no naval establishment.

Jamaica and St Lucia, considered together, were listed fourth. Here Nugent dwelt on the necessity at that time of protecting British prosperity in the Caribbean and the future trade potential of a proposed Panama Canal. Jamaica had naval establishments, but the Windward Islands' naval dockyard was situated at Antigua. King George Sound was classed fifth: a good harbour strategically placed on the exceptionally long sea route from the Cape to Melbourne. This ranking was bolstered by a panegyric on the industry and loyalty of the Australasian peoples.[71] There was no naval establishment at King George Sound.

The sixth choice, Trincomalee, would come before Mauritius only as long as Suez remained open. Nugent obviously realized the need for a strong position in Ceylon, but he suggested that Galle, a roadstead more conveniently placed with regard to the great trade routes, might be a more convenient coaling station despite the costly prospect of the move from Trincomalee.[72] The latter possessed naval establishments and had been regularly used by the East Indies Squadrons since the mid-eighteenth century. This suggestion, however, illustrates how little attention Nugent gave to naval opinion in his assessments – for despite his recommendation he admitted that Galle would necessarily be replaced by Trincomalee as a trade rendezvous in wartime.

Mauritius, ranked seventh, would jump to third place were the Suez Canal unusable, but in any event its importance was relative to the number of foreign warships operating in the Indian Ocean. Eighth-ranked Esquimalt, on Vancouver Island, received an unenthusiastic endorsement. Nugent had little sentiment for Canada, and the selection of Esquimalt was his sole complete concession to naval opinion. The navy had to have a north Pacific base, and it was the 'only British place at present available'.

Stanley Harbour in the Falkland Islands ranked ninth because it was the only possible position from which the Cape Horn trade could be defended in wartime, 'far away as it is from Great Britain'. The navy had no coal there – although Milne had in 1874 suggested it might be used for coaling – and it possessed no naval establishments although the Pacific Steam Navigation Company maintained coal stocks there. Ascension Island with its obvious position *vis-à-vis* trade between England and the Cape, and its naval docking and medical establishments, came next. Nugent's final recommendation was Suva Harbour in Fiji, and he expressed the hope that Honolulu or some such place might soon become British to complete lines of communication across the Pacific. The Defence Committee recommendations followed Nugent's prioritization, save that St Lucia was separated from Jamaica and independently ranked below the Falkland Islands and above Fiji.

Certainly Nugent's attempt at classification was an important accomplishment. Regardless of the Defence Committee's assertion that all the bases were so important that it was difficult to assign precedence, some order of priority was necessary before any systematic action could be taken. The criteria, moreover, on which the priority was based were generally sensible. Trade, naval proximity and probability of attack were the most rational means of judging importance. Nugent's exact classification could be criticized on matters of detail, but the romantic notion that pounds spent on defence should be in rough proportion to the annual floating trade value passing a certain point, caught the attention of those responsible for coaling station defence planning, and remained their main yardstick until modern times.[73] Nugent's greatest difficulty was that the standard of naval squadron proximity was not a static thing. It could not be measured by quick reference to the closest naval base or, more properly, squadron headquarters. Knowledge of the disposition of naval squadrons in time of war – also contingent on planning – was a prerequisite to reaching conclusions about coaling station defence, and Nugent did not possess that information. It is doubtful, indeed, whether the Admiralty could have furnished answers, had they been put, and the lack of co-operation between the two departments assured that that state of affairs was not liable to immediate change.

The War Office scheme was excellent, but so long as it continued to deal with essentially naval matters without consulting the Admiralty, effectiveness would be circumscribed. The responsibility for this state of affairs rested squarely on the Admiralty, which held rigid views on what was navy business, and whose representatives on the Defence Committee lacked the wit or interest to advise the fortifications specialists on naval needs. Only in 1878 did some interdepartmental co-operation develop – at the instigation of the Colonial Office.

NOTES

1. *Daily Telegraph* (London), 24 February 1874. The previous day the *Daily News* commented in the same vein, urging the value of colonial possessions to the mother country. *The Times* did not speculate on the government's colonial intentions.
2. Robert Blake's standard modern biography treats the Crystal Palace appeal as a fundamentally cynical exercise in political symbolism: 'Disraeli said something, though tantalizingly little, about his concept of empire ... [He] foreshadowed the imperial policy of Joseph Chamberlain and others at the turn of the century, but his ideas seem to have been thrown out more-or-less casually and without any special appreciation of their significance. He barely mentioned India.' Blake, *Disraeli* (New York: St Martin's Press, 1967), p. 523. Stanley Weintraub, however, makes much more of the occasion: 'A theme had been sounded and the Conservative Party released from its malaise. Dramatically contrasting the timid, tuppence-minded Liberal attitude with the imperial mystique, Disraeli had articulated values that would govern Britain as far into the future as World War II.' Note, though, that Weintraub avoids speculating on Disraeli's motives and sincerity. See Weintraub, *Disraeli: A Biography* (New York: Truman Talley/Dutton, 1993), p. 505. Disraeli's post-1872 pro-imperial rhetoric has typically been contrasted with his earlier pronouncements in a very different vein – colonies as 'millstones around our neck' – in support of the assertion that his 'conversion' represented political expediency rather than ideological conviction. More recently, some have suggested that his imperialism took root earlier and was more sincere – at least as it applied to domestic appeal – than has generally been accepted. See in particular Freda Harcourt, 'Disraeli's Imperialism 1866–1868: A Question of Timing', *Historical Journal*, 23, 1 (1980): pp. 87–109.
3. Used in the connotation that pro-colonial meant willingness to formulate and set on policy aimed at the well-being and possibly the extension of the empire.
4. Entertainment of colonials by top-ranking British politicians was rare. Carnarvon was a notable exception, and the members of the Canadian Confederation Delegation 'graced' the table at his seat, Highclere, at Christmas 1866. See Arthur Hardinge, *The Life of Henry Howard Molyneux Herbert, Fourth Earl of Carnarvon*, 3 vols (London: Oxford University Press, 1925), Vol. 1, Chs 14–15, especially p. 337.
5. [Ed. note: One should probably not make too much of the split, at least as it concerned Disraeli's political attitude toward Carnarvon. Lord Salisbury, another of the 1867 Cabinet defectors and a harsh public critic of many of Disraeli's policies, was in 1874 rewarded for his disloyalty with the India Office and ultimately replaced the 15th Earl of Derby at the Foreign Office at the height of the Eastern Crisis. Disraeli's private thoughts about Carnarvon and Salisbury (especially about the latter) may not invariably have been charitable, but he realized pragmatically that they were far too important to the party to be excluded and far too much of a threat to himself on the outside.]

CONSERVATIVE BEGINNINGS: 1874-80

6. The main colonial problem during 1874–78 was, of course, South Africa and the Boer Republics, a subject scrupulously avoided here.
7. Carnarvon to Hardy (copy), 12 December 1875, PRO 30/6-12. A letter from Carnarvon to Dufferin (31 October 1874) outlining the former's ideas in detail is quoted in Hardinge, *Life of the Fourth Earl of Carnarvon*, Vol. 2, pp. 96–8.
8. Carnarvon to Disraeli (copy), 30 November 1875, PRO 30/6-11.
9. Robinson to Carnarvon (enclosing Parkes' letter), 22 September 1875. PRO 30/6-25. Hercules Robinson (1824–97): Governor St Christopher, Hong Kong; Ceylon; New South Wales 1872–79; New Zealand 1879–80; Governor Cape Colony and High Commissioner for South Africa 1880–89, 1895–97; knighted 1859; GCMG 1875; PC 1882. Henry Parkes (1815–96): New South Wales politician; began life as manual worker in Birmingham; to Sydney 1836; newspaper editor 1850; premier 1872–75, 1878–82, and 1887–89. KCMG 1877; GCMG 1888.
10. Dufferin to Carnarvon, 6 March 1875, PRO 30/6-26. Frederick Temple Blackwood, First Marquis of Dufferin and Ava (1826–1902): diplomatist and administrator; earldom 1871; Governor-General of Canada 1872–78; ambassador St Petersburg 1879–83; Governor-General of India 1884–88; ambassador Rome 1889–91; ambassador Paris 1891–96; KCB 1861; GCMG 1876; GCB 1883; marquisate 1889.
11. Dufferin to Carnarvon, confidential memorandum, 'Troops', 24 July 1875, PRO 30/6-26.
12. Dufferin to Carnarvon, confidential memorandum, 'Vice Royalty', 24 July 1875, PRO 30/6-26. Carnarvon did not discuss this and the preceding memorandum with Dufferin or anyone else, at least on paper.
13. Carnarvon to Gathorne-Hardy (copy), 12 December 1875, PRO 30/6-12.
14. Carnarvon to Disraeli (copy), November 1875, PRO 30/6-11.
15. Disraeli to Carnarvon, 8 December 1875, PRO 30/6-11. Quoted in Hardinge, *Life of the Fourth Earl of Carnarvon*, Vol. 2, p. 98.
16. Carnarvon to Hardy (copy), 12 December 1875, PRO 30/6-12. Gathorne Gathorne-Hardy, 1st Earl of Cranbrook (1814–1906): President of Poor Law Board, 1866–67; Home Secretary, 1867–68; Secretary of State for War, 1874–78; Secretary for India, 1878–80; Lord President of Council, 1886–92; earldom 1892.
17. Ibid., 'You will remember our conversation as to the restoration of troops …'
18. Gathorne-Hardy to Carnarvon, 13 December 1875, PRO 30/6-12.
19. Gathorne-Hardy to Carnarvon, 6 March 1876, PRO 30/6-12.
20. Carnarvon to Gathorne-Hardy (copy), 16 March 1876, PRO 30/6-12.
21. 16 March 1876. Hardy to Carnarvon, PRO 30/6-12.
22. On 21 March 1876. See Hardinge, *Life of the Fourth Earl of Carnarvon*, Vol. 2, p. 98 and Gathorne Gathorne-Hardy, *The Diary of Gathorne Hardy, Later Lord Cranbrook, 1866–1892: Political Selections*, ed. Nancy Johnson (Oxford: Clarendon Press, 1981), p. 267, entry for 22 March 1876. The plan was rejected despite a second plea by Carnarvon for the prime minister's support. According to Hardinge, the reason given by Gathorne-Hardy was that it was difficult to recruit enough men even for home defence. Hardinge derides the Conservative government for allowing a surplus to dwindle away.
23. Carnarvon to Hardy (copy), 13 April 1876, PRO 30/6-12.
24. Screw-propelled of 673 tons.
25. Carnarvon to Ward Hunt (copy), 18 March 1875, PRO 30/6-5. The colony offered to pay £2,000 for the vessel.
26. Yet she was overhauled for further service that autumn, see Milne's

57

'Memorandum to First Lord', November 1875, PRO 30/6-115.
27. 25 March 1875. Carnarvon to Ward Hunt, PRO 30/6-5.
28. Carnarvon to Duke of Cambridge (copies), 10 and 14 December 1874, PRO 30/6-14. This practice was repeated in the case of the Duke of Cambridge's recommendation of General Airey for the governorship of Malta. Carnarvon objected that Airey was unsuitable since he was a bachelor: the social duties required of the governor could best be carried out by a married man. Carnarvon to Duke of Cambridge (copy), 22 June 1875, PRO 30/6-14. Again in the case of General Colborne's appointment as commander of troops at Hong Kong, Carnarvon objected that the nominee was personally unsuited for the task. In this case he was proved right, since Colborne, whom the Duke described as a 'quite reliable officer', totally refused to co-operate with the Governor. See Duke of Cambridge to Airey, 12 November 1875, RA ADD.MSS. In all of these instances Carnarvon was overruled.
29. Gathorne-Hardy to Duke of Cambridge, 2 February 1877, RA ADD.MSS.
30. [Ed. note: to say nothing of the Duke of Cambridge's attitude, for although the Commander-in-Chief found his office removed from Horse Guards to Whitehall he resolutely continued to address his correspondence 'Horse Guards'. He also zealously resisted all attempts to subordinate his authority to civilian administrators.]
31. See the official *Army List* (published monthly). This information was taken from March 1877.
32. Also subordinate to the Surveyor-General of Ordnance were the Directors of Supplies and Transport, Artillery and Stores, and Army Contracts and Clothing. It will be noticed that the arrangement allowed for closer political supervision of material expenditure.
33. See *The War Office List* (published quarterly). This information was taken from November 1872.
34. Jervois, 'Memorandum by the Inspector-General of Fortifications on the Defenceless Condition of the Commercial Harbours at Home, and of the Coaling Stations Abroad', 9 December 1875. Attached to 'Memorandum by the Defence Committee at their Meeting of the 5th of June 1877 with Reference to the Defence of Commercial Harbours at Homes, and of Coaling Stations Abroad', 5 June 1877 (hereafter referred to as memorandum, 5 June 1877), PRO 30/6-122.
35. Duke of Cambridge, 'Memorandum by His Royal Highness the Field Marshal Commanding in Chief on the Defenceless Condition of certain Coaling Stations Abroad', 12 December 1875, attached to ibid.
36. Ibid., forwarded 26 December 1875. These memoranda of December 1875 were probably considered by the Cabinet. See Hardinge, *Life of the Fourth Earl of Carnarvon*, Vol. 2, p. 99.
37. J. L. A. Simmons, 'Memorandum by the Inspector-General of Fortifications on the Defenceless Condition of the Commercial Harbours at Home, and of the Coaling Stations Abroad', 30 June 1876, attached to memorandum, 5 June 1877, PRO 30/6-122.
38. Duke of Cambridge to Gathorne-Hardy, 5 December 1876, printed in Willoughby Verner, *The Military Life of HRH George, Duke of Cambridge*, 2 vols (London: John Murray, 1905), Vol. 2, p. 111.
39. Note the word 'imperial', as opposed to 'colonial'.
40. War Office to Admiralty, 12 December 1876, PRO: WO 148/7896. In future submarine defence was to be overseen at the Fortifications Branch in the War Office.

41. Nathaniel Barnaby, 'The Fighting Power of the Merchant Ship in Naval Warfare' (read at the 18th Session of the Institution of Naval Architects, 22 March 1877), published in *Transactions of the Institution of Naval Architects*, 1877, pp. 1–23.
42. At least no evidence indicating co-operation could be found in War Office files at PRO.
43. George Bowen (Governor of New Zealand) to Kimberley, 19 November 1872, KP PC/A/27.
44. This study makes no pretence of assessing the degree or amount of public support for united empire in Australasia yet it is *suggested* that pro-empire feeling was more pronounced than its opposite.
45. See Bowen to Carnarvon, 25 January 1877, PRO 30/6-25; Carnarvon to Duke of Cambridge (copy), 2 January 1877, PRO 30/6-14; Gathorne-Hardy to Duke of Cambridge, 2 February 1877, RA ADD.MSS; F. Weld (Governor of Western Australia) to Carnarvon, 12 May 1877, PRO 30/6-25. Enthusiasm was especially pronounced in New Zealand, and Jervois was sent to assess Australasian defences.
46. Carnarvon, 'Memorandum on Fiji' (copy), October 1876, PRO 30/6-51. Jervois' memorandum was passed to the Colonial Office, 6 March 1875.
47. Through correspondence with Donald Currie who had spoken at the Royal United Services Institution on the subject. The paper dealt with the need for a complete empire system of telegraphs, coaling stations and graving docks. Currie mentioned the Cape especially when he wrote to Carnarvon on 30 October 1875 and again on 11 January 1876. Carnarvon (27 January 1876) replied that the matter was under consideration. Although no action was taken immediately, Currie seems to have believed that Carnarvon had been impressed. See Currie, 'Maritime Warfare', *Royal United Services Institution Journal*, 21 (1878): pp. 228–47, especially pp. 233–4.
48. Carnarvon to Duke of Cambridge (copy), 14 February 1877, PRO 30/6-14.
49. Carnarvon to Hunt (copies), 3 and 4 May 1877, PRO 30/6-5.
50. No evidence has been found to suggest that Carnarvon discussed his troop restoration scheme with the Colonial Office Permanent Undersecretary, Robert W. G. Herbert.
51. Currie, 'Maritime Warfare', *Royal United Services Institution Journal*, 21 (1878): pp. 228–47.
52. Information contained in Carnarvon memorandum, 8 March 1877, PRO 30/6-51.
53. *Daily Telegraph* and *Pall Mall Gazette* clippings, PRO 30/6-51. Naval officer Cyprian Bridge wrote anonymously for the *Pall Mall Gazette* and seems a likely author of that paper's editorial.
54. Colomb spoke at the Royal United Services Institute on 25 May 1877, on the problems of Pacific strategy, thus once more giving his views that amount of publicity which the Institute provided. See Colomb, 'Russian Development and our Naval and Military Position in the North Pacific', *Royal United Services Institution Journal*, 21 (1878): pp. 659–707.
55. C. H. Nugent, 'Memorandum on the Relative Importance of Coaling Stations', 1 April 1877, attached to memorandum, 5 June 1877, PRO 30/6-122. Nugent succeeded Jervois as Deputy Director of Works for Fortifications in the spring of 1875. He had joined the Fortifications Department as Assistant Director of Works in 1872.
56. The Hawaiian Islands were annexed by the United States in 1898.
57. John Lintorn Arabin Simmons, RE (1821–1903): Field Marshal, Crimean War; British Consul at Warsaw 1858–60; commanding Royal Engineers at Chatham 1865–68; Commandant Woolwich 1869–75; Inspector-General of Fortifications

1875–80; Carnarvon Commission 1879–82; Governor Malta 1884–88; GCMG 1887.
58. J. L. A. Simmons, 'Confidential memorandum on the Length of Time Required for the Russian Army to Invest Turkey', 19 April 1877, PRO 30/6-115.
59. Gathorne-Hardy to Duke of Cambridge, 30 April 1877, RA ADD.MSS.
60. J. L. A. Simmons, 'Memorandum Drawn up by the Inspector-General of Fortifications' (in response to Defence Committee Request and Relative to the Defence of Coaling Stations), and idem, 'Memorandum by the Inspector-General of Fortifications on the Defenceless Condition of Simons Bay, and Other Coaling Stations Abroad', 30 June 1876, both attached to memorandum, 5 June 1877, PRO 30/6-122.
61. C. H. Nugent, 'Memorandum upon the Defences of the Commercial Ports and Anchorages of the United Kingdom', 23 April 1877, attached to memorandum, 5 June 1877, PRO 30/6-122. This memorandum was accompanied by a chart showing the routes of invasions of England back to, and including, Roman times. In it Nugent at one point stated 'I apprehend that the territorial extent and influence of the British Empire would be very limited indeed if the naval force was required to guard and defend the coast – *That force must be assisted by works on shore.*' This was traditional British strategy. Reference to it betrayed his lack of appreciation of its real meaning. The Duke had not mentioned invasion, but rather the protection of commercial ports from isolated attacks. For a recent survey of this question see Michael Partridge, *Military Planning for the Defence of the United Kingdom, 1814–1870* (Westport, CT: Greenwood, 1989).
62. Memorandum, 5 June 1877, PRO 30/6-122. These recommendations were based on the idea of permanent rather than temporary fortifications.
63. Howard D'Egville, *Imperial Defence and Closer Union* (London: P. S. King, 1913), p. 19.
64. As such, it was especially valuable as a retreat for vessels serving on the fearfully unhealthy West African Station.
65. As of 1874. See the *Navy List*, April 1874.
66. Ibid.
67. A fact clearly demonstrated by the Coronel and Falkland Island operations of November–December 1914.
68. Nugent, 'Memorandum on the Relative Importance of Coaling Stations', 1 April 1877, attached to memorandum, 5 June 1877, PRO 30/6-122.
69. See C. Northcote Parkinson, *War in the Eastern Seas, 1793–1815* (London: George Allen & Unwin, 1954), *passim*.
70. Nugent, 'Memorandum on the Relative Importance of Coaling Stations', 1 April 1877, attached to memorandum, 5 June 1877, PRO 30/6-122.
71. In comparison with the Canadians, whom he did not like.
72. Galle did not possess a natural harbour.
73. See D. H. Cole, *Imperial Military Geography* (8th edn, London: Sifton Preed, 1935), especially Ch. 8.

4

Milne's Colonial Defence Committee: 1878–79

On 5 March 1878 an interdepartmental Colonial Defence Committee held its first meeting. It would continue to sit until 28 April 1879.[1] Although the initiative behind its formation came largely from the War Office, the actual appointment and instruction of the committee was the work of the Colonial Office.

There was, of course, nothing novel with the Colonial Office's interest in matters concerning colonial defence. Lord Kimberley, after all, had taken a leading part in the implementation of Cardwell's troop-withdrawal policy in the early 1870s. It has also been seen that Carnarvon attempted to alter Cardwell's colonial military policy – or want thereof – in 1876–77, and that his failure stemmed in large part from the absence of machinery for the exchange of War Office and Colonial Office opinion. The governors of the Australian colonies were likewise commanders-in-chief of their respective colonies, and in similar fashion the Governor-General of Canada still retained the dignity of Commander-in-Chief in Prince Edward Island.[2] In these ways the Colonial Office, despite the traditional practice of consulting the War Office and Admiralty on most service matters, was of considerable importance in any schemes of colonial or imperial strategy. Probably the only reason that imperial defence schemes hatched in the office of the Inspector General of Fortifications did not excite Colonial Office or Admiralty jealousy was the fact that Gathorne-Hardy, the Secretary of State for War, was loathe to share them: in fact they hardly left their nest. Serious Colonial Office consideration of the problem, in Colomb–Jervois terms, seems only to have emerged with Lord Carnarvon's aroused interest in early May 1878, when the subject was discussed in Cabinet, and the Colonial Secretary took cognizance of Donald Currie's gloomy warnings about Cape Town. And it was evidently Carnarvon's interest which spurred defence-consciousness at the Colonial Office and provided the initiative for formation of the new Colonial Defence Committee.

61

The actual proposal, however, came from Gathorne-Hardy. The first three years of his secretaryship had been marked by his impatience with questions involving colonial defence, and hence it is difficult to understand his motive.[3] Possibly, he wished to rid himself of an unpleasant duty by turning the subject over to a committee, but it is more likely that he was impressed by Simmons' explanation of the importance of imperial defence to the Cabinet late in April 1877, and that he then began to confer with Carnarvon on the subject, as his letter proposing a defence committee (8 November 1877) suggests.[4]

He began by admitting that he considered the whole question extraordinarily difficult, but held that it was desirable 'to have some kind of enquiry upon it for our own information'. There were many questions to be settled. What was most important? What was colonial, what imperial, and what mixed? What contributions could be 'demanded of colonies' regarding works, guns and manning? How much could the Admiralty assist? The War Office, Admiralty, Colonial Office and the Treasury should, he stated, be represented on the committee. More significantly, he claimed that professionals were not best qualified to judge such matters: 'Soldiers and Sailors had better be heard than hear and probably a lay tribunal would be best but I am not fixed upon this.' Gathorne-Hardy's disdain for professional participation and simultaneous willingness to be flexible on the issue seem quintessentially British. Carnarvon's reply was generally favourable, although he did not share the Secretary of State for War's anti-professional bias, and furthermore deprecated the involvement of the Treasury, which might have an early cramping effect on the investigations.[5] He in turn suggested that the India Office should be represented and that the naval representative be Vice-Admiral Lord Gilford.[6] This reply showed the same mixture of enthusiasm and lack of realism that had distinguished his troop restoration initiative. In any event, no further correspondence on the subject ensued during the short term.

At the end of January 1878 tension in the Middle East heightened. The government's firm support of the Turks was signalled by ordering the Mediterranean squadron to Constantinople – ostensibly to protect British lives and property – and applying to parliament for a £6 million vote of credit for military purposes. These actions caused Lord Carnarvon's resignation.[7] His place at the Colonial Office was taken by Sir Michael Hicks Beach.[8] Despite Carnarvon's concern for empire and its proper defence, difficulties with Disraeli had occupied him constantly since the past autumn, and there can be little doubt that his conduct of affairs at the Colonial Office suffered.[9] Re-emergence of the crisis mentality of the previous spring, however, meant revived attention to colonial defence, Carnarvon or no. Hicks Beach had hardly kissed hands when Robert Herbert, the Permanent Undersecretary at the Colonial

Office, wrote to the War Office suggesting that colonial defence deserved immediate attention.[10] An interdepartmental committee was necessary 'in view of the fact that many of the more important Colonial ports are now unprovided with any adequate system of defence, it would be advisable to cause an inquiry to be held and a report to be made as to the most pressing requirements of this nature and the best means of meeting them in any sudden emergency; in order that Her Majesty's Government may be in a position to consider any demands from the Colonies for assistance in this matter, and any action it may be necessary to take on the subject'.

Imperial defence ultimately came to mean a world-wide system of defended supply bases designed to assist the fleet in the performance of its duties and to provide wartime refuge for commercial vessels. The successful creation and operation of this system ideally involved the formulation of a general theory of imperial defence strategy, co-operation between the various responsible departments of state in the formulation and implementation of the scheme, fostering co-operation between home and colonial governments to allow for its practical application, and, finally, the firm control of strategy and co-operation – political, economic and military – by representatives of the government of the day, urged forward by informed public opinion. This ideal situation was not realized even by 1887. What was accomplished, though, owed much to this Colonial Defence Committee. On the surface, it was no more than an advisory body to the Colonial Office. Its creation did, however, signal partial political recognition of Colomb's and Jervois' imperial defence principles. Furthermore, its constitution indicated a recognition of the interdepartmental co-operation essential to applied empire defence. Finally, it probed the difficulties involved in securing co-operation between home and colonial governments.

The War Office, Colonial Office and Admiralty were represented. The War Office nominated the Inspector General of Fortifications, General John Simmons, who brought to the committee what organized knowledge existed of the problems involved in imperial defence. The Admiralty nominated Admiral Sir Alexander Milne, retired First Naval Lord and, as has been indicated, the first senior officer of either service to give serious attention to the coaling station problem. He had instigated official study of the problem by his request to Jervois in 1874, and was thus ultimately responsible for Simmons' accumulation of knowledge on the subject. Appropriately, Milne was chosen president of the committee. The Colonial Office was represented by Sir Henry Barkly, late Governor of the Cape Colony, and hence an experienced hand at the complexity of empire defence problems.[11] The War Office provided the secretary, Lieutenant H. Jekyll, RE, and the Colonial Office served as clearing house for the committee's correspondence. It was a strong committee, which worked in the exciting atmosphere of possible war until the Treaty of Berlin (July 1878) ended the sense of emergency.

Two problems immediately faced the committee. First, the amount of ordnance immediately available for temporary defences was pitifully small. It appeared that no stock of harbour-defence torpedoes – to be fired from the shore – existed. Equally alarming, the 34 guns which could be requisitioned for land defence works would be exhausted in arming Simons and Table Bays (Cape Colony), Hong Kong, Singapore, Port Louis (Mauritius) and Trincomalee, all of which were at that moment virtually defenceless. Unless these places, comprising as they did the navy's major coal storage depots, were defended, fleets and squadrons operating from them risked being rendered ineffective. Nor was this the only cause for grave concern, for the committee quickly discovered that even if the meagre stock of guns were sent out, they would be of use only against unarmoured ships.[12]

Second, the terms of the committee's reference, as set by Herbert's letter, were insufficiently clear. The problems were so large and numerous and the means for dealing them so inadequate that Milne and his colleagues did not know where to begin. Thus, further clarification of instructions was requested.[13] Were they to deal with permanent or temporary measures? Through Herbert, Hicks Beach replied that the committee was to address itself primarily to the immediate emergency: to determine what military supplies were instantly available and where these supplies could be most profitably expended.[14] It was to consider places involving both imperial and colonial interests first, crown colonies next, and finally the towns and seaports of self-governing colonies. These instructions clearly indicated that Hicks Beach conceived of the committee as a special advisory body to assist him in assessing colonial difficulties and commitments in the event of war, rather than one to formulate broad principles of imperial strategy.

Its brief thus clarified, the Defence Committee promptly set to work, quickly recommending that the 34 available guns be immediately sent out and adding that a circular letter suggesting emergency measures, such as raising local forces, securing coal supplies, removing Channel buoys, posting look-outs and enjoining the prompt telegraphic relay of important information be sent to all colonial governors.[15] The committee issued its initial reports between 1 and 17 April, which hastily set forth, as requested, the most urgent temporary measures to be taken.

The first report dealt with the Cape, Mauritius, Ceylon, Singapore and Hong Kong.[16] Since all available guns had been designated for those places the previous month, there was little for the committee to add except to recommend the distribution of guns that might materialize in the future. Hence, it was suggested that the armaments of the priority ports be increased. Moreover, Galle (Ceylon) was added to the list because large coal stocks were kept there and recommendations for its defence already drawn up. Generally, the committee acknowledged that its conclusions were based almost solely on the assumption that Russia was the probable enemy, and that, therefore, any attacks would be mounted by unarmoured cruisers, against which medium-sized British 7-inch (7-ton) guns would be sufficient. It also pointed out the difficulty of providing submarine defences when the care and maintenance of such devices required the services of experts, and speculated on the possibility of training colonials for the work.

The second report dealt with Australasian defences.[17] Since Jervois was then on leave in England, the committee had had the opportunity to hear first-hand his opinion on these works, and had been convinced that it was being done in such a manner as to relieve the home government of any anxiety. On the other hand, the committee was of the opinion that the best thing to do at King George Sound was to remove the coal stocks and abandon it, a conclusion completely at variance with the high importance that Colonel Nugent and the Duke of Cambridge's Defence Committee had attached to it.[18] It also deprecated any idea that a ship be permanently established in New Zealand waters.[19] This recommendation was in line with Milne's naval strategic principles, i.e., that warships should never be tied down by inflexible peacetime commitments, but should instead be completely free for use at the discretion of the senior naval officer in the area.

The third report considered Esquimalt, Vancouver Island, and recommended that some guns be sent there, to be manned by local forces, implying that its defence was partially a colonial responsibility.[20]

The fourth report surveyed Heligoland, St Helena, Sierra Leone, Barbados, Jamaica and Newfoundland.[21] St Helena had stocks of coal, but since ships could only coal there in fine weather the Committee recommended that little be done to improve its defences. Sierra Leone was more important because of its value as an alternative coal station to the Cape Verde Islands, Spanish possessions which might be denied the navy in wartime. Guns were recommended for Barbados, but rather unenthusiastically since security there would require large expensive works. As the chief West Indian station, Jamaica required rather heavy defences. St John's Newfoundland, the Committee recommended, should provide two seven-inch guns for its own defence.

Beyond these specific suggestions the committee pointed out the difficulty of discovering a system of reference that suited all cases.[22] Canada, for instance, possessed eastern ports more important than some of those surveyed, but no action had been taken since they were informed that these were dominion responsibilities.[23] Aden was passed over because it was administered by the Indian government, even as Ascension had not been considered because it was entirely the responsibility of the Admiralty.

Furthermore, they did not extend the scope of their inquiry to 'the defence of ports which, though of little commercial value, may under certain circumstances become of great importance strategically as coaling stations for Her Majesty's Ships'. These sites included Fiji and the Falkland Islands; 'the former being the only British territory between the Australian colonies and the west coast of America, and latter between the West Indies and British Columbia'.[24] And they did not consider 'it their duty to make enquiries or report on the military stations Malta, Gibraltar, Bermuda and Halifax, the defences of which as fortresses are especially provided for by the War Department'.

Quite aside from the fact that none of the ordnance, save that apportioned by the first report, existed when the reports were issued, their tentative language indicates that the committee had little confidence in its handiwork because of the restricted terms of reference. The reports, however, were admittedly produced in a rush to satisfy immediate requirements of the emergency and it should occasion little surprise that the judgements in them were not infallible. More important was the year of solid work that the committee subsequently undertook as the standing advisory body on colonial defences.

In the case of the various colonies of Australia and Tasmania, the Colonial Office was pleased to discover that self-defence there was so far advanced that it would not be necessary for the home government to give much assistance.[25] It remained only to compliment the colonies concerned on their activity and to add an assurance that the defence of their common concern, King George Sound, would be urged on the Admiralty.[26] Yet the Australians were unknowingly at the centre of an interdepartmental correspondence in London regarding submarine defence. In studying general defensive dispositions, Milne's Colonial Defence Committee suggested that 25 of the available 49 Whitehead torpedoes should be sent to Australia, despite the heavy cost that sending two trained torpedomen with each torpedo entailed.[27] In late May 1878, while the Eastern crisis still boiled, the Colonial Office suggested hopefully that the Admiralty might pay for and maintain the torpedoes for Australia.[28] The Admiralty refused, based on three considerations: the Whitehead torpedo was too complicated a mechanism to explain to colonials, secrecy might be violated, and to send two men to look after each torpedo would encourage laxity and lack of fitness.[29] The Colonial Office agreed that the Whitehead was too complicated and the subject dropped, the situation in the East having by this point all but subsided, but for the Admiralty's offer to supply outdated torpedoes not requiring a trained crew.[30] This interdepartmental manœuvring could not cloak the financial considerations behind it, nor the fact that the Colonial Office, while grateful for efforts made by the Australian colonists in their own defence, was not prepared to express any gratitude in terms of pounds sterling.

This same devotion to the tactic of verbal gratitude was evidenced by Colonial Office reaction to the problem of King George Sound. Milne's Colonial Defence Committee recommended its abandonment in its second report, but in the meantime the Colonial Office heard of Australia's self-defence efforts and realized that the colonists would not be pleased by news that the imperial government did not intend to defend the one point Australians regarded as their greatest weakness. Moreover, since King George Sound lay outside any of the self-governing colonies, logically its defence should have devolved upon London.[31] Hence, when it thanked the Australian and Tasmanian governors for colonial promptitude, the circular which did so suggested that despite the committee's recommendations the Colonial Office would try to persuade the Admiralty to take responsibility for the Sound.[32] On the same day a curt note went to the Admiralty stating that in light of the Committee's recommendation, if the navy wished to use the Sound as a coaling station the cost of its defence would have to be paid out of the navy estimates.[33] Not surprisingly the Admiralty declined the offer, and despite the possibility of ruffling colonial sensibilities, the Colonial Secretary informed the Governor of Western Australia that the Sound would be abandoned.[34] The Governor, Harry St George Ord, pointed out in reply that it was the best-situated refuelling station for the steamship line connecting Perth with Adelaide – Western Australia's only regular link with the outside world. Such a move would foster Colonial dissatisfaction and, not surprisingly, added Ord, his own standing would be confounded.[35] The Colonial Office was unmoved. Ord wrote again, this time stating bluntly that if a major war came Britain would 'find that her responsibilities for the protection of her Colonies is in as full force as ever' and that the call might come at an awkward time. At King George Sound only light defences were required and, referring to the damage its loss would cause to Western Australia, Ord stated that it 'cannot be supposed that the Imperial Government would demand such a sacrifice from any Colony, least of all from one whose existence is a struggle, to which it could effectually put an end'.[36] This argument impressed the Colonial Office sufficiently for the matter to be referred back to Milne's Defence Committee. The latter unbent a little, acknowledging that Governor Ord's general views on colonial security might interest a permanent Colonial Defence Committee – Milne and his colleagues advocated such a body be created – and suggesting that the Admiralty be shown his letter.[37] Naturally enough the Admiralty saw in this appeal to the Colonial Office no reason to change its naval arrangements, and Western Australia was so informed.[38]

The whole of these negotiations regarding King George Sound reveal the Colonial Office's desire to avoid responsibility, financial and otherwise. Western Australia was a very poor colony, one as yet lacking its own responsible government. The colony could not afford to protect its own lifeline and the Colonial Office did not feel compelled to do so, secure in the knowledge that without self-government Western Australian objection would be politically insignificant. The Colonial Office thus avoided responsibility, not to mention expense, on the pretext that its own ideas on strategy were subordinate to Admiralty policy.

With regard to New Zealand, after an interview with Premier Sir Julius Vogel, the Colonial Defence Committee determined that defence arrangements there were inadequate and recommended an outlay of £44,000 to mount guns at five principal ports.[39] The New Zealanders promptly agreed, and asked that guns be ordered on their behalf.[40]

Canada responded to the emergency in a patriotic spirit, but the reasons did not have much practical effect nor did defence consciousness there long survive the pacific results of the Congress of Berlin. There were two major areas in the dominion meriting defence preparation: the east coast ports and Esquimalt on Vancouver Island. With regard to the former, Milne's committee was unhelpful, stating first that these fell outside its terms of reference, and later, when pressed, that local defence was purely a matter for negotiation between the navy and local authorities.[41] The committee finally issued a report on the Canadian east coast ports, but only when pressed by the Colonial Office.[42] By the time it did the Eastern crisis had passed and so had Canada's co-operative spirit. It is probable that the committee's neglect was founded on the ideas that Canadians were not really 'British' and, besides, Canada itself was indefensible. In line with the first of these suppositions, when in June 1878, while the Eastern crisis still hung in the balance, the Canadian government offered to raise a whole division in case of war, Secretary of State for War Sir Frederick Stanley minuted that the offer should be kept quiet and that the Colonial Secretary had already returned an appropriately cool answer.[43] The British mentality was, of course, also in line with the general assumption that volunteers could not stand up to regulars in battle, an assumption which did not die until the First World War.

Their offer should not suggest that Canadian politicians were alive to the responsibilities placed on their shoulders by the withdrawal of the garrisons. Instead of putting their politicized militia in proper order, the first response was a request for more navy cruisers to protect east coast shipping.[44] In reply the Canadians were properly put in their non-contributory place. The Admiralty, they were informed, had its dispositions for dealing with an emergency, and it would be Her Majesty's government in London, not in Ottawa, who would decide where and when cruisers would be stationed when an emergency arose. It was further suggested that a country with a merchant marine larger than any in Europe save Britain's might, with profit, consider arming its own fast vessels.[45] The Admiralty may have been slightly overdoing it in this last recommendation, but the first two were well-merited raps over Canadian knuckles. The last point, moreover, did not annoy the Canadians: they themselves thought that such armament was desirable, although, like the Governor of Western Australia, they viewed it as a British responsibility.[46] When the crisis was at its height, however, the Canadian government, urged by the Governor-General, took some steps to put harbours such as Sydney (Cape Breton), Charlottetown (Prince Edward Island) and Saint John (New Brunswick), in some state of defence.[47] The preparations were made by Sir Edward Selby Smyth, commander of the Canadian militia. A subsequent check, however, revealed that although he was to be congratulated upon the fine 'spirit' of the militia, the guns he had recommended for harbour defences would not penetrate the thinnest armour afloat. The work was therefore largely useless.[48] This judgement was not surprising, given the rapid change in gunnery, but the rebuke to Selby Smyth quickly doused the remaining embers of Canada's interest in the problem of east coast defence, since, on his advice, they had already ordered guns from Woolwich.[49]

Esquimalt, on the Pacific Coast, was considered at greater length both during and after the emergency, and the course of the discussion surrounding it sheds interesting light on the ramifications of defence preparations.[50] By recommending that the garrison there be supplied locally, Milne's committee implied that the Canadians were or should be responsible for its defence. The War Office had been cool towards Esquimalt, partly because the scarcity of passing trade meant that it failed to qualify for consideration under Nugent's formula, but more probably because it meant garrisoning an outpost of empire cut off from home control in every way except through the navy. Possessing establishments there, the Admiralty was more convinced of Esquimalt's importance and asked the Colonial Office to solicit Canadian assistance.[51] In so doing the Admiralty flourished its major argument for harbour defence: the squadron must keep the sea from the enemy and could not be expected to reduce its effective numbers for that purpose by dispatching vessels to guard its shore-based supplies. But the Duke of Cambridge's Defence Committee had defined Esquimalt as serving a purely imperial purpose. Hence the Colonial Office reminded the Admiralty that the base's defence concerned the War Office, Admiralty and Treasury.[52] What Canada's position would or should be was impossible to say, although the Colonial Office was prepared to request Canadian help at the time of the Russian war scare. Surprisingly, the Canadian government agreed to man and mount guns supplied by the home government.[53] An officer was sent from the Royal Military College at Kingston to supervise the erection of earthwork batteries at Esquimalt. From 12 to 28 men laboured at their construction 12 hours a day until work halted at the end of August.[54] This was a real frontier emergency effort. There was no available ordnance in England. Some guns were eventually borrowed from the navy, although the Admiralty was not pleased with such an arrangement.[55] At the moment the Canadians sent their supervisor to oversee the work at Esquimalt, the Colonial Office was taunting the War Office over its lack of preparedness by reference to the naval guns 'which the Dominion Government may require for the defence of this Imperial station'.[56] The War Office admitted that the navy held 'the strongest possible opinion' of Esquimalt, but appeared only too glad to have the responsibility and cost for its defence borne elsewhere.[57] Perhaps it was less pleased upon learning that Canada had been informed that its generous response did not necessarily make it responsible for the whole Esquimalt defence bill.[58]

All went happily for a time and as late in the crisis as 19 June Governor-General Lord Dufferin telegraphed that he had persuaded the Canadian government to erect another battery at Esquimalt.[59] Only the Colonial Office, however, knew how much tact was required to secure colonial co-operation. The Admiralty was hopeless. Having asked for assistance in the first place, in the full knowledge that War Office help could only come on paper, the request for the loan of naval guns for Esquimalt's defence, which could have been anticipated, received only grudging assent. A Canadian suggestion that Nanaimo (Vancouver Island) should be defended was dismissed on the grounds that there was no naval coal there.[60] Since the Esquimalt coal was mined at Nanaimo this line of argument was not strictly true. In July, with the crisis safely passed, the Admiralty refused to lend the ammunition necessary for their own loaned guns, and blandly suggested, despite the Colonial Office's decision not to hold Canada responsible for Esquimalt's defence, that the Canadians should provide their own ammunition dump.[61] Somehow this opinion was forwarded to Ottawa.[62] Yet in September the Admiralty again urged Esquimalt's importance.[63] As in its correspondence with the War Office, the Colonial Office reply was pre-emptory. The Admiralty was bluntly informed that any cost involved in the loan of its *matériel* must be borne by the navy, not by the Canadians or the Colonial Office.[64]

When the crisis passed it dawned on both Milne's Defence Committee and the War Office that they had paid a price for the defence of Esquimalt: they had lost control of an imperial work. In response to a committee request, Hicks Beach wrote to Dufferin for details of what was going on at Esquimalt, and suggested that work at the base be suspended until the report arrived.[65] Selby Smyth's subsequent report did not satisfy the War Office, probably because he was not generally respected by British professionals for his work in Canada. Moreover, the soldiers made it known that they assumed no responsibility for permanent fortifications built by the Canadians unless they first had the opportunity to inspect them.[66] This bickering dragged on through the winter of 1878–79 with the Colonial Office urging that the Canadians not be made to feel unappreciated.[67] Despite the fact that the inspection was managed fairly circumspectly and each government selected an officer for the two-man inspection team, the Canadians saw the bill in the offing and made it clear that permanent defences at Esquimalt could not count on Canadian financial outlay.[68] The Canadians were easily led by sentiment, more easily than most Englishmen realized, but they recognized a financial obligation when they saw it. Their response, in effect, was that imperial needs required imperial funds.

As in the case of Australasia, one sees in the Canadian example and the experience of Milne's Committee, the inability of the army and navy to think in terms outside their own departments. The Colonial Office, while just as successful in avoiding expense, did manifest a degree of tact in its relations with Canada and a certain shrewdness in dealing with military minds. Of the Canadians, all that can be said is that they did more than any one in Whitehall seemed to expect, but that was still little enough. As Canada's merchant marine formed a high proportion of shipping engaged in the Australian trade, perhaps some Canadians appreciated the efforts made to ensure safe anchorages for 'Bluenose' ships in Adelaide, Melbourne and Sydney.[69]

The Duke of Cambridge's Defence Committee had judged the Cape Colony the most important of Britain's strategic bases overseas, save the four imperial fortresses.[70] During the year of activity by Milne's Committee, however, it was hardly treated in a manner commensurate with this verdict. The latter suggested that ten guns each be sent to Table Bay (Cape Town Harbour) and Simons Bay (the Royal Navy anchorage), but as only ten guns were immediately available, Simons Bay should have preference.[71] It was also recommended that local forces should be provided by the colonies to man the works projected. The ten guns were duly sent to Simons Bay and the War Office suggested that since the guns would be useless without proper works something should be done.[72] The Colonial Office obtained a reluctant grant from the Treasury to construct the works.[73] At Simons Bay the batteries took some time to erect. Only in December 1879 was the Governor, Sir Bartle Frere, able to invite members of his government to watch five of the guns tested. Embarrassingly, two of the five were disabled on being fired: the locals were probably not over-impressed.[74] In addition, the government of Cape Colony was certainly not anxious to add to its already considerable military commitments and did not volunteer large forces, but the Cape Mounted Rifles, an efficient local force under 1,000 strong, were available.[75] Yet despite this flurry of activity the actual defence arrangements were slightly farcical in view of both the lack of available ordnance in England and the Committee's ignorance of the Cape's defence possibilities.[76]

Some further progress was made by June 1878 when Milne's Committee accepted the opinion of the Colonial Secretary that Simons Bay was a wholly imperial responsibility, while the valuable harbour of Cape

Town ought to be the joint responsibility of home and colonial governments.[77] Despite this decision, further action was postponed until the spring of 1879 when Lord Chelmsford reported on the requisites for defence of the Cape Peninsula, and it was agreed that a local defence committee should be established at the Cape to produce additional information.[78]

Milne's Committee also considered the defence of St John's Newfoundland, although that self-governing colony was not mentioned by the Duke of Cambridge's Defence Committee in its assessment of important bases.[79] In April 1878 Hicks Beach expressed concern about its defence and attempted to ascertain its importance. The War Office and the Treasury were accordingly asked for their views on the question.[80] While their answers were awaited, the anxiety of the Colonial Office was further increased by the colony's declaration that it would gladly supply manpower for the defences but could not afford to pay for guns and works.[81] On receipt of this statement the Colonial Office proclaimed itself willing to bear the total cost, less manpower, subject to Treasury approval.[82] The War Office reply dampened this enthusiasm with the opinion that St John's was not an imperial concern.[83] Hence, guns alone should be supplied by the home government, an opinion soon echoed by a suspicious Treasury.[84] By this point – early August – the immediate war danger was past and the Colonial Office attempted to obtain a more permanent definition upon which the sharing of defence expenditure could be based.[85]

St John's became a test case because the Colonial Office maintained generally that the imperial government should fund imperial posts, that prosperous colonies should pay for their own local defence wherever possible, and that naval support alone would be sufficient for poorer colonies.[86] In the case of in-between places like St John's, however, it was difficult to apportion definite responsibility. It was not essential by an imperial definition and it could not afford to do the whole job itself, yet a successful attack on it would be 'humiliating' in an imperial sense. In the face of Treasury opposition, though, no further discussion took place.

Singapore, Mauritius, Trincomalee and Hong Kong were also sent allotments of available guns, and these were rendered as effective as old ordnance could be by the full or partial erection of local defence works.[87] The Admiralty showed its usual resentment at having its set priorities disturbed when naval guns were grudgingly loaned for the land defence of Hong Kong.[88] It was also forced into unwanted action by news of 70,000 tons of undefended coal at Singapore; three additional vessels were immediately added to the Pacific fleet.[89] Singapore itself was not tardy in contributing towards its own defence, and Jervois' tutelage as Governor showed itself in a colonial grant of £4,200 and the donation of land for artillery placement.[90]

Cardwell's reforms, however, had left the army less flexible for emergencies far afield, and the problem of local forces to man defences caused some concern. In the case of Hong Kong, proposals for organizing Chinese forces were considered and despite Foreign Office objections that an efficient coolie force might be dangerous, such a proposition was under consideration by a local Hong Kong Defence Committee – at the instigation of the Colonial Office – when Milne's Defence Committee itself was dissolved.[91] A proposal respecting Singapore's garrison created similar difficulty, partly because it involved the Indian Army and partly because nobody trusted locals unless they were both white and British.[92] The island of Labuan, north Borneo, also generated problems. When the Colonial Defence Committee was informed that coal was mined there and hence defences might be useful it fell back on its stock remedy for complications: the coal mines should be closed.[93]

Nothing was ever settled with regard to defences in the West Indies because of the usual departmental divergences. Port Royal Harbour, Jamaica, contained a naval dockyard, and therefore the Admiralty favoured its defence, recommending that Barbados be left undefended.[94] Since the latter contained West Indian military headquarters that suggestion was poorly received at the War Office.[95] The Colonial Office was more concerned for the security of the Bahamas. A request for naval assistance there generated the standard reply that naval dispositions were matters of Admiralty concern, implying that all would be cared for in the natural operation of its wisdom.[96]

From this detailed examination discussion of how colonial/imperial defence was handled by the Colonial Office during the year of the Milne Defence Committee's existence, several conclusions may be drawn. First, the Russian 'scare' of 1878 clearly caught the British Empire woefully unprepared for coaling station defence though both the War Office and the Admiralty had previously recognized it as a matter of grave importance in any future war. Not only were defences for the major overseas bases largely non-existent; the want of systematic knowledge regarding local colonial conditions and the lack of spare ordnance at home made even the committee's modest recommendations appear ludicrous. The real value of its labours, therefore, lay not so much in its proposed allocation of unavailable materials, but in its exploration of the problems involved in imperial defence.

Oddly enough, the most salient practical results of the year were those generated by the self-governing colonies in Australasia and Canada. Cardwell's assertion that his withdrawal policy would induce self-reliance in matters of colonial self-defence was probably justified to a greater extent than he could have honestly anticipated. There can be no doubt that local Australasian acceptance of defence burdens relieved the mother country of grave naval support problems in that area, and the remaining problem became largely one of coordination and consultation regarding the actual machinery of defence. Indeed, Australasian efforts compared more than favourably with the home government's accomplishments regarding the defence of bases defined as imperial responsibilities. Similarly, Canadians demonstrated an unexpected readiness to stand by in an emergency, a spirit of co-operation which promised well for the future.

The committee's efforts clearly showed the diversity of the problems involved in imperial defence. In the beginning there had been simply a naval request for assistance, and various ill-defined naval principles determined Jervois' assessment in his memorandum of the strategic importance of particular places. Jervois' criteria had in turn been supplanted by the War Office's choice of particular bases by reference to a standard predicated partially on naval needs and partially on statistical records of passing trade values. When Milne's Defence Committee was seated it must have been difficult enough to reconcile these two departmental views. Furthermore, the committee was forced to show even greater breadth of comprehension because the Colonial Office was not merely represented but had become the controlling department. Thus, in addition to naval needs and trade value, the matter of colonial necessity became a third determining factor. Consequently, the problems of defending strategically secondary but colonially important places such as King George Sound, Colombo, Table Bay, the Bahamas and St John's came to complicate the terms of reference originally established by the defence planners. As has been shown, reactions to these problems varied in each case and so led to the convenient principle enunciated by the Colonial Office: the defence of each borderline case should be determined according to its individual merits. These complicating factors were clearly revealed in correspondence regarding the committee's terms of reference, and that surrounding the defence of specific bases.

There was, furthermore, a fourth confounding factor: the Treasury, the intransigence of which lay at the very root of the difficulties defence planners confronted, before, during and after the Milne Committee's existence. By the end of May 1878 the committee had disposed of its available armament and dispatched its emergency recommendations to overseas posts. Yet even at this early date difficulties arose, for the Treasury agreed to defence expenditure only in the most reluctant manner. Thus, on 2 May the Colonial Office was baldly informed, 'My Lords [of the Treasury] must ... reserve to themselves the ultimate decisions as to the apportionment of the expenditure between the Imperial and Colonial Governments, and they desire that it be clearly understood that the Imperial Government is not in any way committed with regard to any permanent outlay.'[97]

'My Lords' of the Treasury also observed that, with the exception of

Trincomalee and Hong Kong, expenditure seemed to be more for the protection of local rather than imperial interests. This was 'Treasury control' *par excellence*, when parsimony operated under the guise of expert Treasury oversight of the strategic decisions of mere military professionals. In reply to this *tour de force* the Colonial Office meekly suggested that Singapore perhaps had some imperial significance as well.[98] On 18 May the Colonial Office applied for funds for the furtherance of Cape defences at Simons Bay.[99] Again the circumstances of the immediate emergency produced Treasury acquiescence, albeit without enthusiasm, accompanied as it was by a lecture on the evils of creating precedents and a plea for great care in financial recommendations.[100]

This Treasury obstructionism caused a brief flurry of speculation as to the real and proper purpose of Milne's Committee.[101] As early as 1 May 1878 the Secretary of State for War realized the extraordinary difficulties posed by the work of a committee representing so many different departments and involving places where immediate information was generally not available to the investigators.[102] Advice came to the committee on 1 June from both the Chancellor of the Exchequer and the First Lord of the Admiralty.[103] The former endorsed the importance of the subject of inquiry but took the view that a general determination of principle was outside the scope of the committee's labours. It should instead confine itself to pointing out the proper course of action in the immediate emergency, leaving further investigation to a more permanent body that should be appointed in the future. Obviously the Cabinet had not discussed the question, for the First Lord of the Admiralty informed Milne that the committee ought to receive a Treasury guarantee of financial support before it agreed to carry out its work.[104]

Simultaneously the Colonial Office, which seemed to regard Milne's Committee almost as a part of its regular establishment, pressed it to recommend apportionment of costs as between imperial and colonial governments.[105] In other words the Colonial Office requested a professional committee to perform a non-professional function in order to bolster requests to the Treasury for financial support. On 7 June 1878 Milne informed the Colonial Secretary that the committee was prepared to continue and to attempt an estimation of a cost division on the specific understanding that they were only recommending defences for the emergency, based on naval requirements.[106] Yet in actual fact, excepting Table Bay, the committee avoided this duty religiously. Hence on 25 June the Treasury replied to a request for a financial outlay for Hong Kong with assent coupled with the usual lecture on frugality and precedents, pointing out the proposed division of cost should be made without further delay, since, when the emergency was over, the colonies concerned would not be at all anxious to help, and that only the emergency could justify assent to the committee's recommendation in the first place.[107] To this Hicks

Beach replied coolly that he did not anticipate the difficulties that caused the Treasury such concern.[108]

When Treasury help was not forthcoming for the expense of fortifying St John's Newfoundland – admittedly not a point of importance from the War Office's view and one which even Milne's Committee regarded lightly, but about which the Colonial Office was concerned – another attempt to determine principles of dividing the cost was made. It occurred in a much calmer atmosphere, since the emergency was safely past. A Colonial Office letter to the War Office indicated concern over the lack of firm principles in consideration of imperial defence matters.[109] First, it was suggested each case should be decided on its merits – hardly an indication of deep thought in the face of recent difficulties with the Treasury. Second, in cases where strategy was the overarching consideration, the home government must pay – a rather loose statement in view of the fact that the whole of defence supposedly hung on imperial strategy, and that, with the sole exception of St John's Newfoundland, the fortification of colonial commercial ports had not been considered, except in that they were links in the great imperial chain for naval commerce protection. Third, since Australasian trade was local, it should be defended by Australasians. Since the Australasians had, by that time, admitted their liability for all local defence except that of King George Sound, this assertion was not a question of theory or principle, but of simple fact, although the King George Sound problem was by no means settled. Fourth, poor colonies should be left to the sole care of the Royal Navy, and, although non-strategic colonies ought to defend themselves, they nevertheless represented an opportunity for an enemy to damage British prestige, a point which imperial authorities should not forget. Collectively this represented an attempt by the Colonial Office not merely to define principles of cost division on the basis of naval requirements or on the basis of value of passing trade, but also to enunciate the still broader principle that the British government was in varying measure responsible for the defence of all its colonies on a simple possession and responsibility basis.[110]

The War Office reply, which took the form of a memorandum by the Inspector-General of Fortifications, cut through much of this woolly thinking.[111] 'It was now realized', Simmons said, 'how narrowly we had missed being caught unprepared in our overseas defence.' The Russian scare had so impressed members of Milne's Defence Committee, that they, at least, were prepared to admit home defences should take second place to overseas needs. Furthermore, some sort of permanent investigating committee was needed, one that would base its task on the goal of freeing the navy from the duty of harbour defence, and on the general assumption that colonies would be responsible for this task. The main work of this committee should be to decide which places were strategically important, in order that they might receive permanent defences. Simmons' letter, in turn, provided the point of departure for the Royal Commission on the Defence of British Possessions and Commerce Abroad appointed the following year. The immediate legacy of Milne's Defence Committee, therefore, was that in wrestling with the complexities of imperial defence planning it led to official realization of the need for further detailed investigation.

NOTES

1. Milne to Colonial Office, 12 March 1878, PRO 30/6-124.
2. An antiquated remnant of the old Captain-General system. The Commander-in-Chief, Canada, was the Commander-in-Chief, Halifax. At that time Lieutenant-General Sir William O'Grady Haly occupied the post. His position should not be confused with the Officer Commanding the Canadian Militia, an imperial officer responsible to the Canadian government. General Haly was an imperial officer responsible to the British government. See *Army List*, March 1877.
3. Aside from the troop restoration affair discussed above there is a good deal of evidence of Gathorne-Hardy's impatience with any colonial drain on the military, especially regarding South Africa, in Carnarvon's Papers: PRO 30/6-12.
4. Gathorne-Hardy to Carnarvon, 8 November 1877, PRO 30/6-12. This body was distinct from and should not be confused with the Duke of Cambridge's Defence Committee.
5. 8 November 1877. Carnarvon to Hardy (copy). PRO 30/6-12.
6. Richard James Meade, Lord Gilford, later 4th Earl of Clanwilliam (1832–1907): educated Eton; served China (Second Opium) War with distinction, wounded 1858; junior lord at Admiralty, 1874–80; Commander-in-Chief North America 1886; KCB, 1887; Commander-in-Chief Portsmouth, 1891–94. Gilford was a staunch proponent of sails.
7. Carnarvon's resignation was caused by different views between himself and the prime minister on foreign policy *vis-à-vis* Russia, rather than colonial matters.
8. Michael Hicks Beach, 9th baronet, and 1st Earl St Aldwin (1837–1916): Conservative politician, statesman; Chief Secretary for Ireland, 1874; seat in Cabinet, 1876; Secretary of State for Colonies 1878–80; Chancellor of the Exchequer, 1885; President of Board of Trade, 1888–92; Chancellor of the Exchequer, 1895–1902; viscount, 1906; earldom, 1915.
9. See Arthur Hardinge, *The Life of Henry Howard Molyneux Herbert, Fourth Earl of Carnarvon* (London: Oxford University Press, 1925), Vol. 2, Ch. 27.
10. CO to WO (copy), 16 February, 1878, PRO 30/6-124.
11. Sir Henry Barkly (1815–98): colonial governor; British Guyana 1848–55; Jamaica 1853–56; Victoria 1856–65; Mauritius 1863–70; Cape Colony 1870–77; opposed Lord Carnarvon's attempt to federate South Africa; KCB 1853; GCMG 1874; FRS 1864. Barkly had impossibly illegible handwriting.
12. Milne to Herbert, 12 March 1878, PRO 30/6-124, no. 8.
13. Milne to Herbert, 12 March 1878, PRO 30/6-124, no. 9.
14. Herbert to Milne (copy), 14 March 1878, PRO 30/6-124, no. 10.
15. Milne to CO, 14 March, PRO 30/6-124, nos 11–12.
16. 'Report of a Colonial Defence Committee on the Temporary Defences of the

Cape of Good Hope, Mauritius, Ceylon, Singapore and Hong Kong', 4 April 1878, PRO 30/6-124. The reports are inserted at the back of Carnarvon's volume containing the Committee's correspondence.
17. 'Second Report of a Colonial Defence Committee on the Temporary Defences of the Australian Colonies, Tasmania, and New Zealand', 12 April 1878, PRO 30/6-122.
18. See memorandum, 5 June 1877, PRO 30/6-122. The problem of King George Sound was not to be disposed of so easily.
19. Lobbying for a ship permanently stationed in New Zealand waters was not new in 1878. A colonial request for such a vessel was turned down in 1870 because the Admiralty refused to scatter its forces. See Paul Knaplund, *Gladstone and Britain's Imperial Policy* (London: Allen & Unwin, 1927), p. 97.
20. 'Third Report of a Colonial Defence Committee on the Defence of Esquimalt', 17 April 1878, PRO 30/6-124.
21. 'Fourth Report of a Colonial Defence Committee on the Defences of Heligoland, St Helena, Sierra Leone, Barbados, Jamaica, and Newfoundland', 17 April 1878, PRO 30/6-124.
22. Ibid.
23. Milne's committee did draw up a short 'Report on the Principal Canadian Atlantic Ports', but not until another month had elapsed (18 May 1878). See PRO 30/6-124.
24. 'Fourth Report of a Colonial Defence Committee', 17 April 1878, PRO 30/6-124.
25. Colonial Defence Committee to CO, 17 April 1878, PRO 30/6-124, no. 43. Although this work does not discuss the defence of specific Australasian harbours, it is worth noting that the promptness and energy displayed in fortifying them owed much to the efforts of Sir William Jervois, who had become Australian defence adviser in April 1877.
26. CO to Governors of Australia and Tasmania (copies), 26 April 1878, PRO 30/6-124, no. 53.
27. Milne to CO, 20 May 1878, PRO 30/6-124, no. 116.
28. CO to Admiralty (copy), 31 May 1878, PRO 30/6-124, no. 138.
29. Admiralty to CO, 27 June 1878, PRO 30/6-124, no. 312. (Author's note: all points I thought silly in 1955 and to which I now subscribe.)
30. Admiralty to CO, 30 September 1878. PRO 30/6-124 no. 124. The navy offered to supply the 'outrigger' type, which trailed from a vessel, rather than the self-propelled Whitehead variety.
31. Western Australia did not obtain responsible government until 1890.
32. CO to Governors of Australia and Tasmania (copies), 26 April 1878, PRO 30/6-124, no. 53.
33. CO to Admiralty (copy), 26 April 1878, PRO 30/6-124, no. 54.
34. Admiralty to CO, 10 May 1878, PRO 30/6-124, no. 86; Hicks Beach to Governors of South and West Australia, 22 May 1878, PRO 30/6-124, no. 120. He also stated that in event of war a determined effort should be made to destroy any coal that remained there.
35. Ord to Hicks Beach (telegram), 20 June 1878, PRO 30/6-124, no. 181. Harry St George Ord (1819–85): colonial governor and major-general RE; reported on Ascension defences, 1850; Governor Bermuda, 1860–66; Straits Settlements 1867–73; Western Australia, 1877–79; CGMG, 1881.
36. Ord to Hicks Beach, 28 August 1878, PRO 30/6-124, no. 347.
37. Milne to CO, 4 January 1879, PRO: CO 812/14, no. 1.
38. Admiralty to CO, 12 February 1879, PRO: CO 812/14, no. 12; Hicks Beach to

Ord, 20 February 1879, PRO: CO 812/14, no. 13.
39. CO to Normanby (Governor, New Zealand) (copy), 25 April 1878, PRO 30/6-124. Julius Vogel (1835–99): Premier New Zealand; emigrated 1861; Premier 1870–76; New Zealand Agent-General in London 1876–84; knighted 1875.
40. Normanby to Hicks Beach (telegram), 9 May 1878, PRO 30/6-124, no. 76.
41. 'Fourth Report of a Colonial Defence Committee', 17 April 1878, PRO 30/6-124.
42. The Canadian government was worried about these ports. Dufferin telegraphed Hicks Beach on 6 May 1878. See PRO 30/6-124, no. 72. The Colonial Office then pressed the Colonial Defence Committee to consider the matter. See CO to Milne (copy), 11 May 1878, PRO 30/6-124, no. 87 and Milne to CO, 18 May 1878, PRO 30/6-124, no. 111. For the committee's consideration of the east coast ports, see 'Report of a Colonial Defence Committee', 10 August 1878, PRO 30/6-124, no. 280, Incl. I. This report dealing with Canada's eastern ports was not signed by Milne: only by Barkly and Simmons.
43. Stanley minute, 28 August 1878, PRO: WO 32/120-7696. Frederick A. Stanley, 16th Earl of Derby (1841–1908). Financial Secretary to the War Office, 1874–77; Secretary of State for War, 1878–80; Secretary of State for the Colonies, 1885–86; Governor-General Canada, 1883–93; KG 1897; GCVO 1905.
44. Dufferin to Hicks Beach (telegram), 6 May 1878, PRO 30/6-124, no. 72. For the extent of political influence in the Canadian Militia, see Selby Smith (General Officer Commanding the Canadian Militia) to Duke of Cambridge, 1 February 1876, RA ADD.MSS. Selby Smith complained of the way Canadians played politics with army positions and supplies. Dufferin also stressed the poor state of Canada's militia. See Dufferin to Carnarvon, 26 March 1874, PRO 3/6-26.
45. Admiralty to CO, 10 June 1878, PRO 30/6-124, no. 166.
46. Lord Lorne (Governor-General of Canada) to Hicks Beach, 5 June 1879, PRO: CO 812/16, no. 1.
47. Nothing very expensive. The guns recommended were outdated, hence their availability. See Selby Smyth, 'Report on Canadian East Coast Defences', 29 May 1878, PRO 30/6-124, no. 168.
48. See 'Report of a Colonial Defence Committee', 10 August 1878, PRO 30/6-124, no. 280, Incl. I.
49. Hicks Beach to Dufferin (copy), 9 August 1878, PRO 30/6-124, no. 277. The Colonial Secretary suggested that Canada ought not to buy guns until it saw the report of the Colonial Defence Committee (available the next day). This hint hurried the cooling off of the little Canadian enthusiasm that existed.
50. To give some idea of imperial strategy from a peripheral point of view the history of Esquimalt and Empire Defence 1868–87 is recounted in the Appendix.
51. C. H. Nugent, 'Memorandum on the Relative Importance of Coaling Stations', 1 April 1877, attached to memorandum, 5 June 1877; Admiralty to CO, 26 April 1878, PRO 30/6-124, no. 50.
52. On 10 April 1878. See also CO to Admiralty (copy), 1 May 1878, PRO 30/6-124, no. 65.
53. Dufferin to Hicks Beach (telegram), 11 May 1878, PRO 30/6-124, no. 88A. British officialdom did not expect much from Canada. This was indicated in Nugent's 'Memorandum on the Relative Importance of Coaling Stations', and by the fact that in emergencies Canada was approached very carefully – as this particular case indicates.
54. Ibid. See also F. V. Longstaff, *Esquimalt* (Victoria, BC, Canada: The Victoria Book and Stationary Co., 1941), pp. 43–4. The officer dispatched was

IMPERIAL DEFENCE 1868-87

Lieutenant-Colonel de la Chevois T. Irwin, RA. He left smartly on 13 May and arrived in Esquimalt on 27 May.
55. Admiralty to CO, 15 May 1878, PRO 30/6-124, no. 101.
56. CO to WO (copy), 18 May 1878, PRO 30/6-124, no. 109.
57. WO to CO, 7 June 1878, PRO 30/6-124, no. 163.
58. CO to WO (copy), 13 June 1878, PRO 30/6-124, no. 171.
59. Dufferin to Hicks Beach, 19 June 1878, PRO 30/6-124, no. 180.
60. Admiralty to CO, 26 June 1878, PRO 30/6-124, no. 207. The Admiralty view was technically correct since coal did not become navy coal until it entered navy bins.
61. CO to Admiralty (copy), 9 July 1878, PRO 30/6-124, no. 227.
62. Hicks Beach to Dufferin (copy), 14 August 1878, PRO 30/6-124, no. 286.
63. Admiralty to CO, 6 September 1878, PRO 30/6-124, no. 327.
64. CO to Admiralty (copy), 19 November 1878, PRO 30/6-124, no. 351.
65. Hicks Beach to Dufferin (copy), 6 September 1878, PRO 30/6-124, no. 325.
66. WO to CO, 10 December 1878, PRO 30/6-124, no. 357.
67. CO to WO (copy), 19 December 1878, PRO 30/6-124, no. 359.
68. Lorne to Hicks Beach, 19 May 1879, PRO: CO 812/14, no. 33; Lorne to Hicks Beach, 28 May 1879, PRO: CO 812/14, no. 30; WO to CO, 30 June 1878, PRO: CO 812/14, no. 33. The officers were Lieutenant-Colonel T. Bland Strange (Canada), Instructor at Kingston and Colonel Lovell (WO), Commanding Officer Royal Engineers stationed at Halifax, Nova Scotia.
69. Frederick W. Wallace, *Wooden Ships and Iron Men* (London: Hodder & Stoughton, 1925).
70. Memorandum, 5 June 1877, PRO 30/6-122.
71. 'Report of a Colonial Defence Committee on the Temporary Defences of the Cape of Good Hope, Mauritius, Ceylon, Singapore and Hong Kong', 4 April 1878, PRO 30/6-124.
72. WO to CO, 15 May 1878, PRO 30/6-124, no. 102.
73. Treasury to CO, 22 May 1878, PRO 30/6-124, no. 126.
74. Frere to Carnarvon, 16 February 1880, printed in John Martineau, *The Life and Correspondence of Sir Bartle Frere* (London: John Murray, 1895), Vol. 2, p. 369n. Frere questioned a member of Sir Garnet Wolseley's staff about the incident and was told, 'You probably are not aware that the recoil apparatus which has been furnished to you for those guns has been long since condemned in our own service, and would never be put in a battery in Europe.'
75. Milne's Defence Committee was probably not aware of their existence. They were formed to relieve troops during the Indian Mutiny and were available again in 1878 in case of war with Russia.
76. 'Report of a Colonial Defence Committee on the Temporary Defences of the Cape of Good Hope, Mauritius, Ceylon, Singapore and Hong Kong', 4 April 1878, PRO 30/6-124. Ten 6.5 ton guns were recommended by Milne's Committee and sent to Simons Bay, a further ten such guns were recommended for Table Bay. Other recommendations included a *Comet*-class gunboat, six 64-pdr muzzle-loading guns; recruiting a local force of 1,500 infantry, 250 artillery and 150 mounted scouts, all to be under British command.
77. Milne to CO, 7 June 1878, PRO 30/6-124, no. 157.
78. WO to CO, 18 April 1879, PRO: CO 812/14, no. 19; CO to WO (copy), 30 June 1879, PRO: CO 812/14, no. 39. Frederick Augustus Thesiger, 2nd Baron Chelmsford (1827-1905): Indian Mutiny, Deputy Adjutant-General; Bombay presidency 1861-62; Abyssinia, with Napier 1868; Adjutant-General in East Indies 1869-74; command South Africa 1878-July 1879; KCB 1878; GCB 1879.

79. See memorandum, 5 June 1877, PRO 30/6-122.
80. CO to WO (copy), 30 April 1878, PRO 30/6-124, no. 61; CO to Treasury (copy), 30 April 1878, PRO 30/6-124, no. 59. The Colonial Defence Committee's views were also solicited. See CO to Milne (copy), 14 May 1878, PRO 30/6-124, no. 96.
81. John Glover (Governor of Newfoundland) to Hicks Beach, 16 May 1878, PRO 30/6-124, no. 131.
82. CO to WO (copy), 29 May 1878, PRO 30/6-124, no. 136.
83. WO to CO, 21 June 1878, PRO 30/6-124, no. 184. This was an example of soldier-thinking. St John's was the responsibility of the North Atlantic Squadron based at Bermuda. It only came north after the ice broke up in June each year.
84. Treasury to CO, 17 August 1878, PRO 30/6-124, no. 296.
85. CO to WO (copy), 29 August 1878, PRO 30/6-124, no. 314.
86. CO to WO (copy), 4 September 1878, PRO 30/6-124, no. 323.
87. Milne to CO, 14 March 1878, PRO 30/6-124, no. 11; WO to CO, 15 March 1878, PRO 30/6-124, no. 13.
88. Admiralty to CO, 30 April 1878, PRO 30/6-124, no. 64.
89. W. C. Robinson (Governor Straits Settlements) to CO, 29 March 1878, PRO 30/6-124, no. 21; Admiralty to CO, 12 April 1878, PRO 30/6-124, no. 21. The vessels added were *Ruby*, *Shannon* and *Diamond*.
90. WO to CO, 21 February 1879, PRO: CO 812/14, no. 14.
91. CO to Pope Hennessy (Governor of Hong Kong) (copy), 23 June 1879, PRO: CO 812/14 no. 36; FO to CO, 17 October 1878, PRO 30/6-124, no. 346.
92. CO to WO (copy), 7 June 1878, PRO 30/6-124, no. 157. The proposal was not acted upon.
93. Ussher (resident of Labuan) to CO, 7 May 1878, PRO 30/6-124, no. 73; Milne to CO, 29 May 1878, PRO 30/6-124, no. 145.
94. Admiralty to CO, 28 June 1878, PRO 30/6-124, no. 213.
95. CO to WO (copy), 29 August 1878, PRO 30/6-124, no. 314.
96. CO to Admiralty (copy), 11 July 1878, PRO 30/6-124, no. 233; Admiralty to CO, 19 July 1878, PRO 30/6-124, no. 242.
97. Treasury to CO, 2 May 1878, PRO 30/6-124, no. 67.
98. CO to Treasury (copy), 4 May 1878, PRO 30/6-124, no. 71.
99. CO to Treasury (copy), 18 May 1878, PRO 30/6-124, no. 110.
100. Treasury to CO, 22 May 1878, PRO 30/6-124 no. 126.
101. Carnarvon (out of office) wrote to Cape Governor Frere on 23 July 1878, deploring government inertia in imperial defence matters: 'The real vice of the situation is that it is impossible to persuade the Treasury to sanction any expense which is not at the moment popular with Parliament; and as Parliament cannot know what is necessary the ordinary and essential precautions are neglected.' See Hardinge, *Life of the Fourth Earl of Carnarvon*, Vol. 2, p. 99.
102. Frederick Stanley to Duke of Cambridge 1 May 1878, RA ADD.MSS.
103. Stafford Northcote, 'Memorandum on Defence Committee Function', 1 June 1878, NMM: MLN/163/1.
104. W. H. Smith to Milne, 1 June 1878, NMM: MLN/163/1.
105. CO to Milne, 31 May 1878, PRO 30/6-124, no. 140.
106. Milne to CO, 7 June 1878, PRO 30/6-124, no. 162.
107. Treasury to CO, 25 June 1878, PRO 30/6-124, no. 197.
108. CO to Treasury (copy), 5 July 1878, PRO 30/6-124, no. 221.
109. CO to WO (copy), 4 September 1878, PRO 30/6-124, no. 223.
110. A point of view voiced by the Duke of Argyll years previously: 'It is not because of the *usefulness* of our Colonies that we defend them. It is because we *must*

defend them. It seems to me mere folly to discuss the particular value of each Possession we have. I admit that *commercially* our colonies might be quite as valuable to us if they were independent. But this is a proposition, which, whether true or false can have no particular bearing on the question of defence.' See Argyll to Kimberley, 26 July 1873, KP: PC/A/19.

111. J. L. A. Simmons, *Memorandum on Colonial Defences*, 17 September 1878, PRO: CO 812/14 no. 4.

5

The Working of the Royal Commission: 1879–82

The conclusion that a proper assessment and distribution of the burdens of imperial defence required a basic body of knowledge that could only be acquired by a more permanent committee operating under different terms of reference, was apparent to Milne's Defence Committee at an early stage in its work. This opinion was echoed, appropriately, by the Chancellor of the Exchequer, and, after the crisis had passed, achieved a more reasoned and complete form in General Simmons' memorandum, issued on 17 September 1878, advocating a standing committee on colonial defence.[1] Hence the first steps towards the formation of the forthcoming Royal Commission were taken in the War Office, where the Russian 'war scare' had brought home the fact that an imperial war would probably mean a drain on home and Indian armies for garrison duty in imperial posts.[2] Since it was also clear that there would be very few troops to spare as a result of Cardwell's far-reaching reforms, and a great demand for ordnance, colonial defence in the case of a general war would present very serious difficulties. The Cardwell system had not reduced the size of Britain's general military responsibility, though it had cut down the actual means for meeting that responsibility as well as having reduced expenditure.[3] It was undoubtedly this anticipated strain on its resources, that moved the War Office to advocate an investigation of military requirements in the hope that strong evidence of shortcomings would induce greater preparedness and cut the speculative risk. There was similar apprehension at the Admiralty, where the problem of trade protection had inspired a proposal by the Director of Naval Construction to cease building battleships altogether in favour of fast, armed, merchant cruisers with specially strengthened bulkheads.[4] This radical proposal was not adopted, but the fact that it was seriously put forward by such a responsible person showed a great lack of confidence in the navy's ability to protect adequately Britain's trade and empire. Certainly Milne's Defence

Committee itself was under no illusions as to the necessity for something more permanent, and early in 1879, when the War Office was pressing Simmons' memorandum on the Colonial Office as evidence of the need for a new and permanent committee, so Milne's Defence Committee itself suggested that something along the same lines be set up.[5] Hicks Beach agreed to the formation of a new committee in February but, remembering the inadequacy of purely professional opinion when it came to convincing the Treasury, he moved cautiously and suggested the inclusion of a politician, a point with which Stanley, at the War Office, agreed.[6] Copies of Simmons' memorandum were circulated to Milne's Defence Committee and, one suspects, to the Cabinet, and negotiations for a new committee with Milne as president continued right up to the dissolution of his original committee.[7] In fact, plans were underway for Sir Henry Barkly and Lord Cadogan to represent the Colonial Office on the new body.[8]

What induced Hicks Beach to substitute a Royal Commission for the proposed committee is not clear.[9] As late as 10 July the latter was mentioned in correspondence with the Treasury, but on 24 July Carnarvon was requested to preside over a Royal Commission on colonial defence to be established shortly.[10] It is possible that Colomb's most recent advocacy of a Royal Commission penetrated the walls of the Colonial Office, or it may simply be that Disraeli (now Lord Beaconsfield) suddenly interested himself in the problem and, characteristically, quickly realized that the subject was too vast for a mere committee.[11] Whatever the impetus, it is clear that the Conservative government recognized the importance of the subject in a striking way some time in July 1879.

Carnarvon, who at once tentatively accepted the presidency, thus became the central figure around which imperial defence schemes and labours revolved for the next ten years. He was, as should be evident, a natural choice. Even while out of office he had addressed the prime minister on the defenceless state of the Cape of Good Hope, and the very mention of colonial defence must have brought 'Twitters' (Carnarvon) to the Tory chief's mind.[12] Disraeli, it is true, had little regard for Carnarvon as a political supporter in times of stress, but he had great respect for his ability.[13] He must also have appreciated that Carnarvon was well fitted to deal with matters of empire defence, a subject that some years ago Disraeli had himself characterized as involving 'matters of high policy'.

Hicks Beach's proposal to Carnarvon suggested that the inquiry should determine what places should be defended wholly or partially with imperial funds; what works, armament and garrisons were required in those places; the estimated cost of such fortification, and how that cost should be divided between imperial and colonial governments.[14] These were the principal problems, and he supposed that Carnarvon probably knew 'all about it already without further enquiry'. This was a friendly confidence, but acting upon it was not to prove so easy.

Carnarvon at any rate knew his own mind. His suggestions for the composition of the Commission were promptly made and were broad enough.[15] The two Liberals he suggested were Thomas Brassey, self-appointed representative of naval interests in parliament, and Hugh C. E. Childers, First Lord of the Admiralty in Gladstone's first administration.[16] A second Conservative representative would be Sir Henry Holland, who boasted considerable experience with Colonial Office affairs.[17] General Simmons should continue as 'representative of Military opinion'. Admiral Lord Gilford (the Earl of Clanwilliam) should represent Admiralty opinion, since Milne was 'worn out'. At this point breadth of view ceased, for Carnarvon wrote that 'representation of Colonial opinion is ... best away'. It was a portentous decision, and one hard to reconcile with his exercise of tact and solicitousness in previous dealings with Canada in the Dominion negotiations.

The commissioners had their numbers increased by the addition of Robert G. C. Hamilton, whom Hicks Beach put forward as Treasury representative.[18] Carnarvon would go no further than accepting him as a financial expert, feeling that a specifically designated Treasury man would hamper free inquiry.[19] Aside from this addition, and the fact that the Colonial Office selected Milne rather than Gilford as naval representative, the composition of the Commission stood as Carnarvon wished. Captain Jekyll, who had been secretary to Milne's Defence Committee, was appointed to that position in the new Commission. It is interesting to note that Hicks Beach tried again to secure colonial representation, suggesting the Canadian High Commissioner, Sir Alexander Galt, and Sir Julius Vogel, New Zealand agent-general.[20] He argued that the Commission's report would 'be more likely to be acted on by these colonies, if the Commission included some Colonists', and that 'a Commission so constituted might not be without its political effect, as representing the Empire'. The Colonial Secretary was not alone in his doubts concerning the wisdom of excluding the colonials, for Holland, writing later in the year, stated that perhaps the colonials should be tactfully informed that they were not forgotten.[21] Nevertheless, Carnarvon kept colonial representatives out.

Interestingly enough, the man who had argued most tirelessly both for a Royal Commission on imperial defence and for colonial representation upon it, and whose participation might have helped the Commission enormously, attempted to enter the select ranks. On 10 September 1897, when news of the Commission's appointment was public, Colomb called on Carnarvon to urge his 'claims' for joining its ranks. Carnarvon told him there were no 'claims' and that the Commission was already large enough. To Hicks Beach he stated that Colomb 'would add no weight to the Commission' and 'it is unfortunately common in these cases that there are really persons who desire to be added to these Commissions not for the sake of any public services which they can render but as a tribute to their own supposed merits or claims'.[22] The Colonial Secretary replied that Colomb was 'perpetually striving on this subject in magazines and newspapers' and that he was 'pushing and mischievous but nonetheless clever, and probably felt like a small dog that had had its bone taken away by a bigger one'.[23] Doubtless, Colomb was not bashful, yet what the Commission gained in 'weight' it lost in potential information. In heralding the Commission's appointment, the *Morning Post* simultaneously picked its flaws neatly: no colonial representation and no imperial defence pioneers, such as Colomb. It was, in truth, Carnarvon's Commission.[24]

The official charge of the Royal Commission Appointed to Enquire into the Defence of British Possessions and Commerce Abroad was issued on 12 September, although the commissioners as a whole did not signify their willingness to serve until 22 September.[25] The Commission had, however, held an informal meeting on 14 August.[26] There some general principles were decided upon. The commissioners requested that India be explicitly excluded from their deliberations, expressed their determination to handle the sensitive self-governing colonies with tact, and requested that information be obtained on the state of Australasian defences. More important, however, was a resolution calling for secrecy, for the commissioners wanted a guarantee that their reports be for the eyes of the Cabinet alone. This stipulation was easily obtained, for political secrecy on matters involving large military expenditure is never difficult to acquire. It was, however, important in the history of the Carnarvon Commission and its influence, and not solely in the manner intended by its authors.

On 13 September Carnarvon sent Childers a definite scheme of procedure, selecting the consideration of imperial trade routes as the first duty of the Commission.[27] The method of study strongly endorsed the War Office means of measuring priority. Sufficient data having been obtained about trade routes, attention would be given to the manner in which the Admiralty proposed to defend ships on these routes in case of war. Next, the War Office would be called into consultation regarding the actual mechanics of fortifying places selected for new or improved shore defences. The Commission would then define matters of general principle and discuss matters arising out of the evidence. Carnarvon indicated that he was aware of some of the potential dangers involved in too much secrecy when he suggested that the report be divided into public and private sections. Finally, almost as an afterthought, he acknowledged the need for obtaining colonial information.

Carnarvon's brief underscored how far imperial defence had wandered from its original impelling force – coal – but in his reply, former First Lord Childers restored the perspective somewhat by advocating discussion with the Admiralty on coaling stations and the problems involved in their defence.[28] Childers, who had spent time in Australia prior to entering parliament, was also wise enough to see that the self-governing colonies could not be treated in quite the cavalier way indicated by Carnarvon. It was perhaps inevitable that such a large subject should have its investigation get off to a jerky and confused start. Indeed, the first practical work was done by Hicks Beach. Without waiting for a direct request from the Commission, he recognized the special expertise of Sir William Jervois, now Governor of South Australia, by asking him for a report on the defensive arrangements of all the Australasian colonies.[29] This much was already accomplished when regular meetings began in October and an official statement of the Commission's existence was given to all colonial governors. The Commission was also given a base, 13 Delahay Street, from which to work.[30] A shorthand secretary, a draughtsman and a messenger were added to the staff, and the Commission's printed work was let out to the Foreign Office printers.[31]

Carnarvon was astounded by the breadth of the inquiry as its potentialities unfolded. Only two weeks after he had written to Childers suggesting that the Commission could complete its work in a year, he was having second thoughts.[32] In fact there was so much to be done that it was difficult to know where to begin. Carnarvon had for some time been impressed with the importance of the Cape, and there a definite start was made. Not only did the Colonial Office request a local professional committee's report on Cape defences: Carnarvon also wrote personally to Cape Colony Governor Frere stating the urgency of the case for security at the Cape.[33]

Before the New Year Milne and Carnarvon exchanged views as to the Commission's mode of procedure. There can be little doubt that the former resented being displaced as a leader of imperial defence inquiry by even so eminent a patrician and politician as Carnarvon. Equally so, it is clear that Carnarvon had little respect for Milne's ability. When the former First Naval Lord was invited to join the Commission he volunteered his views on what should be its main concern, only to be told by Carnarvon that the time was not ripe for such expression.[34] Meanwhile, Carnarvon was formulating a plan of procedure with Simmons in London, even as he later took Childers into his confidence.[35] This was not an auspicious beginning. Milne could not be present during the October and November sittings, and late in the latter month he again put forward his views by post.[36] In his characteristically disjointed way, he stressed several critical points. First, since an enemy could be blockaded in European waters, the Commission's calculations need only be based on the threats of small squadrons or single raiding vessels. Second, the problem of local volunteers and militia to man the forts was very important. Third, in situations where colonial defence contribution was hoped for, previous consultation with those concerned would render co-operation more likely.[37] These sound suggestions indicate that he had profited from the lessons of Treasury intransigence and had grasped the central army problem of general troop shortage. Carnarvon's reply revealed some sympathy with these ideas. He noted that Jervois' drawback as a defence adviser was a tendency to thoroughness without regard to cost. The Commission chairman also agreed regarding the difficulty involved in the scarcity of troops. Australasian defences, he maintained, should be undertaken by colonists. The chief difficulty would arise over questions of cost apportionment at places like the Cape, Esquimalt and various crown colonies.[38] Unfortunately, Carnarvon's views, however sympathetic, were accompanied by the remark that Milne's letter would best have been addressed to the Commission's secretary. Courtesy was not among his strong points, and this cavalier treatment of Milne was to have major repercussions on the ultimate work of the Commission.

At the beginning of 1880 the commissioners patiently sifted the available evidence on trade routes and colonial defences as they waited for the Cape report which was held up by lack of co-operation between Frere and Sir Garnet Wolseley, the local Commander-in-Chief.[39] The report did not arrive until 12 March, and supplementary local information concerning political attitudes toward defence questions not until April.[40] This delay impressed upon the commissioners the scheduling problems involved in collecting colonial information, and on 20 February they determined on dealing with defence in the responsible government colonies of Australasia, Canada and the Cape during the ensuing summer.[41] Yet despite the halting start Carnarvon was not displeased with the progress made, for on the same day he informed the Colonial Secretary that the composition of the Commission was excellent and that it was getting on at the rate of three meetings a week.[42]

Unfortunately, his sanguine mood was to disappear rapidly. In late March the Commission received a blow, the seriousness of which was not immediately appreciated. A Liberal government replaced the Conservative one following the 1880 general election, and Gladstone returned to 10 Downing Street. Across the road at the Colonial Office, Lord Kimberley again took charge. The consequences might have been predicted. Milne sensed the portent and offered to resign, but was persuaded to stay on by Lord Northbrook, the incoming First Lord of the Admiralty.[43] Poor communication between the Colonial Office and Delahay Street soon convinced Carnarvon that the new government was not interested in the defence inquiry, and he wrote to Kimberley on 28 May to request support.[44] In his strange pompous way Carnarvon attempted to place the matter on a non-political plane. Was the Commission to continue?, he asked. Upon what terms? Who would replace Childers, now Secretary of State for War, and Brassey, now Civil Lord of the Admiralty? He hoped the replacements would be important men. Did the Cabinet appreciate the magnitude of the task? In conversation Kimberley had hinted at restriction of facilities, to which Carnarvon stated that nothing less than full and complete government support would suffice if the work were to be properly done. Carnarvon's fears were amply justified. Kimberley was cool toward the project, and requested a memorandum from the Colonial Office staff giving details of the Commission's formation and progress.[45]

The new Colonial Secretary took the subject to the Cabinet on 8 June 1880. He told his colleagues that he had been alarmed to find the scope of the Commission so wide, and had been shocked to discover that it was the Colonial Office's practice to use the Commission's prestige 'with a view ... "of fortifying" the Office with their authority in applying pressure on other departments for imperial expenditure in the Colonies'.[46] Such behaviour was, he stated with characteristic Liberal concern about departmental accountability and responsibility, a deplorable interference with the 'executive function' of the government on the part of an 'irresponsible body'. Kimberley argued that the defence of commerce was properly a War Office and Admiralty problem that the Commission had usurped. He spoke of the 'difficulty of resisting the demands of the Colonies for public money' and that in this connection Carnarvon was inclined to urge views unacceptable to 'ourselves or our supporters'. Yet despite his numerous reservations or outright objections, Kimberley was of the opinion that the inquiry could not be stopped, since some colonials had been already interviewed by the Commission, and hence knew something of its purposes. Such knowledge might generate adverse publicity for the government were it to scrap the investigation unceremoniously. It would be politically safer to limit the Commission's scope to negotiation with the colonies regarding the division of defence costs between home and colonial governments. Were the entire commerce protection problem withdrawn, 'Carnarvon would probably resign'. Lord Northbrook agreed that the inquiry should be limited and recommended that the ministry should 'put on the Commission two men [upon] whom we can thoroughly depend to be reasonable in their views as to the expenditure of money upon fortifications whether Carnarvon approves of them or not'.[47] Childers, now Secretary of State for War, was less hostile to the Commission's inquiry, although he thought Carnarvon had too much power.[48] Nonetheless, he objected to withdrawing the coal station problem from its consideration, although maintaining that it should not discuss the acquisition of new bases. No Cabinet decision was reached. Yet if Kimberley's views had hinted at radical distaste for colonial defence preoccupation, the authentic voice was heard next day when John Bright denounced this 'fitting outcome to the folly or madness of our predecessors' who 'undertake to defend half the world'.[49] 'We are not', he declaimed, 'proposing to make war but to maintain peace. I suggest that the whole of this insane scheme be given up.'

The bulk of the Cabinet was more subtle, however, and on 12 June Gladstone wrote that, although distasteful, the Commission had to continue for political reasons.[50] Give it 'its tether', he wrote, 'let it take its time, and perhaps make itself useless'. Thus, after a further impatient query from Carnarvon, Kimberley gave his assent to continuance.[51] Certainly it was a bare nod. 'As we find the Commission already in existence', wrote the Colonial Secretary, it was not proposed to change its terms or conditions.[52] The Commissioners could expect all the facilities and information accorded to any similar body. Yet a condition was imposed and Carnarvon began to reap the harvest on his earlier demand for secrecy, for Kimberley insisted upon it. The implication was clear: the Liberal government would let the inquiry proceed, but ensure that its findings did not see the light of day. The provocation was equally clear, and that Carnarvon swallowed his pride and dispatched a frosty but polite letter of acceptance was emphatic testimony that his failings lay more in lack of tact than in lack of devotion to his task.[53] He must have known that the future course of his work would be thorny, and had he known that almost at that moment his former Commission colleague Childers was ensuring that the vital problem of troop dispersal was being withdrawn for the Commission's view, his heart might have failed him.[54]

On 27 June 1880 Simmons wrote to Secretary Jekyll, 'I am glad to hear that the Government have come to a decision to complete the Commission notwithstanding they appear to have done it in an ungracious manner. I am very glad Lord Carnarvon did not send too stiff a reply, as it might have tended to create difficulties on our future proceedings.' A dangerous moment had passed, but the commissioner's outlook could hardly have been buoyant. Yet in the midst of its tribulations support came from one interested quarter. The Queen heard of the Commission's difficulties with the new government, and, through Foreign Secretary Lord Granville, questioned the prime minister.[55] Since the royal letter came after the Cabinet had extended its reluctant assent, Kimberley was able to inform Victoria – rather disingenuously – that any delay was due to Lord Carnarvon's absence and to enlisting of the services of two new commissioners, Samuel Whitbread and the Earl of Camperdown, both ex-Civil Lords of the Admiralty and both staunch Liberals.[56] By August, Childers too had hit upon the proper way to limit the Commission's influence. By enforcing the secrecy upon which Carnarvon was so insistent, he wrote to Kimberley, any damaging revelations of the Commission could be squelched: 'Great caution should be used not to allow this restriction of the work of the Commission to get abroad.'[57] The implication in Gladstone's earlier decision was now explicit.

Notwithstanding the tenuous nature of its existence, during the spring and early summer, the Commission heard evidence from the Duke of

Cambridge and Australasian representatives, excepting those of Western Australia (who were not invited) and of New Zealand.[58] The Prime Minister of Canada, Sir John A. Macdonald, also gave testimony to the Commission. Further, the commissioners requested information from the War Office on the nature and prospects of nearly all actual and potentially important strategic points in the empire, exclusive of those for which the Australasians and the Canadians had assumed direct and complete responsibility. The places listed were differentiated; first priority being given to those that served both as coaling stations and 'ports of refuge', while lesser importance was assigned to those whose possibilities did not extend beyond the storage of coal.[59]

After hearing Macdonald's evidence, the Commission, with the exception of a few days in October spent collecting personal evidence, did little until the following spring. Lord Carnarvon was ordered by his doctor to Madeira during the winter for reasons of health, and in any case little could be done until the War Office produced requested information regarding coaling station defence.[60]

Jekyll, however, kept the Commission alive as he toasted his feet at 13 Delahay Street. He must, in truth, have had little else to do since the Colonial Office was so prudent about sharing defence information with the Commission. Throughout 1880, proposals came to the Colonial Office from the Canadian Governor-General regarding the possibility of establishing a permanent regular army reserve in Canada.[61] Although War Office officials were privileged to assist in pronouncing the scheme 'impracticable', a similar opportunity was denied the defence investigators.[62] The same was true of a proposed scheme to use Chinese volunteers at Hong Kong, which, when it received the tentative approval of the Duke of Cambridge, was passed on to the Commission in the form of a *fait accompli*.[63] Also those whose duty it was to determine the strategic position of Mauritius were not informed when the Governor, Sir George Bowen, ordered rifles for the volunteer militia.[64] The Commission was, however, allowed to rubber stamp a War Office opinion that standardization of military equipment amongst the colonies would be useful.[65] It was also allowed to arbitrate a wrangle between the Colonial and War Offices on the merits of colonial as opposed to imperial Commanders-in-Chief in the various colonies. That imperials should always command was, not surprisingly, the view of the Duke of Cambridge, who used correspondence with his army 'trusties' to keep a finger in every military pie he could.[66] Having had some experience of giving *carte blanche* to military authorities, the Colonial Office, while acquiescing to the general policy, suggested that the final decision in each case be made dependent upon particular circumstances.[67] After all, there was the telegraph. The Royal Commission scored procedurally in its reaction to this honour, replying that such an important question was outside its scope but that it was prepared to lay down the rule that imperial posts should always be commanded by imperial officers.[68]

The commissioners entered 1881 confident that their labours would soon cease, but unaware that the government they served was discussing troop reductions in the imperial fortresses.[69] The latter finally showed its true face early in the New Year, however, when it reduced the commissioners' travelling expense grant from £1,000 to £800; although they probably never knew that Kimberley himself was responsible for this particular courtesy.[70]

During the winter Milne was prevented from doing any effective work by serious eye trouble. By April an operation had relieved his distress so that his offer of resignation could be refused.[71] This personal trouble, however, was the occasion of an extremely friendly exchange of letters between the elderly Admiral and Carnarvon that, for a time, dispelled the frost of their relationship on the Commission, although Carnarvon could hardly have regarded the former's absence as restricting its work.[72]

What did restrict it was the revelation that, despite an additional personal appeal from Carnarvon to Childers in December 1880, the War Office had taken no effective action on the request for information on the various coaling stations made the previous summer. On 3 May 1881 reports on the indicated places did arrive but they were quickly discovered to have been compiled in the Inspector-General of Fortifications' office and based on no more evidence than that already available to the Commission.[73] True, the War Office was not completely inactive. On 25 February the Colonial Office was informed of plans to secure information through a personal investigative officer.[74] Yet that officer did not depart until June 1881, and no attempt was made to inform the Commissioners of the huge delay, much less explain it.[75] On receipt of the inadequate reports the Commission sent a sharp protest to the Colonial Office complaining that War Office inaction had delayed its work for at least six months.[76] A Colonial Office functionary uncharitably charged that this protest was intended to cover the Commission's own tardiness, and no formal complaint was forwarded to the War Office.[77]

Carnarvon's displeasure could hardly have been eased by clashes with the Colonial Office over the relative strategic importance of Galle and Colombo, Ceylon. The Commission attached greater importance to the former, the Colonial Office plumped for the latter, and when a War Office interim report sided with Carnarvon and his colleagues, the Colonial Office noted that 'the War Office seems to be blindly following the lead of the Royal Defence Commission'.[78] Jekyll was called over to the Colonial Office for a 'little talk' and the commissioners were forced to confess that judgements concerning the merits of various Ceylonese harbours were beyond their scope.[79] This outcome was legitimate, perhaps, but cramping and on the large view ridiculous, and only the encouragement of his co-workers and his sense of the importance of the work kept Carnarvon from resignation.[80]

Despite the winter's inactivity and frequent clashes with departments of state, the Commission took more evidence during the spring and summer of 1881, and its first report, dealing in general with Britain's dependence upon overseas trade and particularly with the strategic importance of the Cape, was in its proof stage in July and ready by September.[81] To ensure some circulation, Carnarvon wisely informed the Queen of its existence.[82] Kimberly's reaction was certainly slight. Carnarvon received no reply to his personal letter to the Colonial Secretary covering the first report and pressing its importance.[83] Indeed Colonial Office acknowledgement came only as backwash from Carnarvon's strategy with the Queen, for he was asked that no further reports be sent out without its consent.[84] Victoria nonetheless received her copy. At the Colonial Office itself the first report was compared to an 1881 memorandum on imperial defence dashed off by Colonel Charles 'Chinese' Gordon, then commanding the Royal Engineers at Mauritius.[85] True, his memorandum flashed with sparks of genius, but serious comparison of a report embodying the result of six years' expert experience and two years' concentrated investigation with an impromptu effort by Gordon was hardly complimentary to the Royal Commission.

In fact the latter part of 1881 saw the Commission virtually cut off from the latest defence information by the Colonial Office. The question of forming an imperial reserve in Canada did finally reach the commissioners, but evidently Macdonald's depreciation of peacetime defence planning had lessened their enthusiasm for advising or co-operating with the Canadians, and the dominion was ignored despite a plea from Governor-General Lord Lorne to Carnarvon that it receive some notice.[86]

In January 1882 the Treasury, feeling no doubt that a Commission opinion on the question of providing colonial garrisons would probably tend to greater reliance on local talent and hence a long-run saving, asked the War Office to refer the garrison problem to it.[87] The Secretary of State for War again refused, stating that it was not advisable to widen the Commission's scope.[88] Furthermore, Childers deliberately kept consideration of the defences at the four imperial fortresses away from the Commission.[89] Since these places were traditionally War Office responsibilities his action was explicable, but again hardly indicative of government confidence in the Commission.

The investigation concluded in 1882 and the second report, dealing largely with defence recommendations for Australasia, was ready in March.[90] The third and final report with its important strategic summing-up and detailed discussion of imperial bases was delayed, due to a disagreement on the Commission that generated a minority opinion by Milne and Barkly on the defences of Ceylon and Esquimalt.[91] Advance copies were ready in July and the Commission dissolved in early August, although the winding-up process at Delahay Street went on until December when the fully completed third report was distributed.[92]

A sour note marked the conclusion. Carnarvon wrote personally to Kimberley to stress the importance of the reports and to suggest that a CMG for Jekyll might be in order.[93] Kimberley wrote 'doubtful I think' over the suggestion and replied formally through his staff that the reports would receive the attention that the subject deserved.[94] When the usual letter of thanks was prepared Kimberley noted 'why is this to be signed by me instead of the usual form of communication between Departments?'[95] He was at least consistent. Yet despite the joint difficulties of a discouraging government attitude and of a chairman who, despite his high-minded tenacity, could be both erratic and overbearing, there did emerge three reports.

NOTES

1. J. L. A. Simmons, 'Memorandum on Colonial Defences', 17 September 1878, PRO: CO 812/14, no. 4.
2. Stanley Leathes (ed.), *Cambridge Modern History* (Cambridge: Cambridge University Press, 1910), Vol. 12, p. 33.
3. The evidence for this assertion comes from so many bits of information that its stating here is the result of a cumulative impression. Some indication was given by the Secretary of State for War when, during the height of the Eastern Question, he wrote to the Duke of Cambridge stating that the War Office might be able to supply troops to one area of emergency, but that if both South Africa and Turkey called there were neither reserves available nor plans laid to meet the double strain. See Stanley to Duke of Cambridge, 17 October 1878, RA ADD.MSS.
4. See Nathaniel Barnaby, 'Paper by Chief of Naval Construction', 22 March 1877, Milne Papers, NMM: MLN/163/1. This matter was still under discussion in December 1878. See minute by Admiral Henry Boys, 12 December 1878, NMM: MLN/163/1.
5. WO to CO, 16 January 1879, PRO: CO 812/14, no. 4; Milne to CO, 4 January 1879, PRO: CO 812/14, no. 1.
6. CO to WO, 24 February 1879, PRO: CO 812/14, no. 14; WO to CO, 6 March 1879, PRO: CO 812/14, no. 15.
7. CO to Barkly (Colonial Defence Committee), 17 April 1879, PRO: CO 812/14, nos 20 and 21; Milne to CO, 28 April 1879, PRO: CO 812/14, no. 24. The War Office wanted Milne to continue. See WO to CO, 6 March 1879, PRO: CO 812/14, no. 15.
8. CO to WO, 29 April 1879, PRO: CO 812/14, no. 26.
9. In June 1878 Thomas Brassey spoke at the Royal Colonial Institute. He praised and seconded the agitation of J. C. R. Colomb toward setting up a Royal Commission to investigate the empire defence situation. Yet it is unlikely that the Colonial Office was much guided by opinion at the Royal Colonial Institute. See T. Brassey, *A Colonial Naval Volunteer Force* (London: Longmans, Green, 1878), p. 3.
10. CO to Treasury, 10 July 1879, PRO: CO 812/16, no. 3.

11. Colomb spoke at the Royal Colonial Institute on 28 March 1879.
12. Carnarvon to Beaconsfield, 6 July 1878, printed in Arthur Hardinge, *The Life of Henry Howard Molyneux Herbert, Fourth Earl of Carnarvon* (London: Oxford University Press, 1925), Vol. 3, p. 99. See also Eric Walker, *A History of South Africa* (London: Longmans, Green, 1947), p. 363.
13. Disraeli was highly pleased with Carnarvon's conduct of Colonial Office affairs and friendly with him until the Eastern Question divided them. See Benjamin Disraeli, First Earl of Beaconsfield, *The Letters of Disraeli to Lady Bradford and Lady Chesterfield*, ed. Marquis of Zetland (London: Ernest Benn, 1929), Vol. 1, pp. 161, 164, for appreciative comments by Disraeli. Yet Carnarvon was a difficult personality: 'Carnarvon is in Somersetshire and worries me to death with telegrams of four pages; he is a very clever fellow. But the greatest fidget in the world' (ibid., Vol. 1, pp. 312–13). For Disraeli, cleverness without compatibility of view was not enough during Eastern Question tension, and he wrote of 'the platitudes of Highclere' (Carnarvon's home). (Ibid., Vol. 2, p. 152.)
14. Hicks Beach to Carnarvon, 24 July 1879, PRO 30/6-52.
15. Carnarvon to Hicks Beach (copy), 5 August 1879, PRO 30/6-52.
16. Thomas Brassey, 1st Earl Brassey (1836–1918): Politician and naval advocate; author of numerous works on the Royal Navy and its administration; Civil Lord of Admiralty 1881–84; Parliamentary Secretary at Admiralty, 1884–85; founder of Brassey's *Naval Annual*, 1886; 'but his productions, while full of facts, seldom led up to any concrete conclusions and the effect of them was rather to ventilate the subject than to produce any tangible results' (Vincent Wilberforce Baddeley, in *Dictionary of National Biography*, 1912–21 Supplement, p. 63). KCB 1881; earldom 1911. Hugh Culling Eardley Childers (1827–96): Liberal politician; Trinity, Cambridge; Inspector schools Melbourne, Victoria 1851; agent-general for Victoria in London 1857; MP 1860–85; First Lord Admiralty 1868–71; Secretary of State for War 1880–82; Chancellor of Exchequer 1882–85; Home Secretary 1886.
17. Henry Thurstan Holland, 1st Viscount Knutsford (1825–1914): legal adviser at Colonial Office 1867 (appointed by Carnarvon); Assistant Undersecretary for Colonies 1870–74; Financial Secretary to Treasury 1885–86, 1886–87; Secretary of State for Colonies 1887–1892; PC 1885; GCMG 1888.
18. The Cabinet wanted a finance representative. See Hicks Beach to Carnarvon, 12 August 1879 and 15 August 1879, PRO 30/6-52. Robert G. C. Hamilton (1836–95): public servant; Assistant Secretary to Board of Trade 1872–78; accountant-general of navy 1878; Permanent Secretary to Admiralty 1882; Permanent Undersecretary for Ireland 1883–86; Governor of Tasmania 1886–93; KCB 1884.
19. Carnarvon to Hicks Beach (copy) 17 August 1879, PRO 30/6-52.
20. Hicks Beach to Carnarvon, 12 August 1879, PRO 30/6-52.
21. Holland to Carnarvon, 30 October 1879, PRO 30/6-52. He added, however, that much factual material should be first gathered before the colonists could be practically useful.
22. Carnarvon to Hicks Beach (copy), 10 September 1879, PRO 30/6-52.
23. Hicks Beach to Carnarvon, 12 September 1879, PRO 30/6-52.
24. Clipping dated 12 September 1879, preserved in Carnarvon Papers, PRO 30/6-52.
25. 12 September 1879, PRO: CO 812/16, no. 22 (enclosure); Carnarvon to CO, 22 September 1879, PRO: CO 812/16, no. 29.
26. J. L. A. Simmons, Memorandum, 14 August 1879, PRO 30/6-52. Milne was not at the meeting on 14 August. See Carnarvon to Milne (copy), 13 August 1879,

PRO 30/6-52.
27. Carnarvon to Childers (copy), 13 September 1879, PRO 30/6-52.
28. Childers to Carnarvon, 19 September 1879, PRO 30/6-52.
29. Beach to Jervois, 22 August 1879, PRO: CO 812/16, no. 16. Hicks Beach asked for individual defence reports from all the colonial governors, including Jervois, who was also to report on all Australasian colonies. All reports were to be collected and sent on by Jervois.
30. Delahay Street skirted the southeastern corner of St James Park, connecting Duke Street with Long Ditch. It disappeared early in the twentieth century when the area was cleared to make way for government buildings to house the Board of Trade, Ministry of Health and Education Department.
31. Carnarvon Commission, 'Circular to all Colonial Governors' (copy), 2 October 1879, PRO: CO 812/16, no. 44; Treasury to CO, 11 October 1879, PRO: CO 323/340; Only the title of the Royal Commission was communicated to colonial governors, and they were warned of its secret nature. Colonial Office printing was usually done by Eyre and Spottiswoode, but on this occasion the Foreign Office was used – again for secrecy. See Carnarvon to Hicks Beach (copy), 5 November 1879, PRO 30/6-52.
32. Carnarvon to Hicks Beach (copy), 5 November 1879, PRO 30/6-52.
33. Carnarvon to CO, 9 October 1879. PRO: CO 812/16, no. 35; Carnarvon to Frere (copy), 31 October 1879, PRO 30/6-52.
34. Milne to Carnarvon, 10 August 1879, PRO 30/6-52; Carnarvon to Milne (copy), 13 August 1879, PRO 30/6-52.
35. See J. L. A. Simmons, Memorandum, 14 August 1879, PRO 30/6-52.
36. Milne to Carnarvon, 10 August 1879, PRO 30/6-52; Milne to Carnarvon (copy), 8 November 1879, NMM: MLN/163/2.
37. Milne to Carnarvon (copy), 28 November 1879, NMM: MLN/163/2.
38. Carnarvon to Milne, 16 December 1879, NMM: MLN/163/2.
39. Although Frere sent a personal report. See CO to Carnarvon Commission, 10 January 1880, PRO: CO 812/16, no. 94. To get the Cape Committee report, the Colonial Office was finally forced, on the Commission's recommendation, to ask the War Office to instruct Wolseley to co-operate with Frere. See Carnarvon Commission to CO, 20 January 1880 (Passed on to War Office, 22 January), PRO: CO 812/16, no. 106.
40. Frere to Hicks Beach, n.d. (received at CO 12 March 1880), PRO: CO 812/16, no. 172; Frere to Hicks Beach, n.d. (received at CO 1 April 1880), PRO: CO 812/16, no. 191 (enclosure).
41. Carnarvon Commission to CO, 20 February 1880, PRO: CO 812/16, no. 135.
42. Carnarvon to Hicks Beach (copy), 20 February 1880, PRO 30/6-52.
43. Milne to Jekyll, 8 May 1880, PRO 30/6-52. It is not certain exactly why Milne contemplated resignation. It may have been dislike of Carnarvon. Yet the fact that Milne, through being First Naval Lord (1872–74), had some experience of Liberal attitudes to defence, points to the explanation suggested above. Thomas George Baring, first Earl of Northbrook (1826–1904): Undersecretary for War 1868–72; Viceroy of India 1872–76; First Lord of Admiralty 1880–85.
44. Carnarvon to Kimberley (copy), 28 May 1880, PRO 30/6-52.
45. Robert Blake, 'Memorandum on the Progress of the Royal Commission', 1 June 1880, PRO: CO 323/356 – 1884. Blake (not the historian) prepared the memorandum especially for Kimberley.
46. Kimberley, Cabinet memorandum, 8 June 1880, KP: PC/B/24.
47. Northbrook, Cabinet memorandum, 8 June 1880, KP: PC/B/24.
48. Childers, Cabinet memorandum, 8 June 1880, KP: PC/B/24.

THE WORKING OF THE ROYAL COMMISSION: 1879-82

49. Bright to Kimberley, 9 June 1880, KP: PC/B/24.
50. Gladstone to Kimberley, 12 June 1880, KP: PC/B/24.
51. Carnarvon to Kimberley (copy), 15 June 1880, PRO 30/6-52.
52. Kimberley to Carnarvon, 17 June 1880, PRO 30/6-52.
53. Carnarvon to Kimberley (copy), 18 June 1880, PRO 30/6-52.
54. In reply to a Treasury request that the colonial garrison problem be referred to the Royal Commission, Childers replied that this was a question of government policy and that it was not proposed to widen the scope of the inquiry to include questions of policy. See WO to Treasury (copy), 23 June 1880, PRO: WO 32/88-7512.
55. Granville to the Queen, 19 July 1880, RA D29, no. 41.
56. Kimberley to Sir Henry Ponsonby (Private Secretary to the Queen), 20 and 21 July 1880, RA P25, nos 111 and 112. These two new members officially joined the Commission on 2 August 1880, although Carnarvon invited Whitbread to hear the evidence of Sir John A. Macdonald (29 July 1880). See Carnarvon Commission to CO, PRO: CO 812/21, no. 48; Carnarvon to Whitbread (copy), 26 July 1880, PRO 30/6-52.
57. Childers to Kimberley, 10 August 1880, KP: PC/B/24.
58. From 'Digest of Evidence' attached to 'Third and Final Report of the Royal Commissioners Appointed to Enquire into the Defence of British Possessions and Commerce Abroad' (hereafter Carnarvon Commission Third Report), 25 May 1880, PRO 30/6-126, 612-13.
59. See Carnarvon Commission to CO, 26 July 1880, PRO: CO 812/21, no. 42. (1) Coal and Refuge Harbours: Table Bay and Simons Bay at the Cape; Port Louis, Mauritius; Colombo and Trincomalee, Ceylon; Singapore; Hong Kong; Port Royal, Jamaica; Esquimalt; Aden; Falkland Islands. (2) Coal Harbours only: Sierra Leone; Gambia; St Helena; Ascension; Cyprus; Perim; Galle, Ceylon; Diego Garcia, Seychelles; Cocos; Penang; Labuan; Thursday Island (Northern Australia), Fiji; King George Sound, Western Australia; Barbados; St Lucia; Antigua; Bahamas; St Johns, Newfoundland. Ports of refuge were harbours where unarmed shipping could safely congregate and where warships could expect some refit facilities.
60. Carnarvon to Kimberley (copy), 18 October 1880, PRO 30/6-52.
61. Selby Smyth, 'Memorandum on Imperial Reserve in Canada', 11 November 1880, PRO: WO 32/121-058. The proposal had come to the Colonial Office in the first place. See Lorne (Governor-General of Canada) to Kimberley, 12 September 1880, KP: PC/B/6. For Selby Smith's proposal see Appendix.
62. The decisions were issued in the Colonial Office on 27 November 1880 and in the War Office on 15 December 1880. See CO to WO, PRO: WO 32/120-7696; PRO: WO 32/121-058.
63. This scheme had the benefit of the practised advice of Colonel G. C. Gordon who was visiting in China at the time. He approved the scheme, as did the Duke of Cambridge. Yet it is doubtful whether the Duke approved of Gordon's opinion that 'all rubbish of goose step, right face, etc., which our regular drills delight in, ought to be left untaught'. See Governor Hennessy to Kimberley, 5 July 1880, PRO: CO 812/21, no. 57 (encl.). The Duke of Cambridge thought the experiment might be made with small numbers and great caution. See WO to CO, 6 July 1880, PRO: CO 812/21, no. 32. The War Office suggested that the subject be referred to the Royal Commission. See WO to CO, 23 July 1880, PRO: CO 812/21, no. 421. When the Colonial Office did inform the Royal Commission only this letter and Colonel Gordon's were sent. The rest of the correspondence was withheld. See CO to Carnarvon Commission (copy), 2 August 1880, PRO:

CO 812/21, no. 46.
64. WO to CO, 16 July 1880. PRO: CO 812/21, no. 39. Although Mauritius' offer to form a volunteer force was passed on, the guns were for Mauritius volunteers. See CO to Carnarvon Commission, 15 June 1880, PRO: CO 812/21, no. 19. Mauritius also contributed £21,000 per annum towards its own defence. See WO Memorandum, January 1880, PRO: WO 32/88-7512.
65. Carnarvon Commission to CO, 15 October 1880, PRO: CO 812/21, no. 79. WO to CO, 19 July 1880, PRO: CO 812/21, no. 40.
66. Duke of Cambridge to Major-General Colley (with special reference to South Africa) (copy), 5 January 1880, RA ADD.MSS. The Duke used this steady correspondence with commanders of army units stationed abroad (part of his 'old boy' network) to influence events in the colonies, and to curb reforms he did not like, especially those attempted by 'that desperate reformer', Wolseley. See Duke of Cambridge to General Johnson (Commander-in-Chief India), 17 April 1879, RA ADD.MSS.
67. CO to WO (copy), 4 November 1880, PRO: CO 812/21, no. 92.
68. Carnarvon Commission to CO, 10 January 1881, PRO: CO 812/21, no. 113.
69. Carnarvon Commission to CO, 16 December 1880, PRO: CO 812/21, no. 106; CO to WO (copy), 30 December 1880, PRO: CO 323/347-20301. The Colonial Office had no objection to a reduction of troops in the four imperial fortresses.
70. CO to Treasury, 10 January 1881, PRO: CO 812/21, no. 114.
71. Milne to Carnarvon, 18 April 1881, PRO 30/6-52.
72. Milne to Carnarvon, 7 February 1881, PRO 30/6-52.
73. Carnarvon Commission to CO, 3 May 1881, PRO: CO 323/350-7892.
74. WO to CO, 25 February 1881, PRO: CO 323/350-3489.
75. WO to CO, 15 June 1881, PRO: CO 323/350-1065.
76. Carnarvon Commission to CO, 3 May 1881, PRO: CO 323/350-7892.
77. Robert Meade's minute, endorsed by permanent undersecretary Herbert on 5 June 1881, PRO: CO 323/350-7892.
78. Meade minute on WO to CO, 24 May 1881, PRO: CO 323/350-9216
79. Ebden minute on ibid.; Carnarvon Commission to CO, 21 June 1881, PRO: CO 323/350-10888.
80. Whitbread to Carnarvon, 24 September 1881, PRO 30/6-52.
81. Evidence was taken from Lord Northbrook (5 July 1881) which Carnarvon personally preserved (PRO 30/6-52), Donald Currie, shipowner; Sir Charles Bright, telegraph engineer; Sir Bartle Frere, late Cape Governor; and Lieutenant-Colonel Drury of the Queensland Artillery Company. See Carnarvon Commission Third Report, Digest of Evidence. 'First Report of the Royal Commissioners appointed to Enquire into the Defence of British Possessions and Commerce Abroad', *Parl. Papers*, 1887, Vol. 55, p. 299 (version edited by Carnarvon, published for colonial conference of that year). Also preserved in PRO 30/6-131. Proof dated 9 July 1881, see PRO 30/6-123. Carnarvon to Kimberley, 18 September 1881, PRO 30/6-52.
82. Carnarvon to Ponsonby (copy), 8 September 1881, PRO 30/6-52.
83. Carnarvon to Kimberley (copy), 18 September 1881, PRO 30/6-52.
84. CO to Carnarvon Commission, 19 October 1881. See Carnarvon Commission to CO, 26 September 1881, PRO: CO 323/350-17589.
85. Ebden minute on ibid., 7 October 1881, PRO: CO 323/350-17589.
86. The problem of the proposed Canadian reserve was still being discussed in the spring of 1882 and finally dropped when a decision had to be made as to whether the War or Colonial Office should bear the cost. The excuse given was that the Royal Commission did not recommend anything. See WO 32/121, 7698/476 and

THE WORKING OF THE ROYAL COMMISSION: 1879–82

WO 32/121, 058/816; CO to Carnarvon Commission (copy), 1 February 1881, PRO: CO 812/21, no. 121. Macdonald gave evidence on 29 July 1880. See Carnarvon Commission Third Report, Digest of Evidence. See also Alice R. Stewart, 'Sir John A. Macdonald and the Imperial Defence Commission of 1879', *Canadian Historical Review*, 35, 2 (June 1954): pp. 121–39. For Lorne's plea, see Lorne to Carnarvon, 3 December 1881, PRO 30/6-52.
87. WO to Treasury, 1 January 1882, PRO: WO 32/88-7512.
88. Ibid. 'But the larger question of the general military organization of the various Colonies, and their arrangements for land defences, as well as the relations between the Mother country and the Colonies in reference to these matters had not been referred to this Commission nor does Mr Childers think it desirable so to extend the scope of their enquiry.'
89. WO to CO, 24 November 1881, PRO: CO 323/350-20577.
90. See 'Second Report of a Royal Commission appointed to enquire into the Defence of British Possessions and Commerce Abroad', 23 March 1882, PRO 30/6-131. Subsequently printed in Parl. Papers, 1887, p. 56, Section 7D of Vol. 2 (Appendix).
91. Carnarvon Commission Third Report, PRO 30/6-126.
92. Carnarvon Commission to CO, 24 July 1882, PRO: CO 323/353-13068; Carnarvon to Kimberley, 4 August 1882, PRO: CO 323/353-13864; Jekyll to Milne, 5 December 1882, NMM: MLN/163/2.
93. Carnarvon to Kimberley, 4 August 1882, PRO: CO 323/353-13864. (CMG was Commander of the Order of St Michael and St George.)
94. Kimberley minute on ibid., 6 August 1882; CO 323/353-13864; CO to Carnarvon Commission, 2 August 1882, PRO: CO 323/353-13068.
95. Kimberley minute on 6 August 1882, 11 August 1882, PRO: CO 323/353-13864.

6

The Royal Commission Reports

The first report of the 'Royal Commission Appointed to Enquire into the Defence of British Possessions and Commerce Abroad' concerned the defensive priority of the Cape of Good Hope, and the need for police forces in colonies to enable troops to be withdrawn from non-essential imperial work in wartime.[1] It also enunciated some general principles concerning the interrelation of volume trade, coal and steamships in war. The Cape's perceived importance spurred this report's production very early in the proceedings, for the commissioners were so 'impressed by these considerations that they postponed to this one all other questions committed to them, and made Cape defence the subject of their first and most pressing recommendation'.[2] This emphasis was not surprising, considering Carnarvon's past interest in South Africa as a whole and his continuing interest in the necessity of defending the Cape Peninsula in particular. Indeed, his ideas regarding South African policy generally hinged on his appreciation of the colony's location as a vital focal area for ships passing between India and the United Kingdom.[3]

The report underscored the economic importance of the Cape, for it calculated the annual value of passing trade at £150,000,000, assuming the Suez Canal to be unusable.[4] Since there was no secure base for naval operations between the Lizard and the Cape, excepting Gibraltar, the Cape's security in wartime was of vital importance, since it would certainly be a major trade concentration point. Adequately defended coaling facilities was not the sole consideration: the Cape was valued also as a port of refuge for merchant vessels and as a supply point for the relief and supplementation of Indian and Far Eastern defences.[5]

Yet considering the importance the commissioners attached to the area, their recommendations were particularly unsatisfactory. The navy headquarters at Simons Bay, with its secure anchorage, was acknowledged to be 'as indispensable to Your Majesty's Navy' on the recommendation of local experts, despite the fact that Cape Town's harbour at Table Bay possessed docks and jetties offering coaling and repair facilities far in advance of the primitive facilities at the navy site, where little more than fresh water was available. This was a concession to naval habit, and since the naval base displayed no prospects for commercial development, the total cost of fortifying it would devolve entirely on the home government. But the docking and coaling facilities at Table Bay were so good that defence was imperative, meaning that two places in close proximity would have to be fortified, were the commissioners' recommendations heeded. They indicated awareness of the need for some sort of cost division between the home and colonial governments regarding Table Bay, but made no specific recommendations.[6] Numbers of guns or batteries were not specified: only armament type was definitely suggested.[7] Manpower recommendations were not, however, so circumspect. A proposed garrison of 4,000 was to be composed of 3,000 imperials and 1,000 local volunteers. A gunboat for Table Bay and torpedo launches for both Simons and Table Bay completed the recommendations.[8]

If Cape defence was so vital as to require 4,000 soldiers it should have been likewise important enough to the Commission for it to have suggested more specific proposals for proper fixed defences, and some formula for dealing with the imperial relations problem involved in apportioning costs. Probably the report was intended more to alarm the government or force its hand than to provide a detailed solution to the long-term problem. Yet this rather unsatisfactory report should not be interpreted as indicating lack of meticulousness on the Commission's part. Rather its issue in this form can be taken as an indication of the urgency that the members attached to their task in general, and to the critical problem posed by Cape defence in particular. Since the Liberal government had hardly given the Commission a vote of confidence, the production of a report containing such urgent recommendations was probably intended both to ensure continuance of the inquiry and to secure some executive action on imperial defence.

The report also addressed War Office preoccupation with the problem of raising police forces in the colonies to replace regular army garrison forces in the event of their being withdrawn in an emergency.[9] In some colonies the regulars were used as police forces. Colonies in general, and especially British Honduras, stated the commissioners, should have auxiliary police forces ready to replace the regulars, since it would be 'imperatively necessary' to withdraw the latter in wartime. Obviously the commissioners were unaware that Childers had withdrawn the garrison problem from their consideration.

Finally, the commissioners discussed, on a somewhat optimistic note, Britain's relative position with regard to the slow replacement of sail by steam tonnage. Sailing tonnage was, for the moment, neither increasing nor decreasing, while steam tonnage had increased steadily since 1860. The only trade route in the world still dominated by sail was the north

Pacific route (North America to the Far East), and even bulky cheap cargoes, like coal and grain, were now preferably dispatched by steam. The optimism stemmed from the fact that Britain's Merchant Marine equalled those of all the rest of the world taken together, and its steam tonnage was double that of the rest of the world combined. Since most of the fast steamers – those most suited for conversion to auxiliary cruisers for commerce raiding – were under British registry, it would be important to prevent their sale to a possible enemy in an emergency.[10]

By 1881, when the first report was issued, the state of marine engineering was far in advance of its position a decade and half earlier when Colomb first pointed out the centrality of coal to imperial and commercial defence. Hence, the coal problem was slightly eased by the fact that in peace modern steamers could make almost any point-to-point journey in the world without refuelling. Yet, the report stressed, it was more economical for merchant vessels to coal often and maximize valuable cargo space that would be wasted were a full coal load carried, and that warships – owing to a variety of design factors – were not such frugal coal consumers. Hence, despite the increasing steaming radius of merchant ships, the empire must still be concerned about defence of coal supplies.[11]

This, in essence, was the first report. Its primary purpose, quick action at the Cape, was not achieved. A solitary letter to the Governor of British Honduras regarding the inadvisability of using garrisons for police duty likewise produced no result.[12] The only other flicker of interest was shown in a minute by Robert W. G. Herbert, the Permanent Undersecretary at the Colonial Office, to the effect that the Cape seemed to be strategically important.[13] Otherwise, the immediate fate of the report was deposit in the secret cupboards of its recipients.

Its successor was not underscored with the urgent appeal that the Cape's defencelessness had generated. Nevertheless its contents can hardly have been intended to induce complacency. It was divided into two sections: 'The Duties of the Navy' and 'The Defences of the Australian Colonies'.[14] The opening remarks displayed the usual Victorian respect given statistics by citing the annual world-wide value of British trade.[15] The effect created, however, was not nearly so telling as a simple statement submerged in a later paragraph, to the effect that all of Britain's foreign commerce was seaborne.[16] The implication was clear: unfettered access to the sea, both in peace and war, was not merely a question of commercial advantage, but of sheer survival. Living at a time when British naval superiority was assumed rather than assured, however, the commissioners sometimes confused the two.[17] The duty of the navy was, in their eyes, to protect that commerce. Yet the task had seemingly become more difficult, owing to the widely held opinion (outside the Admiralty) that effective blockade of enemy battle fleets and commerce raiders was no longer possible, owing to the liberating effect of steam propulsion.

Reasoning along these lines in turn produced the two most important conclusions in the 'Duties of the Navy' section of the report.

First, it acknowledged in general terms that the navy did not possess enough ships for its tasks, either battleships for the home fleet or cruisers for foreign stations.[18] But rather than attempting to specify the types or numbers of ships which should be constructed, the commissioners contented themselves with a general expression of concern about the adequacy of the fleet. This was a tactful approach, presumably calculated to appeal to the natural sympathies of the professionals at the Admiralty, as was the bare assertion that since the country was spared matching the size of foreign armies the requirements of naval supremacy should not be shirked. Therefore, the only specific recommendation in respect to naval adequacy arose from Director of Naval Construction Nathaniel Barnaby's scheme to draw on the resources of the merchant marine in wartime. The commissioners were sufficiently impressed with his logic to recommend that fast merchantmen, the operational value of whose speed the evidence had brought out, be armed in wartime for commerce-raider interdiction.[19] It was further suggested that suitably large and swift merchant ships be required to conform to certain Admiralty specifications – especially regarding watertight subdivision and protection of the propulsion plant – and that care should be taken to prevent any significant number of these vessels from passing under foreign registry.

The second conclusion following from Britain's unique trading position, was the particular meaning that the commissioners attached to the word 'strategy'. In their report naval strategy was set forth in a truly modern sense, a breakthrough which represented the triumph of the ideas of the officially spurned J. C. R. Colomb.[20] British naval strategy, they held, depended on the assurance of adequate coal supplies for the navy, wherever it might be operating, and the denial of coal supplies to enemy vessels or fleets. Apart from the general observations about warship numbers and types, all of the report's conclusions were firmly rooted in the idea that operational efficiency depended on availability of coal supplies. The only limitation the commissioners were willing to place on the number of Britain's defended overseas coaling stations was that no more should be set up or acquired than could be adequately defended, and the process of acquiring new ones should stop short of causing international complications.

Specific recommendations followed easily. In war, coal supplies of Britain's allies should be defended as far and as soon as possible. International law dictated that belligerents could coal in neutral ports once every three months, but the commissioners speculated that a needy ship close to coal in distant waters would probably not stand upon ceremony. Empire coal storage ports should be defended, and when defences were completed coal should be kept only in these ports. Enemy colliers at sea presented a potentially grave problem and could only be dealt with by naval action in response to reports from vigilant British consuls.[21]

As for how coaling stations and bases were to be defended, the Commission's conclusions represented a triumph for both Colomb's ideas and the navy's 'freedom of action doctrine'. The fleet was required for cruising and could not stay in port to guard its own supplies: 'Our seaports must rely for their immediate defence on local means, leaving Your Majesty's Navy free to act at sea. The more remote parts of Your Majesty's Dominions may in some cases be most effectually protected by the action of the fleet at a distance from the point to which protection is afforded.'[22] They concluded, therefore, that security must be provided by fixed land works, aided by land-based torpedo defences, rather than by floating defences such as turret ships. The commissioners showed their appreciation both of the contemporary political climate, and of the army's shortage of troops, in emphasizing that they had limited their selection of bases as far as they could, consistent with the principle of providing 'adequate bases for the support of the operations of the Navy, sufficiently protected against attack in such force as may reasonably be expected'.[23] This, surely, was a fair statement, even if it offered an easy opening to politicians bent on economy.

Yet with the advantage of hindsight doubts remain as to whether the commissioners fully grasped the implications of their own logic. They concluded the 'Duties of the Navy' section with a warning: 'An increase of the Navy will involve large expenditure' – a straightforward enough proposition but one which they followed with the observation that 'the alternative is a much larger expenditure for fortifications and garrisons of a costly nature'. This suggested that, expensive though it would be, there was an alternative to the Colomb–Jervois approach. On other grounds their reasoning was less heretical for they also stressed the 'grave risk to our positions as the great carrying power of the world' which failure to enlarge the navy would risk, and took the straight Admiralty line in basing all of their defence recommendations 'upon the assumption that your Majesty's Navy will hold the seas, and that provision has to be made against the attack not of large hostile fleets, but of independent cruisers or small armoured squadrons'.[24] And whatever criticism can be levelled at their strategic reasoning, the commissioners certainly demonstrated their understanding of the prevailing political mentality toward government spending in framing their arguments in terms of economy.

Their conclusions with regard to Australasia were, they admitted, based largely on the work done, and information provided, by Jervois.[25] The precept upon which their recommendations were based was that the Australasian colonies should provide for their own harbour defences, and that the Royal Navy should be broadly charged with the duty of protecting their floating trade. This was a general principle, however, not a hard-and-fast rule, since they hinted that it would be 'not unreasonable' for the colonies to make some common contribution to general naval upkeep in the Australasian area.[26] In some unspecified cases the home government might contribute to the maintenance of harbour defences at places where facilities existed necessary for the efficient operation of Her Majesty's ships.

Aside from Jervois' information, the commissioners had before them War Office investigator Colonel Peter Scratchley's reports on New Zealand, King George Sound and Thursday Island.[27] They also interviewed the agents-general of New South Wales, and South Australia, as well as local militia representatives of Queensland, New South Wales and Victoria, and heard the evidence from the Governor of Queensland.[28] Along with these contributions the commissioners had also to consider the Australasian delegates' refusal, at an 1881 intercolonial conference at Sydney, to pass a motion advocating colonial contributions to the navy's Australian Squadron. Indeed the conference delegates made it clear that they considered sea defence entirely the home government's responsibility, a declaration that caused some stir in England.[29]

Since the Australasians had long ago and without question assumed responsibility for the defence of their own harbours, the Commission's specific recommendations need not be discussed here.[30] Suffice to state, Jervois' recommendations were largely followed. Unlike Jervois, however, the commissioners did voice the hope that the Australasian colonies might be induced to contribute to the Royal Navy, and that such assistance, if obtained, should not be made conditional on the constant presence of navy vessels or any other obligation restricting the freedom of the Admiralty and the local naval commander.[31] The strategical reasoning behind this proviso was set forth with the 'Duties of the Navy', but when the Australasians were sent the portion of the second report that pertained directly to them, they were not also provided the 'Duties of the Navy' section that furnished the strategic rationale on which the proposal for colonial contribution to the Royal Navy was based. This omission, unsurprisingly, reduced Australasian enthusiasm for the second report's pertinent portions, since it seemed to ask them for an outlay with no guarantee that it would mean heightened security in the event of a crisis.

Incidentally, the commissioners dealt a death-blow to any hopes of troop restoration. Such an outcome was not surprising in view of Carnarvon's past experience of the subject. A request from Victoria, referred to the commissioners by the Colonial Office, for some 'regular' Royal Artillerymen was rejected, the commissioners stating, 'the terms upon which Imperial troops are desired have not been fully discussed but we think it unnecessary to enquire into them, as we are unable to advise the reintroduction of Imperial troops into the self-governed Australian Colonies'.[32]

Yet notwithstanding this rather brusque dismissal, the commissioners did display some sensitivity to the problems faced by colonial politicians and at times sincerely tried to live up to their stated intention to be tactful in dealing with the self-governing colonies. They admitted, for instance, that colonial politicians also had to justify defence estimates to their colonial legislatures and displayed even greater good sense in suggesting that since a 'large visible force in any Colony would make any politician's attachment to it politically unwise in peacetime, no permanent forces should be formed in the Colonies with the exception of small Artillery sections'. The same breadth of understanding was shown in the commissioners' recommendations on the vexing question of who should command troops stationed in the self-governing colonies. The answer – a colonial in peacetime and an imperial officer in war – showed insight into colonial mentality was well as sensitivity to colonial feelings, as did a recommendation that a proposed imperial instructor/inspector for all the colonies should be designated an adviser rather than a commander.[33]

This last recommendation was complicated by the lack of unity between the colonies. This want of cohesion was, the commissioners opined, the most serious military difficulty in Australasia. A common instructor would generate controversy over salary contribution, and were a military school set up, as they thought it should be, it too would certainly be a source of dispute, as to the percentage each colony should contribute to its building and operation, and even over where the school should be sited.[34] Only a united Australia was likely to rectify the want of co-operation from which these problems largely stemmed. In the meantime, the commissioners generously recommended that any request for an imperial instructor/inspector should be met with prompt and efficient compliance by the War Office.

From the point he began surveying Australasia's defence needs, Jervois had repeatedly recommended that the South Australian coast should be permanently protected by a ship of war especially set aside for that purpose. The commissioners endorsed this suggestion, evidently contradicting their previous strategic argument against restricting the operational freedom of warships.[35] They offered no explanation for the apparent inconsistency, nor showed any appreciation of the dampening effect such an endorsement must have on the request for Australasian contribution to the Royal Navy. In the following paragraphs, however, the report expressed regret that Victoria was the only Australasian colony to have taken advantage of the Colonial Naval Defence Act (1865), implying that their suggestion for permanently stationing a warship off South Australian waters was intended to stimulate naval consciousness in Australasia.[36] If, however, they were at the same time serious in pressing for colonial contributions to the Royal Navy, the concession to South Australia was a tactical blunder of the first magnitude, suggesting that naval protection could be had for nothing.

Having decided, contrary to their stated principles, that the South Australian coast was worthy of permanent naval defence, the commissioners had to confront the additional difficulty that the only place along that coast where coal might be stored in large quantities was, according to the Admiralty, unworthy of defence.[37] Since Milne's Defence Committee had considered – and the Admiralty rejected – the possibility of fortifying it, the Peninsular and Oriental Steam Navigation Company had abandoned King George Sound as a coaling station. The company's offer to sell both the stock of coal and the location had been declined by the Admiralty and the Colony of Western Australia.[38] Yet the commissioners remained concerned about the place. Though the Sound was, officially, of no value to the navy, the commissioners continued to maintain that it might be important in a future war, both as a refuge harbour and coal depot for British shipping, or, if seized by enemy forces, as a base from which commerce raiders could strike at Australasian trade. Thus it was suggested that since Western Australia was too poor to secure the place, all the Australian colonies contribute jointly to its defence.[39] This policy would both promote Australasian unity in security matters and relieve the home government of a small defensive worry. An imperial contribution was also hinted at but not definitely recommended.

The second report ended with a table pointedly indicating the unequal distribution of the financial burden of imperial defence. Australasians, on average, contributed between 7½d and 2s 4d per capita to defence yearly, whereas each Briton paid 15s 7½d. Fortunately for the sake of amicable home–colonial relations the report was more subtle than the implication in the statistical table. Subtle or not, however, it shared the fate of its predecessor. Victoria's Private Secretary Ponsonby remarked in a letter of 24 May that 'The Second Report of the Defence Commission has been safely put away in the Confidential Cupboard with the First.'[40]

The third report was completed and advance copies circulated in July 1882, although the finished bound products did not finally leave Delahay Street until December.[41] A veil of secrecy has, until now, largely hidden the third report.[42] The first and second reports were published in their entirety in the *Parliamentary Papers* concurrent with the 1887 colonial conference, but only extracts of the third report appeared. Its lengthy concealment was due both to the second Gladstone administration's disinclination to act on it, and the secrecy demanded by its detailed description of empire military strength and positions.

The third report was the largest of the three, and included extensive appendices containing the correspondence upon which the report was based, plus a digest of evidence, and, in one case, the actual minutes of evidence. The report proper consisted of detailed recommendations for all of the imperial bases not previously considered, together with a number of concluding general remarks. In the last, the commissioners stated that their detailed recommendations were useless unless the Royal Navy was able to guarantee the safety of British seaborne commerce as it approached home waters, a point already stressed in the 'Duties of the Navy' section of the second report.[43] They then restated their opinion that steam propulsion had revolutionized naval warfare, that warships were useless without coal and that they were more dependent on frequent coaling than were merchant ships. Their conclusions, however, raise doubts as to how fully they comprehended the strategic importance of coal. Empire 'bases', they stated, could be divided into two categories. First, and most important, were those used both for naval refits and as harbours of refuge. Second were those used solely as navy coaling stations. The first, they stated, required heavy defences, the second only light works and guns, suggesting that the commissioners felt that they knew better than the Admiralty how naval war should be conducted. This failure to give Admiralty views due weight, indeed, the failure to make a sustained effort to discover what Admiralty views really were, marked and marred the whole report.

It appeared to the commissioners that one of the most dangerous tendencies they had discovered was the permission granted to private concerns to maintain coal supplies at isolated sites, in the absence of any clearly defined safeguards by the War Office, the Colonial Office, or the Admiralty to ensure that such stocks did not fall into unfriendly hands.[44] Unless a system of control were quickly set up, they stated, the defences recommended would be so much waste paper. Once, however, these recommendations for the protection of coal supplies were carried out, the British Navy would be in an almost invulnerable strategic position.

The commissioners admitted that the garrison problem was vexing, and disapproved of the use of British troops for purely police purposes, advocating instead the use of local levies for these duties whenever possible. Since, unknown to them, the War Office had withheld information on the subject, they could hardly have gone further than that.

The only breath of suspicion that was wafted in the direction of the War Office was a remark to the effect that antiquated or outdated defence works would not suffice if the strategic chain was to hold. In light of that observation it is worth noting that the Commission interviewed Sir Bartle Frere in May 1881, and thus probably knew of the defective guns at Simons Bay. Whether this timely injunction carried much weight at the War Office can best be assessed by looking at how and to what extent these recommendations were implemented.

The commissioners were not prepared to lay down any fixed principle regarding the division of security costs between home and colonial governments, although they made recommendations in specific cases. They probably regarded the problem as insoluble; a realistic conclusion, no doubt, but one affording small comfort to the Colonial Office, where a cost-division principle was necessary for any dealings with the rigidly parsimonious Treasury. In the second report they had already indulged the hope that colonial contributions to the Royal Navy might one day be secured. Here they contented themselves with the observation that naval costs were entirely imperial, and the colonies, generally speaking, ought to undertake the local shore defences of naval stations and commercial harbours, a principle that 'the Australian Colonies have already recognized'. Finally they anticipated that the percentage of colonial defence contributions would increase with advancing colonial prosperity. This general assumption was reasonable enough, but the commissioners failed to indicate that a vital distinction should be drawn between colonies that were free to decide how much they would contribute and those who were not (i.e., representative as opposed to responsible government colonies). This was an inexplicable oversight and must be taken into consideration in any assessment of the thoroughness of their work.[45]

In their detailed recommendations for the defence of particular stations the commissioners first considered the Cape route; embracing the sea lane stretching from the Lizard to the Cape. Cape Town and Simons Bay, already the subjects of recommendations, were excluded, as was Gibraltar, which was beyond the scope of inquiry. This process of elimination left Sierra Leone in west Africa, Gambia in northwest Africa, Ascension and St Helena in the south Atlantic, and Port Elizabeth in the Cape Colony. Of these, Sierra Leone and Ascension were first-class Admiralty coaling stations.[46] The commissioners had before them, along with the reports of local committees and Royal Engineer officers, the opinions of First Naval Lord Astley Cooper Key.[47] The last placed no value upon Port Elizabeth and Gambia and only slightly more upon St Helena. Sierra Leone, he stated, was important as a naval coaling station, and should be defended. He neglected to mention Ascension: an odd omission given that the island was both a naval health resort and an Admiralty coaling station.[48] Notwithstanding the views of the government's senior naval adviser, the commissioners' recommendations made full use of the latitude accorded them. Considering both its coal depot and strategic location with regard to the French base Dakar, Sierra Leone, they stated, ought to be defended by works to the value of £175,400. Owing to the unhealthy climate, however, they preferred that the suggested garrison of 1,600 troops consist of regularly enlisted black troops, a recommendation reflecting how the War Office's failure to provide pertinent information on the garrison situation affected the Commission's judgement. No defences were recommended for Gambia and Port Elizabeth. Nor were fortifications advocated for Ascension, despite its naval importance. The commissioners felt themselves faced with a choice between St Helena and Ascension. They chose the former, suggesting that the navy should move its establishments there, despite Cooper Key's views to the contrary. The choice furthermore indicated the predominance of War Office views in the Commission's deliberations, for although neither island possessed a secure anchorage, Ascension at least had a coal depot. The report suggested that the decision was based on the comparative cheapness of St Helena's defence.[49] This tendency to base recommendations more on army than on navy considerations, evident in the decisions on the Cape route, characterized the whole third report, despite the concluding assertion that it was framed mainly upon the pressing nature of naval requirements.

From the Cape the commissioners turned their gaze eastward, considering the importance and security of Mauritius, Aden and Perim at the entrance to the Red Sea, Diego Garcia in the Chagos Archipelago, the Seychelles Islands and the Cocos or Keeling Islands.[50] Perim, the Cocos and the Seychelles were quickly dismissed, as was Diego Garcia. The last of these places did, however, bring to the commissioners' attention the existence of private British steamship companies' undefended coal stocks.[51] Of the need to defend Aden, strategic adjunct to Suez and second-class coaling station, there was no doubt. Mauritius presented a more interesting problem. The Admiralty regarded it as a second-class coaling station, but interest in Mauritius was not great, since the navy possessed first-class coal supplies locally at Zanzibar, and further afield at the Cape and Trincomalee. Moreover, as yet Mauritius had no telegraphic link with the outside world, a deficiency which substantially reduced its strategic worth.[52] The War Office, however, valued the island as a point of call for coal and other supplies for troop ships bound between the Cape and India.[53] The well-fortified French island of Réunion was also nearby. There was, in addition, something of a military vested interest in the defence of Mauritius, since £45,000 was extracted annually from the colony for the maintenance of a small garrison. The commissioners therefore decided to advocate its defence, explaining that it would be very important should Suez become unusable.[54] Having learned that no British ship regularly called at the island with mail – this duty being in French hands – British mail-service was recommended, as was the laying of telegraph cable. Mauritius furnished another instance of the power that army views exerted over the Commission's deliberations, even if the recommendations were sensible and timely.

The commissioners hardly touched on the defence of the Mediterranean – an unsurprising neglect, given that the imperial fortresses of Gibraltar and Malta were excluded from their survey.[55] They were content to suggest that something might be done on Cyprus but were not enthusiastic enough to be precise.[56]

Among actual or potential bases in the Far East they surveyed Singapore, Penang (Straits Settlement), North Borneo, Hong Kong, Thursday Island on the north tip of Queensland, and Port Hamilton. The last of these was Korean, and the commissioners' recommendations with regard to it furnish one of the few examples of out and out 'imperialism' that the history of these years has to show. The Admiralty having stated that British ownership of Port Hamilton would be useful against Russia, the commissioners agreed and suggested that force might be used if the Koreans objected.[57]

Penang, Straits Settlement, was declared not worth defending and it was recommended that any British regular troops there be moved to Singapore and replaced by local levies.[58] North Borneo was also judged to be of no use. Thursday Island too was rejected, but there the case was not entirely clear-cut. The Admiralty and the War Office investigating officer who examined the place both thought it important. The commissioners declined to recommend defending it 'though the Admiralty may decide upon establishing a second-class coaling station'. Trade on the Singapore–Melbourne route was, they decided, too slight to justify the expense. Moreover, 'although a point of observation from which ships may act to close the Straits', Thursday Island 'does not command the passages now in use'.[59] Again a decision was made contrary to Admiralty opinion.

The case of Hong Kong was clear-cut.[60] It was a first-class Admiralty coaling station and the First Sea Lord stated that no expense should be spared to make the headquarters of the China Squadron secure. The Duke of Cambridge too made it clear that he regarded its defence as imperative, and pointed out how difficult it would be to reinforce the garrison there if ever a monsoon and a sudden war coincided.[61] The commissioners agreed. Extensive floating and fixed defences were recommended at a cost of £370,193. They also stated that they thought it unwise to raise coolie regiments. Instead, the colony ought to pay for barracks and maintenance of any regular troops that might be imported.[62] Singapore's strategic importance was equally clear despite its being only a second-class Admiralty coaling station.[63] The commissioners felt that this focal point of eastern trade should be heavily defended, the colony supplying the land, the imperial government the guns and torpedo boats, and the cost of maintenance being evenly divided between the two.[64]

The recommendations regarding the North America–West Indian route were uneven. The eastern Canadian ports were a colonial concern and the commissioners refrained from detailed recommendation, stating only their opinion that undefended coal in those ports should be removed at the beginning of any war. They furthermore voiced their dismay at not being permitted to discuss the defences of Halifax and Bermuda.[65] Their opinions about West Indian defence may have been guided by Cooper Key's suggestion that it was only expedient to defend one position there, and that since Jamaica was difficult to defend it should be Port Castries (St Lucia).[66] Conversely, the Duke of Cambridge stressed the importance of Jamaica as a military station, and Barbados, which also sheltered an army establishment. This divergence of opinion was a further manifestation of the want of departmental co-operation that had vexed Milne's Defence Committee.[67] The recommendations of Carnarvon's Commission offered a compromise solution.[68] The military establishment in Barbados should be closed down and both Port Royal (Jamaica) and Port Castries defended. Here the War Office came as close as it ever would to having its settled ideas rejected by the commissioners.

There were also three places about which the commissioners disagreed amongst themselves: Esquimalt (Vancouver Island), Ceylon and Labuan. To understand the source and nature of this disagreement, it is necessary to keep in mind the dominance of War Office views and doctrines due to General Simmons' membership of the panel and Carnarvon's general reliance on him for expert advice. It is also necessary to understand Milne's personal relationship with the rest of the Commission, particularly Carnarvon.

On 4 March 1882 Cooper Key gave evidence before the Commission. Perhaps his cool recital of naval necessities made Milne realize that the sort of report envisaged would not meet naval needs as the First Naval Lord saw them. He then must have brought this to the attention of the other commissioners. Rather than acquiescing to the naval view, however, it was suggested to Milne that the navy might be held responsible for some local defence – a suggestion to which he rightly objected. On the basis of previous pronouncements he had every right to assume that the 'freedom of action' doctrine was at the root of all the commissioners' work and recommendations.[69] Doubtless it was a severe shock to Milne to discover that his and Simmons' views were so far apart after such a long association.

When the extent of the divergence dawned on him, Milne protested strongly. He must have been further angered to discover at this point that he stood alone. Only Sir Henry Barkly gave him any support, and only concretely on one particular point. Thus heavily taxed, he instinctively felt that his first duty was to the navy and only second to the Commission. He was very bitter in this fight for the naval perspective. By 20 May Milne spelt out his disagreement with the general recommendations regarding Labuan, Ceylon and Esquimalt, and poured out his bitterness in a letter to Barkly: 'it is Simmons versus the Navy which I won't stand'.[70] A letter from Jekyll on 26 May indicates that the disagreement was not confined to these ports alone: Simons Bay was also mentioned.[71] Jekyll also admitted that Milne's views could probably be met were Carnarvon not bent on concluding the Commission's work quickly. Jekyll personally disapproved of the chairman's haste, but he was not in charge of the investigation. Carnarvon attempted to smooth things over by personal compliments, stressing Milne's great contributions to the Commission's work, but the feeling that he and the navy had been betrayed was too strong in the old Admiral's mind and he expressed himself accordingly in his reply.[72]

The outcome of this disagreement is partially shrouded in obscurity. Milne did not preserve his correspondence systematically, and the Carnarvon Papers at the Public Record Office do not contain this Milne–Carnarvon exchange. The appearance of a precise memorandum by Milne, dated 12 June, giving detailed information as to what coaling stations the Admiralty considered important, and the fact that Milne dropped his opposition to the report on Labuan, north Borneo, suggests that some last-minute peace was arranged.[73] The Commission first intended to leave Labuan defenceless. Milne, however, objected strongly, arguing that during the monsoon season the voyage from Singapore to Hong Kong could not be made comfortably by naval vessels without a stop for coal at Labuan.[74] His views carried the day, and the report therefore recommended that coal on the island be moved inland in wartime and protected by a lightly defended redoubt.[75] This met Milne's objections sufficiently so that he did not protest officially in the report. The cases of Esquimalt and Ceylon were not so easily resolved, however, and Milne signed the third report only on condition that it included his appended dissenting opinion regarding the recommendations for their defences

In Ceylon's case the old problem of the potential value importance of Galle, early urged by the War Office, had been quashed by a strong Colonial Office objection to even discussing the subject.[76] There remained for consideration, however, the important commercial harbour of Colombo and the naval establishment at Trincomalee. The First Naval Lord saw the ticklish nature of the problem and proposed, when interviewed, that both harbours be defended. Of Trincomalee he said: 'An isolated naval station is always preferable to one combined with a commercial port.'[77] The commissioners, with the exception of Milne, disagreed, claiming that 'ships of war lying there would be at a great disadvantage in obtaining information of an enemy's movements at sea'.[78] This blithe dismissal must have annoyed Milne! Yet apart from rejecting the Admiralty's strategic opinion, the commissioners' decision was reasonable. With Hong Kong, Singapore, Mauritius, Calcutta and Bombay earmarked for defence, plus the necessity of doing the same at Colombo, the high cost involved in fortifying and garrisoning Trincomalee was not proportionally worthwhile.[79] They also pointed out, quite logically, that there were no docks or refitting facilities at Trincomalee, and that Colombo harbour, though largely artificial, was being enlarged and improved. Yet whatever the soundness of the commissioners' views, they were based on the recommendations of Sir John Code, Commander-in-Chief of the armed forces in Ceylon.[80] Again, War Office views had triumphed and Admiralty judgement set aside.

Milne's dissenting opinion was mild.[81] He admitted Colombo's importance as a commercial port in peacetime, and therefore confined his objections to endorsing Cooper Key's admonition that the relative importance of the two ports would change radically in wartime. Under such conditions Trincomalee, with its excellent harbour, would prove much more secure than the 'exposed anchorage' at Colombo.

The divergence over Esquimalt was more fundamental, and, although it again displays War Office dominance, there was little to choose between the opinions given, for the site was by no means an ideal position for a fortified post and naval anchorage.[82] It had long been War Office doctrine and accepted political wisdom that Canada could not be held against the United States. Sir John Macdonald endorsed this view in his testimony, although he deprecated the possibility of such an event.[83] There was in addition, as the commissioners pointed out, hardly enough annual trade from British Columbia to make a Russian descent on the area worthwhile. Yet there was some obligation for Britain to defend Esquimalt, at least so Macdonald maintained.[84] Indeed, the Canadian government was obligated to the Province of British Columbia to press the imperial authorities for the construction of a dry dock there.[85] Furthermore, despite its distance from the nearest non-Canadian British territory, Esquimalt was the only naval establishment on British soil between Alaska and Cape Horn on the western coast of the Americas. That it was the only place on that coast was an important point, although not a positive one, for even Cooper Key admitted that in war it would be necessary to procure or seize two intermediate coaling stations between Vancouver and the Falklands if Esquimalt were to be of any real strategic use. True, it was both a first- and a second-class Admiralty coaling station, and for that reason the First Naval Lord favoured defending it. But the defences of Esquimalt seemed to imply the possibility of an attack from the United States, which brought the Commission back to square one, since, according to both the soldiers and Macdonald, there was no defending Canada in general and Esquimalt in particular against a determined US attack.[86]

Weighing these considerations, the commissioners stated that they could not on military grounds recommend that Esquimalt be defended. This reasonable conclusion, however, was marred by another provocative statement. 'We fail to see', they stated, 'how Your Majesty's ships, when deprived of a supply of coals, could continue active operations on the western seaboard of America, and we think it as a matter for grave consideration whether or not the Esquimalt ships should be sent to join the Pacific [i.e., China] Squadron at Hong Kong.' They were, however, impressed by Canada's promise to press for the maintenance of Esquimalt as a naval port and admitted that this constituted a delicate political question – especially since the Admiralty supported Canada's determination. Hence, they added, 'so far from since repudiating the deduction naturally to be drawn from the latter stipulation [Canada's commitment] the Board of Admiralty have encouraged the Dominion Government to commence a dock at the port capable of accommodating Your Majesty's ships on the station, while the War Office has dispatched officers of distinction, one after another, to report as to the best mode of improving the defences'.[87]

The Commission therefore recommended that the British government supply armaments and professional assistance to help the Canadian government while the latter supplied the men and works requisite for Esquimalt's defence. Carnarvon's personal recognition of the importance of good inter-empire relations to imperial defence generally and to Anglo-Canadian relations in particular, undoubtedly produced this statesman-like recommendation.[88] It was further advised that any actual work be preceded by full and frank communications with the dominion government.[89]

In his dissenting statement Milne declared that Esquimalt should be defended in accordance with his Defence Committee's recommendation of 1878. He argued that the station was useful as a base for showing the flag in Pacific waters, and for ferrying diplomatic representatives in peacetime. In war the Pacific squadron would concentrate, ready to act against any attacks on imperial trade. Just how this was to be done from Esquimalt, far to the north of any significant commercial sea lanes, he did not say. It was, however, the majority's suggestion about Hong Kong that really annoyed him. He pointed out that if the squadron were ordered to Hong Kong it would be extremely difficult to steam against the prevailing west winds. It would first have to steer south to latitude 15°N and cross there. Its only coaling *en route* would be the Sandwich (Hawaiian) Islands. The desperation of the old Admiral is revealed in his plaintive warning, 'In fact, this passage would probably have to be made almost entirely under sail', a faint echo of the Admiralty discussions of 1874.[90]

The real substance of his objection, however, was contained in his final remark which probably reflected not only his view on Esquimalt, but on the mentality which dominated the Commission. 'I consider this proposal to remove the Pacific Squadron is not within the scope of the instructions under which the Commission is acting, for it is one which would require the special consideration of the Admiralty and the Foreign Office, and is, in my opinion, an interference with the Executive Departments of the State.'[91] In other words, decisions regarding naval dispositions – and by implication the bases necessary for their support – should be made without reference to the War Office. It was this point with which Barkly concurred.

How much validity there was in Milne's objection it is difficult to say. Since a Royal Commission does not make law – its recommendations being simply strong advisory admonitions to the government – the grounds for his dissent seem rather trivial.[92] What shines through clearly, however, and what Milne could not really state, since it would suggest incompetence on his part, was the fact that Admiralty opinion and policy had not predominated in the work of the Commission.

In emphasizing that the third report's recommendations generally relied too heavily on War Office views, the present author does not imply that the soldiers deserved blame and the sailors praise. This outcome was due to several factors: to the Commission's own oversights, to Lord Carnarvon's character and methods of conducting business, to Milne's personality, to War Office insularity, and, especially, to Admiralty complacency.[93]

Only a very small proportion of the Commission's correspondence was forwarded to the Admiralty for the board's information. Some of the blame for this neglect may be laid at Lord Kimberley's door. When Secretary of State for War Childers wrote to the Colonial Office explaining the delay in sending War Office investigators abroad, he asked that they be supplied with 'such information as may have been collected by the Admiralty – to whom it is assumed a similar communication had been made'.[94] No such communication had ever been sent to the Admiralty from the Colonial Office. Yet such failings can hardly absolve the commissioners, for they had every reason to know, given the frosty correspondence between Carnarvon and Kimberley in 1880, that the latter was unsympathetic to their work. If they wanted naval advice, therefore, they should have requested it directly. This they had neglected to do.

Within the Commission itself Carnarvon must be singled out for attention. Milne's two attempts to express his views on the nature of the inquiry were brushed aside in 1879. More fundamentally, Carnarvon seems to have had little regard for Milne generally, preferring to rely on Simmons for professional advice. Since the latter was easily the Commission's best-informed member on the *details* of imperial defence and perhaps even on many larger aspects, it is easy to see why Carnarvon was impressed, yet in thus aligning himself with the representative of one service in the preparation of a defence report that largely concerned the other he committed a serious blunder. Had the split been one of professional opinion only, danger might have been averted, but since there was some personal pique, concealment, and secrecy within the Commission – as evidenced by Milne's bitter outburst when he discovered how marginalized he was – the combination of professional disagreement and personal factors produced a markedly skewed report.

Milne was a blunt old sailor. He knew a great deal about imperial defence problems – almost certainly more than any other senior naval officer – but his mind lacked precision.[95] His views generally coincided with those of Simmons and Carnarvon, but there were subtle differences and when these produced results differing from those he anticipated, he was mystified. When Cooper Key gave evidence in 1882, Milne must have realized at once from the reaction of his fellow commissioners that he had been sleeping, and probably he was accused by his ex-colleagues at the Admiralty of betraying the service. In June 1882 – the better part of three years after the Commission was constituted – Milne provided the first official list of Admiralty coaling stations that it had seen, a fact which hardly reflects to the credit of his initiative.[96] It was moreover too late to sway the Commission's collective opinion, and the old Admiral only salved his wounded pride with his dissenting opinion. Carnarvon should have been alive to this danger much earlier.

But behind the failure to ascertain Admiralty opinion lay the attitude of the Admiralty itself. Secure in its status as guardian of the *Pax Britannica* and trading on the reputation that Nelson's exploits had conferred, it maintained an attitude of insularity which was a far greater potential detriment in the age of steam than it had been in that of sail.[97] Hence, in an external inquiry set up to help increase naval efficiency, no naval interest in it was taken until the last moment, and then too late. The Admiralty was certainly not ignorant of the existence or charge of the Commission.[98] The War Office–Colonial Office squabble over Galle, Ceylon, had been referred to the Admiralty, and in response the First Naval Lord had stated his preference for Trincomalee, but First Lord Lord Northbrook quashed it on the grounds that he did not wish to interfere in an interdepartmental squabble.[99] This circumspection in 1881 resulted in helpless frustration in 1882 when the report was issued.

When the Admiralty was finally apprised of the fact that its general opinions on defence were desired, the boot was on the other foot. So far from refusing to acquiesce, Northbrook read the correspondence and wondered if 'the Admiralty agree in the opinions expressed, for if not the Defence Commission should be warned, or they are liable to fall into serious mistakes'.[100] But when referred to the Admiralty's professionals this ray of sanity was extinguished.[101] Beyond furnishing the Commission, as requested, with a report on foreign military stations, and sending a circular letter to Commanders-in-Chief asking that they co-operate with the Commission investigators, it maintained its silent tradition.[102] When the Commission's queries did find their way to the Admiralty, they were all immediately referred to the Hydrographer, who disdained comment on what concerned his province and generally settled the whole policy question.

Of the War Office little need be said. Its appropriation of the subject of coaling station defences from 1875 until 1882, not without Admiralty connivance, be it noted, is one of the central factors in understanding how British imperial defence doctrine evolved as it did. The role of the Colonial Office is more difficult to assess. Its original entry into the realms of general empire strategy stemmed largely from the desire to secure some principle of cost division between home and colonial governments, although Hicks Beach's interest in and Carnarvon's concern for problems of defence strategy played significant parts as well. From the standpoint of the permanent Colonial Office staff both Milne's Defence Committee and the Carnarvon Commission were useful in the sense that they relieved the department of a not particularly congenial duty. Indeed, both were used as repositories and consultative bodies for all awkward defence problems.[103] In the end, the original goal remained unachieved: never did the department receive the clear-cut cost division principles it desired.

The work of the Commission and the reports it issued were not perfect. Personal differences, departmental intransigence, and lack of political support all produced flaws. Further, despite the great interest that Canada's Governor-General, Lord Lorne, took in the Commission's work, and his hope that Canada would receive adequate attention, nothing concrete emerged apart from some recommendations on Esquimalt, together with a few general remarks on Canadian east coast ports.[104] Perhaps this oversight was due to the fact that little of the correspondence referring to Canadian defences ever arrived at Delahay Street. Clearly the commissioners were unwilling to comment on the subject after Macdonald indicated Canada's unwillingness to be bound in any rigid defence agreements. Perhaps the lacuna was caused simply by the pressure of time.[105] None of the reports explains or apologizes for this omission, despite the fact that Carnarvon wrote to Lorne late in 1881 promising an eventual report on Canadian defences.[106]

Yet a recital of defects – however numerous – is not the best assessment of the Commission's labours and its achievements. For when the reports were completed, they represented a reasonable approximation of what was necessary for the security of the British Empire's chain of outposts, and if their conclusions at times displayed shortsightedness, the bulky appendices could always be used by the interested as a corrective. The basic requirement of a world girt with a chain of secure bases which would enable the Royal Navy to act almost anywhere was clearly set forth. J. C. R. Colomb's work infiltrated into official circles, via Jervois; and through the thought of the War Office and the energy of the Colonial Office it received exploration and endorsement in the Carnarvon Commission's reports.

NOTES

1. Submitted to the Colonial Office, 18 September 1881.
2. Carnarvon to Henry Holland, 6 June 1887. See 'Papers laid before the Colonial Conference 1887', *Parl. Papers*, 1887, Vol. 56, pt 2 (Appendix), sec. 7, p. 296.
3. Carnarvon's interest in coaling station defence began largely as a result of Donald Currie's urging the importance of the Cape in an empire strategic sense.

THE ROYAL COMMISSION REPORTS

See Ch. 3 above. On 7 February 1881 he wrote to General Simmons that fighting in South Africa – the First Boer War – should be cleared up, but that no matter what else happened we should hold the fortress there or 'every kind of complication, colonial and foreign' would follow. See Carnarvon to Simmons (copy), 7 February 1881, PRO 30/6-52.

4. 'First Report of Royal Commissioners Appointed to Enquire into the Defence of British Possessions and Commerce Abroad' (hereafter cited as Carnarvon Commission First Report). This report and the second and excerpts of the third are included amongst the 'Papers laid before the Colonial Conference 1887', *Parl. Papers*, 1887, Vol. 56, pt 2 (Appendix), sec. 7. All three reports in their complete form are preserved in PRO 30/6-131, to which specific references in this chapter refer. The figure for passing trade was identical to that calculated by Colonel C. H. Nugent in 1877, indicating a reliance on earlier War Office investigation.
5. Carnarvon Commission, First Report, p. 4. Conversely, though this is not mentioned in the report, the very fact that the Cape was such an important focal area for shipping would have drawn enemy commerce raiders towards it, as it did in the Second World War. At the same time, without local bases from which to operate, enemy commerce raiders could do no more than alarm and irritate; the Cape and other such places were safe from serious attack.
6. The Cape government already contributed £10,000 per annum towards Britain's expense in defending it. See 'Confidential War Office Memorandum on Colonial Contribution to Military Expenditure', January 1880, PRO: WO 88-7512.
7. 25 ton, 10.4 calibre guns.
8. Carnarvon Commission First Report, p. 6.
9. Ibid., 6.
10. Ibid., pp. 10, 14–16.
11. Ibid.
12. Robert Meade minute, 15 May 1882, PRO: CO 323/353, no. 9217.
13. Robert W. G. Herbert minute, 18 May 1882, ibid.
14. 'Second Report of the Royal Commissioners Appointed to Enquire into the Defence of British Possessions and Commerce Abroad' (hereafter cited as Carnarvon Commission Second Report), PRO: PRO 30/6-131, to which specific references in this chapter refer. This report was submitted to the Colonial Office in May 1882.
15. £900,000,000, of which £144,000,000 was constantly afloat.
16. Ibid., p. 2.
17. [Ed. note: recent studies have challenged this conclusion. See J. Beeler, *British Naval Policy in the Gladstone–Disraeli Era, 1866–1880* (Stanford, CA: Stanford University Press, 1997), pp. 253–9; Andrew Lambert, 'The Shield of Empire, 1815–1895', in J. R. Hill (ed.), *The Oxford Illustrated History of the Royal Navy* (Oxford: Oxford University Press, 1995), pp. 163–4.]
18. Carnarvon Commission Second Report, p. 2.
19. Ibid., pp. 5–6.
20. Ibid., p. 2.
21. Ibid., pp. 3–4. [Ed. note: enemy colliers were a larger problem in theory than in practice, given the impossibility of coaling at sea under any but the calmest conditions. The Commission did not, however, have the benefit of experience in this respect.]
22. Ibid., p. 4.
23. Ibid.

24. Ibid., p. 6.
25. Ibid.
26. Towards the latter part of 1881 the New South Wales Legislature debated the possibility of making an annual contribution to the Royal Navy Australian Squadron. Cost apportionment presented an insuperable problem. The information was passed to the Admiralty where the professionals welcomed the trend that such a debate indicated, but the First Lord maintained that such a scheme could never be worked satisfactorily owing to the fact that colonies contributing to squadron upkeep would want some voice in its disposition even in wartime. This correspondence was withheld from the Royal Commission. See CO to Admiralty, 8 November 1881, PRO: ADM 1/6604.
27. Peter Henry Scratchley (1835–85): Major-General, RE; Indian Mutiny; Superintendent of defence works at Melbourne, 1860–63; accompanied Jervois to Australia to advise on Australasian defence, 1877; Vice-President of Commission on military defences New South Wales, 1861; KCMG 1885. Scratchley's report was received at the Colonial Office on 1 September 1880. See Carnarvon Commission Second Report, Appendix 4: pp. 161–76. The Admiralty attached little importance to Thursday Island. See CO to Admiralty, 23 December 1881, PRO: ADM 1/6604.
28. 'Third and Final Report of the Royal Commissioners Appointed to Enquire into the Defence of British Possessions and Commerce Abroad' (hereafter cited as Carnarvon Commission Third Report), Digest of Evidence, p. 619, PRO 30/6-126. The evidence of Sir Daniel Cooper, Agent-General of New South Wales was heard on 8 June 1880, that of Sir Henry Blyth, Agent-General of South Australia on 14 October 1880. See ibid., p. 626. The local militia representatives heard were Lieutenant-Colonel E. R. Drury, commanding Queensland Artillery (19 May 1881, ibid., p. 631), Major G. J. Airey, New South Wales Artillery (10 June 1880, ibid., p. 621), and Major P. T. Sargood, Victorian Field Artillery (1 June 1880, ibid., p. 616). Sir Arthur Kennedy, Governor of Queensland, was interviewed on 8 June 1880 (ibid., p. 620).
29. *The Times* (London), 19 March 1881, p. 10. This decision did not please the Secretary of State for War, but he admitted that nothing effective could be done until Australian Federation came about. See Carnarvon Commission Second Report, Appendix 4, p. 99.
30. Their contribution was not small. Between 1878 and 1882, for instance, Victoria spent £120,000 on naval defence – for torpedo boats, gun boats and minefields – exclusive of the upkeep of naval and military forces. See CO to Admiralty (enclosing a report by Scratchley on the defences of Victoria), 24 August 1882, PRO: ADM 1/6644.
31. Carnarvon Commission Second Report, p. 34.
32. Ibid., p. 29.
33. Ibid., pp. 28–31. This would not please the Duke of Cambridge who held the view that high commands in the colonies should invariably be reserved for imperial officers. See Cambridge to General Colley, 5 January 1880, RA ADD.MSS.
34. Carnarvon Commission Second Report, pp. 30–2.
35. Ibid., p. 32.
36. Victoria was training a small naval reserve. The Colonial Naval Defence Act of 1865 was simply a permissive act allowing for the formation of such forces in the colonies. The colony also ordered the coastal defence monitor *Cerberus*, which guarded Melbourne harbour throughout her active life. She was also, incidentally, the first of Edward Reed's breastwork monitors, and thus the direct

precursor of the *Devastation* and, in terms of her armament disposition, of most pre-Dreadnought and Dreadnought battleships. The Commission's apparent reasoning is most plausible in view of the fact that in July 1882 South Australia indicated her willingness to purchase a ship expressly for the colony's defence. See CO to Admiralty, 7 September 1882, PRO: ADM 1/6644.
37. Carnarvon Commission Second Report, p. 33.
38. Admiralty to CO, 11 March 1880, PRO: CO 812/16, no. 170; Governor Western Australia to CO, 9 August 1880, PRO: CO 812/24, no. 54.
39. Carnarvon Commission Second Report, p. 33.
40. Ponsonby to CO, 24 May 1882, KP: PC/B/23.
41. Carnarvon Commission Third Report; Jekyll to Milne, 5 December 1882, NMM: MLN/163/2.
42. The existence of this third report in the Carnarvon Papers was made known, its contents outlined, and its significance speculated on, by Gerald S. Graham in *Empire of the North Atlantic*, pp. 278–88, especially p. 279. [Ed. note: general historical ignorance of the third report and its contents is less now than when Professor Schurman wrote these words in the mid 1950s. W. C. B. Tunstall's 'Imperial Defence 1870–1897', in *The Cambridge History of the British Empire* summarizes all three reports (pp. 232–3); Donald C. Gordon's *The Dominion Partnership in Imperial Defence* likewise furnishes an overview (pp. 62–76), as does Dr Schurman's own *Education of a Navy* (p. 30). The current work, however, remains the most comprehensive treatment of the Carnarvon Commission and its reports.]
43. Carnarvon Commission Third Report, pp. 28–31. To wit:

> But your Commissioners deem the commercial interest to be so vast and the paramount importance of its protection so great, especially in the supply of food and raw material, that they consider Her Majesty's Government ought not to rest satisfied with our fleet being merely on a comparative equity with other nations, which has [sic] few colonies and but a limited trade; but that our Navy should be decidedly superior to that of all other nations not only in our ironclad fleet for home defence as well as any other service which might arise in the Mediterranean, more especially for acting in regard to the Suez Canal, depending on circumstances which may arise in respect to maintaining its state of efficiency; but that in fast and well-armed cruisers we ought most decidedly to be considerably in advance of any nation, especially in regard to the speed and armament of our ships ... Your Commissioners view with some anxiety the existing force of the Royal Navy for affording protection to our great national interests at home, in the Mediterranean, and abroad, and we adhere to the opinions already expressed, that the strength of our Navy in ironclad ships and in cruisers for the protection of commerce should be decidedly in excess of any other nation, and even with a considerable increase great difficulty would be found in affording protection to so extended an Empire and so vast a commerce.

This reference to the need for an increase in the general strength of the Navy was specially inserted to put pressure on Gladstone and the Admiralty for naval increases. See Holland to Milne, 17 June 1882, NMM: MLN/163/2.
44. This concern had been occasioned by the Orient Steamship Company's request to lease one of the Diego Garcia Islands. On the commissioners' recommendation a clause was written into the contract providing for the destruction or removal of the company's coal stocks in the event of war. See CO to Admiralty, 17 May 1882, PRO: ADM 1/6644.
45. The general conclusions ended with a final, and, in the circumstances,

IMPERIAL DEFENCE 1868–87

superfluous admonition to secrecy.
46. A first-class Admiralty coal station was one that stored coal purchased by the Admiralty. A second-class coaling station sold coal to Admiralty ships under local agreement. The Admiralty did not officially draw this distinction for the commissioners until June 1882. See Carnarvon Commission Third Report, Appendix 1.
47. Ibid., Appendix 4, nos 4, 5 and 6; Digest of Evidence, pp. 606–9. Astley Cooper Key (1821–88): Entered Navy 1833; Crimean War 1854–55; at Canton, 1856; Director of Naval Ordnance 1866–69; president Royal Naval College 1873; Commander-in-Chief North America 1876; First Naval Lord 1879–86; GCB 1882; PC 1884. Key gave evidence before the Royal Commission on 4 March 1882.
48. Ascension was completely under Admiralty control. For this reason Milne's Defence Committee had considered it outside its frame of reference. Cooper Key may well have thought that in the same way the Commission was unauthorized to deal with it.
49. Carnarvon Commission Third Report, pp. 2–4.
50. Ibid., pp. 4–11. It was the possibility of cable-cutting at the Cocos that lured the *Emden* to her fate there on 9 November 1914. See Julian S. Corbett and Henry Newbolt, *Official History of the War: Naval Operations* (London: Longmans, Green, 1920), Vol. 1, pp. 380–4.
51. The commissioners' reasoning against leasing islands without provision for the removal or destruction of any coal stocks in event of war was seconded by the Admiralty. See CO to Admiralty, 17 May 1882, ADM 1/6604.
52. During the Russian war scare of 1878 Royal Navy vessels were forced to stay at Aden because of lack of cable communication with Mauritius. See F. N. Boone (Mauritius) to Hicks Beach, 13 April 1880, PRO: CO 812/16, no. 201.
53. In early 1880 the Governor of Mauritius wrote to Hicks Beach that, during the past six months, five Indian troop transports had stopped at Mauritius for coal and supplies. See Bowen to Hicks Beach, 24 February 1880, PRO: CO 812/16, no. 184.
54. The population of Mauritius was largely of French origin, a fact that must have complicated consideration of its defence, especially considering the proximity of Réunion, for France was perceived as a most likely future enemy.
55. And the fact that, as imperial fortresses, Gibraltar and Malta were presumably well defended.
56. Carnarvon Commission Third Report, p. 11. [Ed. note: Cyprus had been acquired from the Ottoman Empire in 1878, one of the consequences of the Congress of Berlin, following the Eastern Crisis. Disraeli's government hoped that it would furnish a base of operations for navy vessels operating in the eastern Mediterranean, Malta being too far away to fulfil adequately the function for steamships. British hopes were disappointed, not because of the location of Cyprus, but owing to the lack of a suitable harbour on the island. This deficiency must have been evident to the commissioners, and probably explains their lack of enthusiasm for the subject. With the occupation of Egypt in the year of the third report's completion, the British secured their eastern Mediterranean base: Alexandria.]
57. On the 2 April 1885, in the midst of the Russian war scare over the Penjdeh incident, the British flag was hoisted over Port Hamilton, The occupation ended on 27 February 1887. See 'Correspondence Respecting the temporary Occupation of Port Hamilton by Her Majesty's government', *Parl. Papers*, 1887, Vol. 41, p. 185.

58. Penang had the advantage of direct cable communication with Singapore, yet this link did not help much when the *Emden* raided it on 28 October 1914 and sank a Russian light cruiser and a French destroyer in the harbour. See Julian S. Corbett and Henry Newbolt, *Official History of the War: Naval Operations*, Vol. 1, p. 337.
59. Carnarvon Commission, Third Report, p. 18.
60. In 1881, 26,501 registered vessels called at the port.
61. Carnarvon Commission Third Report, Digest of Evidence, p. 612.
62. Ibid., pp. 15–16.
63. Its annual trade was valued at £67 million, £25 million being with Great Britain.
64. After the 1878 Russian war scare Singapore had voted an extra £4,200 towards improving its defences and gave the necessary land free of charge. See WO to CO, 21 February 1879, PRO: CO 812/14, no. 14.
65. Carnarvon Commission Third Report, p. 18.
66. The annual trade passing through the West Indies was then £21,000,000. See ibid., Digest of Evidence for the views of Cooper Key and the Duke of Cambridge.
67. In 1878 the situation was more complex since not only had the Admiralty and War Office put forward their particular defence needs: the Colonial Office wanted the Bahamas defended as well.
68. The Commission did not collect extensive evidence on the West Indies. The main concern was the prospect of laying a strategic cable between Halifax and Bermuda. Since both places were, as imperial fortresses, outside the Commission's scope, the cable connection subject was not dealt with in their recommendations.
69. Milne to Barkly, 16 March 1882, NMM: MLN/163/2.
70. Milne memorandum (copy), 20 May 1882, NMM: MLN/163/2; Milne to Barkly (copy) (enclosing memorandum), 20 May 1882, MLN/163/2.
71. Jekyll to Milne, 26 May 1881, NMM: MLN/163/2.
72. Carnarvon to Milne, 1 June 1882, NMM: MLN/163/2; Milne to Carnarvon (copy), 5 June 1882, MLN/163/2.
73. Carnarvon Commission Third Report, Appendix 1.
74. Milne memorandum, 20 May 1882, NMM: MLN/163/2.
75. Carnarvon Commission Third Report, p. 14. This recommendation was obviously not intended seriously and was a sop to Milne. The idea was Simmons'. He also suggested that a miniature railway be constructed between the redoubt and the dock. See the Third Report, Appendix 2.
76. This occurred in 1881. See WO to CO, 24 May 1881, PRO: CO 323/350-9216.
77. Carnarvon Commission Third Report, Digest of Evidence, p. 607.
78. Ibid., p. 9.
79. The Ceylonese were uneasy when the Commission was formed, for fear of being called upon for a greater financial contribution. The government of Ceylon already contributed £121,000 per annum to military upkeep. See *Ceylon Observer* clipping, 13 December 1879, preserved in NMM: MLN/163/2 and War Office memorandum, January 1880, PRO: WO 32/88-7512.
80. Carnarvon Commission Third Report, Appendix 4, no. 57.
81. Attached to the Third Report.
82. Carnarvon Commission Third Report, pp. 23–5, 31–3.
83. Since Canada was almost totally neglected by the Commission, except in this reference to Esquimalt, Macdonald's evidence was important. He stated that war with the United States was unlikely; and that Canadians would not vote defence money in peacetime. The strength and frankness with which he put

these views forward probably convinced the Commissioners to avoid specific recommendations for Canadian defences. For Macdonald's evidence see Alice R. Stewart, 'John A. Macdonald and Imperial Defence', *Canadian Historical Review*, 35, no. 2 (1954): pp. 121–39.
84. Ibid., p. 136, question no. 3879.
85. Ibid. See also G. P. de T. Glazebrook, *A History of Canadian External Relations* (Toronto: Oxford University Press, 1942), p. 265.
86. War Office memorandum on Esquimalt, 14 December 1880, printed in Carnarvon Commission Third Report, Appendix 4, no. 130.
87. Ibid., p. 24.
88. It was well that the commissioners allowed more than War Office strategy to influence their final conclusion. In December 1882 the Canadian government protested against even the temporary absence of the Royal Navy Squadron from British Colombian waters and cited the promise to that province to keep up the navy base. The Admiralty refused to be fettered, but the incident showed the strategic wisdom of a tactful handling of the Esquimalt problem. See CO to Admiralty, 14 December 1882, PRO: ADM 1/6644.
89. As late as 1888, however, the War Office had not worked out exactly which officer was responsible for Esquimalt, and there was no regular army communication with it. See PRO: WO 32/262-256-64.
90. Carnarvon Commission Third Report, p. 33.
91. Ibid.
92. In any event constitutionality was not a common basis for argument amongst admirals.
93. This complacency is well illustrated by an incident that occurred some years later. In 1888 the Admiralty withdrew some of its ships from the Red Sea without consulting either the military or political people in Egypt, and protests from the military authorities went unheeded. Lord Wolseley minuted thus:

> His Royal Highness considers this correspondence a fresh proof of how very desirable it is that the Army and Navy should be under some one authority. In no other way does it seem to be possible to combine the action of these two services to the best advantage of the State.
>
> That a commodore in the Navy should have the power to remove the ships of war from a port situated as Suakin now is, without consulting the general Officer commanding in Egypt, or Her Majesty's Representative in that country, is a condition of things that is fraught with serious danger to the Empire.
>
> However, until this big general question is seriously taken up by the Cabinet, there is little use in remonstrances on the part of the Commander-in-chief. The Admiralty will not even deign to consider our views, and invariably refuse all concessions.

He argued that the matter was one to be settled by the Cabinet. See Wolseley minute of October 1888 attached to Admiralty to WO, 20 September 1888, PRO: WO 32/265-7700/6358.
94. WO to CO, 25 February 1881, enclosed in CO to Admiralty, 14 March 1881, PRO: ADM 1/6604.
95. Obvious from a study of his private papers. Probably a great deal due to old age and ill-health. [Ed. note: While First Naval Lord Milne produced numerous very specific memoranda on naval dispositions and the requisite number of cruising vessels for protection of British trade in time of war. I would thus amend this assertion slightly. Milne's thought could be very precise indeed, but he often expressed his views in convoluted fashion. I concur with Professor Schurman

that the effects of age and ill-health may well have played a part in his marginalization within the Commission.] [Author's note: The problem was not precision about remembering detailed service statistics, but the fact that Milne, like many military people, lacked the power of distinction in argument – the power to distinguish – and hence he (and they) sound flat in the world of the College, the Bar and the Board Room.]
96. Suggesting also that the other commissioners thought that Milne's views reflected official Admiralty opinion.
97. Although it must be admitted that the adjustment problems occasioned by the revolution in naval architecture were enormous. The War Office had no comparable *matériel* difficulty to overcome.
98. On 30 November 1881 the Colonial Office forwarded the military reports on the defences of St Helena to the Admiralty. The only minute upon it, made by the First Naval Lord, carefully refrained from commitment. 'No opinion is asked for in this report', Cooper Key noted, and none was given. See Cooper Key minute on CO to Admiralty, 30 November 1881, PRO: ADM 1/6604.
99. Northbrook minute, 10 May 1881, attached to CO to Admiralty, 19 April 1881, PRO: ADM 1/6604.
100. Ibid.
101. The First Naval Lord drafted a letter on the importance of Trincomalee for the Royal Commission. It was never sent. See Cooper Key minute, 10 May 1881, attached to CO to Admiralty, 19 April 1881, PRO: ADM 1/6604.
102. See minutes of 12 June and 25 June 1881 on WO to Admiralty, May 1881, PRO: ADM 1/6604.
103. Lord Kimberley wrote in 1880 that it was the practice of the 'Colonial Office to refer every question, great and small, as to colonial defence to the Commission with the view ... "of fortifying" the office with their authority in applying pressure on other departments for Imperial expenditure in the colonies'. See Kimberley Cabinet Memorandum, 8 June 1880, KP: PC/B/24.
104. Lorne to Carnarvon, 3 December 1881, PRO 30/6-52. John Douglas Sutherland, styled Lord Lorne, 9th Duke of Argyll (1845–1914): Married Princess Louise, fourth daughter of Queen Victoria (1871); Governor-General Canada, 1878–83; Unionist MP, 1895–1900.
105. The time factor is strongly supported by the fact that, although not mentioned in the text proper, Appendix 6 of the Third Report contains correspondence relating to a proposal to establish an imperial reserve army force in Canada.
106. Carnarvon to Lorne (copy), 6 December 1881, PRO 30/6-52.

7

Aftermath of the Commission

BEGINNINGS OF GOVERNMENT ACTION

The degree of enthusiasm with which the three reports of the Carnarvon Commission were greeted in political circles might have been predicted by anyone knowing Gladstone's indifference to the subject and Kimberley's and Childers' manifest lack of enthusiasm for the Carnarvon inquiry during the final two years of its existence. In combination with the repeated injunctions to secrecy, these attitudes all but ensured that the reports produced neither a sense of urgency nor any immediate result.[1]

The first report produced only perfunctory comment from the civil servants at the Colonial Office. Little more resulted from the second, which was circulated in customary leisurely fashion between May and July 1882. In minuting the report for his superiors, Robert Meade, second undersecretary at the Colonial Office, noted that the warning about using regular army troops for police duties in British Honduras had been passed along to the governor, who, in reply, pleaded the dearth of dependable local forces as an objection to withdrawal.[2] This was the only immediate reaction to the second report. On 18 May R. W. G. Herbert noted that the reports were 'interesting' and 'important' but that no immediate response was necessary, adding, however, that the Colonial Office should attempt to secure some action regarding defences at the Cape. If a war caught the empire unprepared the Colonial Office would get the blame for the Cape's defenceless state.[3] He also suggested that the different sections of the reports be considered *separately*, indicating how little he grasped the commissioners' intent – to say nothing of the concept of unified imperial defence – or perhaps how adept he was at avoiding any recommendations likely to cause friction with his chief. Meade was more persistent, and on 25 May he again forwarded the reports to Kimberley.[4] They were returned to Herbert's tray on 1 July and the permanent undersecretary tactfully minuted that haste was unnecessary because the third report had not yet been produced, and that the Colonial Secretary would take them all home to study in the parliamentary recess.[5] The Secretary of State agreed and noted that action would be considered in the new session after contemplation and consultation between Lord Northbrook, Childers and himself.[6] As has been shown, the Secretary of State's reaction to the conclusion of the Commission the next month did not lend much hope to this promise.

Yet the government was quite prepared to take action that involved purely colonial expense, and with Jekyll's parting blessing, it was decided to send the Australian section of the second report to the colonies it concerned. This step was accordingly taken on 11 January 1883.[7] The whole subject had, however, really reverted to its pre-1878 status, and depended largely on departmental humour. On 6 December 1882, for instance, the Admiralty requested information on colonial coast defence in North America, the East and West Indies, China, the Cape, West Africa and Australia. This initiative pleased the Colonial Office since it did not clash with the Carnarvon Commission reports (indeed, it ignored it).[8] The Colonial Office did not bother to reply to this query, even to the extent of suggesting that those at the Admiralty interested in the subject might profitably read the Commission's reports.

In December 1882 Kimberley left the Colonial Office for the India Office, and Lord Derby took his place.[9] Ironically enough, it was from Kimberley's new office that a request came to the Colonial Office on New Year's Day 1883 to inquire into cost division between the imperial and the Indian governments for the defence of Aden.[10] Herbert noted for his old chief that any such apportioning was dependent upon the Cabinet's decision as to what was to be done with the Commission's reports.[11] Another small reminder of the existence of the reports came when Blake's 1880 memorandum for Kimberley on the progress of Carnarvon's Commission surfaced at the Colonial Office, and Herbert noted that it should be circulated with the reports.[12]

The days of Colonial Office control of imperial defence, however, were nearly over. Sometime in the opening months of 1883, certainly prior to mid July, the Cabinet decided to return the whole imperial defence problem to the Inspector-General of Fortifications. On 14 July Lord Hartington – who had succeeded Childers at the War Office – recommended an extension of the retirement age for Sir Andrew Clarke, the Inspector-General of Fortifications, on the grounds that he was engaged in preparing schemes in connection with the Royal Commission's report.[13] Hartington's request was forwarded to Queen Victoria, who minuted 'immediate'.[14] The War Office, and through it Gladstone and Liberal economic ideals, now largely controlled the fate of imperial defence.[15]

The crucial figure at the War Office was Clarke himself. He was appointed Inspector-General of Fortifications in June 1882, over the heads of four colonels senior to him. He was, moreover, both a staunch

Liberal and a personal friend of Hugh Childers, then Secretary of State for War. Not surprisingly, his appointment occasioned some comment. There is no proof to back widespread contemporary speculation that it was a political 'job', but there is likewise no doubt that, although held in high professional regard, Clarke had Liberal acquaintances in high places and shared their political views, and in the 1880s Garnet Wolseley was a shining example of what Liberals would do for a soldier who did military things without spending too much money.[16] With retirement facing him in 1883 – before his temporary rank of major-general became permanent – his disposition may well have inclined him toward accommodating his political masters. Childers' 'Submission Paper' to Queen Victoria states the reasons for Clarke's appointment, mentioning his undoubted qualifications and the need for his professional commentary on the Royal Commission's reports. Almost in the same sentence, however, Childers asserted that he required Clarke's assistance in wisely allocating the 'several millions' that the Liberal government intended to spend on colonial defence.[17] In light of Gladstone's, not to mention Childers', well-documented attitude toward defence expenditure, the latter's claim stretches the bounds of credulity. Clarke had his virtues as an Inspector-General of Fortifications, yet an understanding of his peculiar position is necessary to appreciate his action on the Carnarvon Commission's reports.

Of course, the reports themselves were not completed until December 1882. Little, if anything, was done with them for the next five months, for in May Carnarvon addressed the House of Lords, apprising the peers of the reports' existence and chiding the government over its lack of action.[18] This criticism evidently spurred the administration to motion – albeit languidly – for Clarke produced a memorandum on the commissioners' recommendations the following month.[19] Its contents were, however, only vaguely in accord with the views expressed in the three reports and involved less expense, again suggesting that the Inspector-General of Fortifications may have owed his appointment at least in part to extra-professional considerations.

Clarke was complacent regarding the urgency of defending particular places. He agreed that Mauritius needed fortifications, but stated that work should not begin on them until conditions were 'pressing'. The present time was 'not propitious'. He found Singapore's proposed defences too ambitious, on the grounds that the British Far East squadron would never be far removed. He argued, furthermore, that no enemy commander would dare 'throw away' shot at Singapore. He was inclined to abandon Esquimalt due to the slightness of the local trade. He came down heavily for the importance of Jamaica and considered St Lucia of little value since it was not as *economically* important as Jamaica. He agreed with Milne regarding Trincomalee's importance. In short, he obviously disregarded the carefully worked-out strategic basis for the Royal Commission's conclusions, and personally judged each case by his own criteria. His strategic reasoning thus seemed muddled.

Easier to understand, given his politics and connections, was his view that the expense of imperial defence would be lower than the Commission's envisaged figure. He argued, for instance, that garrisons could probably be formed from local volunteers when an emergency arose. Indeed, Clarke evinced little faith in fortifications, full-stop. In 1885 he advised the Australians that defence funds would be better spent on naval preparations than on fixed works ashore.[20] But the overarching rationale for his apparent indifference to the topic was his conviction that a war with European powers would be restricted to Europe. Empire defence, whether naval or land-based, was a secondary, if not a tertiary, matter. Such an attitude was unlikely to induce political support for the concept.[21]

Beyond political and financial considerations, Clarke had a further reason for circumspection. In 1882 the Morley Committee, which had been investigating the defence of commercial ports in the United Kingdom, made its report.[22] Faced with establishing priorities, the Duke of Cambridge, it may safely be assumed, was more inclined to concentrate on home, rather than overseas, defences. Moreover, the Duke had re-established his authority over imperial defence planning by the simple expedient of reviving the old Defence Committee and forcing Clarke to send proposals for both home and overseas defences to that committee for verification.[23] The Inspector-General of Fortifications thus had to be careful to frame his recommendations in such a manner as not to conflict too markedly with the Duke's sensibilities.

The contents of the Carnarvon Commission reports next stirred official interest in March 1884, when the War Office informed the Colonial Office that the Duke of Cambridge's Defence Committee had approved some of the commissioners' recommendations.[24] Specifically, Hong Kong and Singapore were accorded top priority, although the committee added that most of the cost of fortifying those two vital points could in all probability be charged to the colonial governments. The Cape defences were judged next in importance. The War Office letter acknowledged that Simons Bay was entirely an imperial responsibility, but in another manifestation of the spirit of economy which permeated the government, recommended that the Cape government be asked to defend Table Bay since the interests there were 'purely colonial and commercial'. At the same time the India Office was informed by the War Office of a plan for the defence of Aden.[25]

But times were changing, and the imperial stream that was to burst its banks on the news of Gordon's death at Khartoum in early 1885 was already beginning to flow. In May 1884 the Queen asked Gladstone to consider empire defence requirements. The prime minister promised a statement on the subject. On 29 July the Imperial Federation League held its founding meeting. Imperial defence and an imperial customs union were the league's primary practical objects, and the influence of J. C. R. Colomb was writ large in its agenda.[26] For a brief moment in mid 1884 colonial matters became news.

More important in arousing public interest in security matters, imperial defence included, however, were W. T. Stead's 'Truth About the Navy' articles in the *Pall Mall Gazette* which began to appear in September.[27] Stead had gone to the Admiralty and learned first-hand how little Gladstone cared for defence matters. He also obtained a good deal of confidential information from a 'captain R.N.' who trusted his discretion.[28] Although he tended to concentrate upon the inadequacy of the fleet, Stead did not overlook the coaling station situation.[29] The public impact of his revelations was enormous. For the first time since 1859–61 defence requirements became a general topic of discussion, and the government's hand was eventually forced.[30]

The Times was at first unmoved by Stead's agitation, and parliament was not in session when the first of his articles appeared, so there was no immediate government reaction. In October, however, the pace quickened. The Queen was disturbed and badgered Gladstone on the subject of coaling stations.[31] On 18 October the publication of a government paper revealing half-hearted interdepartmental correspondence relating to the implementation of the Carnarvon Commission's recommendations shocked *The Times* into activity. It clearly revealed that even the tentative and incomplete proposals made by the War Office in March had been opposed by the Treasury.[32] The paper's editorial of the same day questioned confident official assurances that slight defences would suffice, and shrewdly speculated on how closely the recommendations of the Inspector-General of Fortifications compared with those of the Carnarvon reports.[33] Firmly, if belatedly, in the saddle as the champion of Britannia's Trident, *The Times* lent its blessing to the coal station agitation by pronouncing it to be above party strife, deeming the subject a 'permanent national concern'. The change in outlook was complete. On 13 October *The Times*' 'special correspondent' for naval matters had praised Admiralty parliamentary secretary Thomas Brassey for elevating questions of naval preparedness above political controversy; on 22 October an editorial took Brassey to task for his complacent attitude toward naval affairs.[34] This agitation had its effect, and on 23 October Gladstone announced that the government's plans for coaling station defence would shortly appear.[35]

On 7 November *The Times* printed an article entitled 'The Imperial Defences', by 'a correspondent'.[36] Carnarvon would hardly write anonymously. 'A correspondent' was thus probably either J. C. R. Colomb, or C. H. Nugent, the only men besides the Carnarvon Commissioners capable of appreciating the controversy in perspective. The author wisely declared that only the Queen's permanent military advisers could prevent imperial defence problems from being considered piecemeal, rather than globally. The subject should, he bluntly stated, be considered as a whole.

Carnarvon, who had no faith in Gladstone's promises to give attention to the subject, gave notice of a question in the House of Lords for 13 November 1884. The threat of an embarrassing public debate, together with the ongoing press agitation, prompted Colonial Office under-secretary Robert Meade to urge that a reasonable 'beginning should be made at once on this much delayed subject'.[37] This plea, in turn, generated a hastily drafted government white paper on proposed defences for Aden, Trincomalee, Singapore, Hong Kong and Simons Bay.[38] Carnarvon had little time to study the proposals before he spoke.

Carnarvon opened by explaining that his scope was limited, since the First Lord of the Admiralty had, prior to the debate, extracted a pledge of secrecy from him concerning the contents of the reports of the Royal Commission.[39] Thus circumscribed, he was nonetheless able to note that the government's proposals for defending the Cape dealt with Simons Bay, but neglected Table Bay. The defence of the one, he stated, was wasted if the other were ignored. He furthermore warned not to expect too much in the way of assistance from colonial governments. He emphasized Britain's dependence on seaborne trade and how the safety of that trade was principally the navy's responsibility. The success of its mission depended, in turn, largely upon the security of its repair and coaling bases. It would not be sufficient merely to increase the fleet. What then was necessary? Here Carnarvon admitted that since he could not make comparisons between the government's proposals and the Commission's recommendations, he could say little definite to answer that question.

He could, however, examine the government proposals on their own merits. The total expenditure envisaged in the government's scheme was £891,000. But by ignoring the defence of Simons Bay, charging the cost for Aden's defence to the Indian government, and proposing to fortify only Singapore and Hong Kong, the figure chargeable to the United Kingdom was reduced to £345,000.[40] He wondered how this priority system was determined. Moreover, by dividing imperial and local charges, the actual chargeable sum was further reduced to £150,000, to be divided on the basis of £103,000 for armament and £47,000 for works. Since the armaments would not be voted until the works were completed, this left an initial outlay of £47,000 from the original £891,000 proposed. Carnarvon obviously knew something of Treasury control.

Not only were the recommendations a farce, he charged: he also strongly deprecated the piecemeal approach adopted. The commissioners, he maintained, had been thorough, and on consideration of the best professional advice they had recommended defences in terms of the empire as a whole. The government's scheme, on the contrary, was 'narrow' and 'departmental'. It was an eloquent testimonial to how the Treasury could use a 'departmental spirit' to secure economy, and Carnarvon deplored the tendency to allow that department to pronounce on matters outside of its natural province, to say nothing of its competence. He wondered if the Admiralty was a subordinate department to the Treasury, and expressed surprise that Brassey, an ardent navalist regardless of his political loyalties, agreed to such a small scheme. He concluded by disclaiming any party motive, and by washing his hands of responsibility for the empire's defencelessness.

Carnarvon's speech left the way open for Northbrook to place the blame on the unsystematic manner in which defence problems were dealt with by the departments, and by so doing to keep the debate on a high level. Perhaps such a course was not acceptable to Gladstone, for Northbrook's reply used this opening as an avenue for discrediting Carnarvon and extricating the government from an embarrassing position. This task was made easy by a request by Liberal Lord and Carnarvon Commission member the Earl of Camperdown that the source of government proposals be indicated.

Northbrook assured his listeners that the importance of coaling stations was generally accepted, but maintained that legitimate doubt remained as to the size of any probable attack upon them in wartime. He deplored the fact that Carnarvon's conclusions were entirely opposed to those of the government, especially at the moment that the question was being seriously considered. The charge of Treasury control, he claimed, amused him. Certainly that great department was not 'vicious'. The government's proposals, he said in reply to Camperdown's query, were based on recommendations by the Inspector-General of Fortifications, but had been referred to and passed by the Duke of Cambridge's Defence Committee, and 'the same praise is due to the work of that Committee which my noble friend applied to the work of that Commission'. Northbrook continued:

> I cannot agree with my noble friend in the remarks he has made about that Committee. I do not know why [he] should depreciate that Departmental Committee and speak in disparaging terms of it. It was composed of men who possessed the greatest knowledge of the subject, and I do not see why the term 'Departmental' should be used of them as a slight when they were dealing with a matter with which their whole professional education qualified them to deal.

Carnarvon interrupted to point out that he said 'Departmental spirit', not 'Departmental Committee', to which Northbrook replied that the Inspector-General of Fortifications had had naval advice, and that the

First Naval Lord was a member of the Duke of Cambridge's Defence Committee. It was, 'after all ... a question of authority, and if I thought the noble Earl was more likely to be right than the Defence Committee I should bow to his authority'. He agreed that Simons Bay was of great importance, but maintained that Carnarvon's claim that defences for Simons Bay were useless without defences at Table Bay 'is a point upon which he will find the general current of professional opinion against him'. He hoped that Carnarvon's words regarding the Cape would not discourage colonial assistance. He concluded by stating that important subjects like this one took time to deal with and that delay would only produce a greater excellence in the finished result. The debate concluded, naturally enough, with a speech by the Duke of Cambridge supporting Lord Northbrook.

Lord Northbrook's defence was transparent but effective. The Duke of Cambridge's Defence Committee was essentially a War Office committee. True, it contained the First Naval Lord, but it is highly unlikely that he had any effective voice in a body presided over by the Duke. In any event, he would be consulted on details rather than on general policy. This would also have been the case with regard to the naval advice that Northbrook stated had been given to the Inspector-General. Northbrook had cleverly manœuvred Carnarvon into a position where further attack must be either bitter in the party sense or else constitute an attack on the military competence of the Duke of Cambridge. *The Times* was not impressed by this stratagem, yet the perils of publicly attacking the Duke prompted the editors to content themselves with stating that Northbrook's reply had neither the dignity nor the power that Carnarvon's thoughtful speech merited.[41] When Carnarvon opposed Cardwell's troop-withdrawal policy in 1870, Kimberley privately implied that he had spoken for strong partisan political reasons and that the Liberals had dexterously 'exposed the artifice'.[42] On the subject of imperial defence in 1884 Carnarvon's speech was grave and rose above party politics almost completely.[43] It was he who 'exposed the artifice' of Northbrook, whose defence was as dexterous as his case was weak.[44]

On 2 December 1884 the leading journal printed a letter from J. C. R. Colomb. He accused the Liberals of quashing the Carnarvon Commission reports for partisan political reasons, since their 'production unaccompanied by a proposal to meet the necessary expenditure would involve grave political consequences'.[45] On the same day, Lord Northbrook announced a supplementary estimate of £3.5 million for the navy. The coaling station recommendations, however, stood as outlined in November.[46] Carnarvon attempted to escape from the corner into which Northbrook had driven him by asking if the Duke of Cambridge's Defence Committee had actually seen the Royal Commission's reports first-hand. Northbrook, however, realized the strength of his position and simply accused Carnarvon of attempting to abolish the Duke's committee. Carnarvon could go no further, although ex-First Lord of the Admiralty W. H. Smith baldly informed the House of Commons that departmental concealment existed and that everybody recognized it except members of parliament.[47] Since the government had been pressured to take action – however modest – the coaling station defence advocates in parliament were forced to rest, if not content, at least quiet.

Yet if the administration appeared to have scored a victory as far as the coaling station problem and imperial defence generally were concerned, superficial appearances were soon belied. Stead's articles and the resultant debates had brought the problem before parliament in such a manner as to raise it above the realm of political partisanship. Lord Carnarvon's lecture on the 'spirit of departmentalism', with the assistance of a new Russian war 'scare' following the Penjdeh (Afghanistan) border incident, prompted the formation of a new interdepartmental Colonial Defence Committee in March 1885.[48] This committee has generally been regarded as marking the beginning of imperial defence planning as it came to be understood between 1897 and 1914, a distinction accorded it largely due to the bottomless capacity of the committee's secretary, George Sydenham Clarke, for publicizing any institution or event with which he happened to be connected. It certainly constituted a landmark, since in operation it devised a regular system for dealing with details of colonial defence.[49] Meetings were held whenever the secretary had collected sufficient information to make a gathering useful. Those with special colonial experience and knowledge were routinely invited to give information. Colonial defence memoranda were circulated to the Colonial Office, War Office, Admiralty and finally, if the approval of all were obtained, to the Treasury. Such a method of proceeding went some way towards counteracting 'Treasury control', since that department now had to deal with the representations of three, rather than one other department.[50] The secretary collected reports coming from local defence committees in the colonies and kept a register of all correspondence. In the two years before the 1887 Colonial Conference, the committee produced 26 memoranda and 57 special recommendations on colonial security.

By its very existence the Colonial Defence Committee partially obviated the greatest difficulty hitherto found in dealing with imperial defence: lack of a permanent body set up to deal with nothing else and using a clearly defined and consistent method of procedure. It also rendered 'Treasury control' a little less rigid, at least in the tone of its manifestos.[51] What it did not do was to place naval functions in their proper relationship to imperial defence, since the committee was heavily weighted in favour of the War Office. Of the six committee members, four represented the army. The Colonial Office and the Admiralty had but one representative each.[52] Given the Admiralty as it then existed, however, together with the peculiar position of the Duke of Cambridge as Commander-in-Chief of the Army, it is difficult to see how this imbalance could have been avoided. It would require an American, Alfred Thayer Mahan, to repopularize the navy so that the reforming zeal of John A. Fisher could not be quenched by conventional methods.[53] But such a time was, as of 1885, still well in the future. From a purely military point of view what was wanted was a general staff, and for this the Colonial Defence Committee of 1885 was a feeble substitute.

Nor was the establishment of a permanent committee to consider colonial security the only manifestation of revived interest in matters of empire. The problem of garrisons for imperial bases recommended for fortification by the Carnarvon Commission was finally considered by a War Office committee formed in October 1885.[54] This committee's report made detailed recommendations on numbers and composition of the military personnel for nearly all of the bases selected by Carnarvon and his colleagues.[55] Their recommendations followed the general principles laid down by the Commission, being pitched at a minimum level, encouraging the formation of local defence forces, and resting on the basic assumption that the joint defence provided, generally by the navy and particularly by projected fortifications, would be sufficient to render a large enemy landing an unlikely contingency.

The fidelity with which this committee accepted conclusions reached by the Carnarvon Commission was remarkable, even in its slight tendency to departmentalism. In considering the garrison needs of Ceylon, for instance, it cleverly avoided making specific recommendations for Trincomalee, which the Commission had suggested be abandoned. Since Canada had agreed to man Esquimalt defences, the committee was spared wrestling with that problem. Significantly, Labuan was not mentioned.

The War Office committee on imperial garrisons did, however, use the opportunity provided to reverse the one judgement of the Carnarvon Commission against departmental custom. It recommended that Barbados be retained as a military post, that the naval port of St Lucia receive only a small artillery detachment, and that spare garrisons for that unhealthy port be kept at British Honduras and the Bahamas.[56] Their recommendations in the West Indies would, first, ensure that dispersal of force that the Commissioners had attempted to avoid, and, second, leave naval needs unsatisfied. Although these recommendations were in accordance with War Office custom, they were directly descended from the army bias that had permeated the Carnarvon Commission's third report. The members of the War Office committee would hardly have been human had they missed the opportunity provided. These were, however, only minor blemishes on a valuable report with a firm strategic basis. It speaks volumes for the authoritative mantle the Carnarvon Commission reports had acquired by 1886, as it does for the appreciation of the importance of imperial defence principles among War Office professionals, that such a departmental committee could so meticulously accept the commissioners' detailed recommendations, together with the strategic reasoning behind them. Since Sir Andrew Clarke was a member of the committee the result is all the more remarkable. Either he was heavily outvoted or else the fall of the Gladstone government (in mid-1885) had some little effect on his views concerning the value of the Carnarvon Commission's ideas as the basis for imperial defence.[57]

Of course, there was a significant difference between concocting imperial defence plans and actually implementing them, and the degree to which the Colonial Defence and War Office Committees' recommendations for the defence of coaling stations were acted upon by various governments after 1884 needs to be surveyed as well.[58] The revised estimates made by Gladstone's government amounted to £976,760 for fortifying the first-class coaling stations of Aden, Trincomalee, Colombo, Singapore, Hong Kong, Cape of Good Hope, Mauritius, Jamaica and St Lucia. Of this, £330,470 was contributed by the Indian and colonial governments, leaving an imperial charge of £646,290. For second-class coaling stations the charge was £178,500, according to Brassey, who announced the figure during the brief third Gladstone ministry of 1886. He himself proclaimed the government's plans and proposed expenditure adequate.[59]

With a Conservative government in office the following year, however, Brassey could afford to be more critical and, perhaps more honest. Moreover, with the appearance of the first volume of his *Naval Annual* in 1886 he had a pulpit from which to espouse his ardent navalism. His interest in imperial defence issues had doubtless become keener since an 1886 cruise during which he visited many of the ports under consideration. Empire defence now meant something concrete to him. By the publication of the second *Naval Annual* he had concluded that both parties' commitment to imperial defence was inadequate, and that public support was needed. Only a large popular outcry could overcome 'Treasury control' and open the public purse.[60] Brassey's conscience may well have been troubled by the partisan necessity of defending the Liberal government for keeping the Carnarvon Commission reports secret. He could, however, give credit to Stead. The reports had been hidden from the public, and consequently there had been no demand for government action. '[But] for the influence of the press the recommendations of the Commission would have been pigeon-holed.'[61]

He also considered empire coaling station defences in some detail in the 1887 *Naval Annual*. Aden had been rendered practically impregnable.[62] Works were under construction at both Trincomalee and Colombo, the latter paid for by the colony of Ceylon, but the armament, since it was to the charge of the imperial government, would probably be years in arriving.[63] Modern fortifications had been constructed at Singapore by the local government, but the guns promised by the home government had not yet been delivered. Defences were going up at Mauritius at the local government's expense, yet here again Britain had not delivered the promised armament. Mauritius, moreover, still lacked cable communication with the outside world. Brassey expressed the conviction that the strategic position of the Cape was 'thoroughly understood in England'.[64] Yet the colonists had totally neglected Table Bay defences and the work undertaken by the imperial government at Simons Bay would be undercut, if not rendered worthless, by the proposed armament of old muzzle-loaders. Works were in progress at St Helens, but no British guns had arrived.[65] The same was true at Sierra Leone. King George Sound and Thursday Island were still undefended.[66] This was the extent to which the recommendations of the Carnarvon Commission had been carried out by 1887.

NOTES

1. The 'secrecy' also meant secrecy about making the reports available to the general public. There were copies specially designated for the members of the commission, the Queen, the Duke of Cambridge, the prime minister, the secretary of state for war, the First Lord of the Admiralty, and the Colonial Office. These, except for a number of rough working drafts, were the only copies printed. See 'Third and Final Report of the Royal Commissioners Appointed to Inquire into the Defence of British Possessions and Commerce Abroad' (hereafter cited as Carnarvon Commission Third Report), Appendix 12, nos 4 and 7, 619, PRO 30/6-126.
2. Robert Meade minute, 15 May 1882, PRO: CO 323/353, no. 9217.
3. Robert W. G. Herbert minute, 18 May 1882, ibid.
4. Meade to Herbert, 25 May 1882, ibid.
5. Herbert minute, 1 July 1882, ibid.
6. Kimberley minute, 2 July 1882, ibid.
7. Jekyll to CO, 18 December 1882, PRO: CO 323/359-17535.
8. Admiralty to CO, 6 December 1882, PRO: CO 323/351-21103.
9. Edward Henry Stanley; 15th Earl of Derby (1826–93): politician; Secretary for India, 1858–59; Foreign Secretary, 1866–68 and 1874–78; Colonial Secretary, 1882–85; Liberal Unionist leader in the Lords, 1886–91; KG 1884.
10. India Office to CO, 1 January 1883, PRO: CO 323/355-48.
11. Herbert minute, 10 January 1883, ibid.
12. Herbert minute, 2 February 1883, PRO: CO 323/356-1964.
13. Spencer Compton Cavendish, Marquis of Hartington, later 8th Duke of Devonshire (1833–1908): politician; Junior Lord of Admiralty, 1863–66; Postmaster-General, 1868–70; Chief Secretary for Ireland, 1870–74; Secretary for India, 1880–82; Secretary of State for War, 1882–85; Unionist, 1886; refused prime ministership, 1886 and 1887; President of the Council, 1894–1902.
14. Hartington to Ponsonby, 24 July 1883, RA: B-35, no. 36.
15. This assertion may overstate the case, but not greatly. The mood of the government towards defence measures can been seen in a *Treasury* proposition

that telegraphic communications be established with West Africa in order to render the West African squadron more immediately effective. The Admiralty felt compelled to refuse this suggestion, for linked with it was a proposal to reduce the numbers of the squadron. Indeed, it was put forward on the 'ground of its economy and importance'. See CO to Admiralty, 23 January 1883, ADM 1/6682.

16. R. H. Vetch, *Life of Lt-General Sir Andrew Clarke* (London: John Murray, 1905), see preface by George Sydenham Clarke, p. vi; George Sydenham Clarke, *My Working Life* (London: John Murray, 1927), p. 26. Many years later, Sir George Sydenham Clarke (Lord Sydenham of Combe) wrote that Sir Andrew was believed to have a personal hold over Childers, and on another occasion he stated that the appointment was widely believed to be a political 'job'. Sir George maintained that both of these interpretations were incorrect. This same conclusion is reached by Sir Andrew's biographer, R. H. Vetch. Since both Vetch and George Sydenham Clarke owed a good deal to Sir Andrew's assistance in the advancement of their careers, such a conclusion is not surprising. One must accept their claim, failing definite proof to dispute it. On the relationship between the army and politicians, see Hew Strachan, *The Politics of the British Army* (Oxford: Clarendon Press, 1997), pp. 92–117.
17. Vetch, *Life of Sir Andrew Clarke*, p. 335.
18. Henry Howard Molyneux Herbert, 4th Earl of Carnarvon, *The Defence of the Empire*, ed. G. S. Clarke (London: John Murray, 1897), pp. 1–11. Carnarvon's speech may have helped to generate the sense of urgency under which it was possible to secure the Queen's approval for postponing Clarke's retirement.
19. Andrew Clarke, 'War Office Confidential Memorandum by the Inspector General of Fortifications on the Report of the Royal Commissioners Appointed to Enquire into the Defence of British Possessions and Commerce Abroad', KP: PC/B/24.
20. Vetch, *Life of Sir Andrew Clarke*, p. 251.
21. Many of Clarke's ideas were sound *if taken by themselves*. But he was also a political appointment and said what his political friends wanted to hear.
22. Vetch, *Life of Sir Andrew Clarke*, p. 235.
23. Duke of Cambridge minute attached to 'War Office Confidential Memorandum by the Inspector General of Fortifications on the Report of the Royal Commissioners Appointed to Enquire into the Defence of British Possessions and Commerce Abroad', KP: B/PC/24.
24. WO to CO (copy), 19 March 1884, PRO: WO 33/42, 447–53. The activity may have been related to a lecture on overseas defence by Colonel C. H. Nugent, Deputy Director of Works for Fortifications until 1881, at the Royal United Services Institution in April 1884. News of Nugent's forthcoming speech probably came to the War Office in March, and since he had much inside information which might prove damaging, it may have prompted the department to take action. Certainly Nugent had more sympathy for coaling station defence than did Clarke, and his speech pressed for action on the subject. He also stated that the weak point of the Carnarvon Commission was want of colonial representation. See C. H. Nugent, 'Imperial Defence: Abroad', *Royal United Services Institution Journal*, 28 (1884): pp. 464–85.
25. WO to India Office (copy), 19 March 1884, PRO: WO 33/42, 447–53.
26. Anon., 'Imperial Federation', in *Report of the Conference, 29 July 1884* (London: Cassell, 1884). The League's members were split on the customs union issue. The protectionist side of the League's activities is described in Benjamin H. Brown, *The Tariff Movement Reform Movement in Great Britain 1881–1895* (New York: Columbia University Press, 1943). For the League generally, see J. E. Tyler, *The*

Struggle for Imperial Unity, 1868–1895 (London: Longmans, Green, 1936); and A. Folsom, *The Royal Empire Society* (London: George Allen & Unwin, 1933). More recently, see D. C. Gordon, *The Dominion Partnership in Imperial Defence, 1870–1914* (Baltimore, MD: Johns Hopkins University Press, 1965). Colomb was an ardent supporter of the Imperial Federation's defence schemes, and the League undoubtedly helped establish the importance of imperial defence through its literature, even as its representations in 1886 did much to bring about the Colonial Conference of 1887, at which defence was the principal topic of conversation.

27. [W. T. Stead], 'What is the Truth About the Navy', *Pall Mall Gazette* (London), 15 September 1884. This was the first article in the series.
28. Frederick Whyte, *The Life of W. T. Stead* (New York: Houghton Mifflin, 1925), Vol. 1, Ch. 7, especially p. 150. See also Arthur J. Marder, *The Anatomy of British Sea Power: A History of British Naval Policy in the Pre-Dreadnought Era, 1880–1905* (repr. edn, New York: Pantheon Books, 1976) and Harvey Blumenthal, 'W. T. Stead's Role in Shaping Official Policy: The Navy Campaign of 1884' (unpublished PhD dissertation, George Washington University, 1984). The 'captain R.N.' was John A. Fisher, probably acting at the instigation of Geoffrey Phipps Hornby.
29. Coaling stations were mentioned in Stead's articles from the first, but in mid October a separate article devoted to the subject was published. See [W. T. Stead], 'The Truth about Our Coaling Stations', *Pall Mall Gazette* (London), 16 October 1884.
30. A supplementary estimate of some £3.5 million was approved to strengthen the navy and its facilities.
31. Gladstone to the Queen, 22 October 1884, RA A78, no. 19.
32. The paper was published in *The Times* (London), 18 October 1884, p. 9.
33. Ibid., p. 9.
34. Ibid., 13 October 1884, p. 3; 22 October 1884, p. 9.
35. Ibid., 24 October 1884, p. 7; see also Hansard's *Parliamentary Debates*, 3rd ser., Vol. 293 (1884), col. 58.
36. *The Times* (London), 7 November 1884, p. 4.
37. Meade minute, 10 November 1884, PRO: CO 323/357-18109.
38. Published in *The Times* (London), 14 November 1884, p. 6.
39. A practical example of Childers' logic that by the simple expedient of insisting on secrecy, the Liberals need never be embarrassed by alarming revelations from the Commission's findings.
40. He could have added, had the pledge of secrecy not prevented him, that the government's order of priorities differed markedly from the Commission's, which had assigned the greatest importance to the Cape, on strategic grounds.
41. *The Times* (London), 14 November 1884, pp. 6, 9.
42. Kimberley, 'Journal of Events under the Gladstone Ministry 1868–73', 22 July 1870, KP: PC/A/42.
43. Hansard's *Parliamentary Debates*, 3rd ser., Vol. 293 (1884). The entire debate occupies cols 1534–56. A report of the debate can also be found in *The Times*, 14 November 1884, p. 6.
44. The First Lord of the Admiralty, rather than the Secretary of State for War, spoke for the government, despite the recommendations for coaling station defence having been drawn up in the War Office. Stead's articles had done something, therefore, to link the coaling station situation with the navy in the public mind.
45. *The Times* (London), 2 December 1884, p. 12.
46. Ibid., 3 December 1884, p. 5.

47. Ibid., pp. 6–7. See also the leader on p. 9.
48. Yet the new committee was founded largely on the initiative of civil servants: Sir Andrew Clarke for the War Office, and undersecretaries Herbert and Meade at the Colonial Office, using the possibility of war with Russia as an excuse to secure some interdepartmental co-operation in colonial defence. See Vetch, *Life of Sir Andrew Clarke*, p. 238, n. 1. Clarke himself assigned most of the credit to Meade. See ibid., p. 367. The accomplishments of the 1885 Colonial Defence Committee are described by George Sydenham Clarke (Lord Sydenham of Combe) in *My Working Life*, and in a paper 'Measures Taken in Relation to Colonial Defence', printed for the 1887 Colonial Conference. See PRO 30/6-131. The description of the committee here relies on the latter source.
49. No evidence has been found to suggest that the 1885 Colonial Defence Committee had access to the complete Carnarvon Commission Reports.
50. The committee tended to trespass on the field of government policy. In January 1893, when its proper sphere of activity was considered by Gladstone's government, it was defined as existing to deal with details of colonial defence only. Formulation of large items of policy belonged properly to the Admiralty and War Office working in concert. See 'Confidential Regulations of Colonial Defence Committee', PRO: WO 32/236-40261.
51. Treasury letters largely ceased to evaluate army and navy strategic decisions.
52. The War Office representatives were the Inspector-General of Fortifications (initially Sir Andrew Clarke), the Assistant Director of Artillery (Colonel H. Geary, RA), the Deputy Director of Works for Fortifications (Captain George S. Clarke) and the Quartermaster-General (represented by the Assistant Quartermaster-General, Lord W. Seymour). The Admiralty representative was the Chief of the Foreign Intelligence Division, Captain T. S. Jackson, and the Colonial Office member Assistant Undersecretary for the Colonies, Robert Meade.
53. Later Admiral of the Fleet Baron Fisher of Kilverstone.
54. It members were Hon. G. C. Dawnay, Surveyor-General of Ordnance; General Sir A. Herbert, Quartermaster-General; Major-General Sir A. Clarke, IGF; Major-General Sir R. Buller, VC, Deputy Adjutant-General; Major-General R. J. Hay, Deputy Adjutant-General RA; R. H. Knox, Esq., Accountant-General; John Branston, Esq., representing the Colonial Office; Secretary, Colonel Maurice, RA.
55. 'Report of a Committee on Colonial Garrisons', 16 August 1886. PRO: CO 323/366, 3-38.
56. See Chapter 6 above.
57. In 1884 he deplored the tendency to base government action on the Carnarvon Reports. See 'Confidential Paper by A. Clarke for Lord Hartington', 24 November 1884, PRO: WO 33/42, 771-5.
58. That coaling station defence did not consume large Treasury grants during these years was partly due to the fact that the 'Fortress England' idea was still in competition, for in 1888, a system of fortifications was erected around London. See J. K. Dunlop, *The Development of the British Army 1899–1914* (London: Methuen, 1938), p. 12. Also there was argument amongst professionals as to what constituted the best type of harbour defence. See George Sydenham Clarke, *Fortifications* (London: John Murray, 1890), especially pp. 176–85.
59. Thomas Brassey, *Naval Annual 1886* (Portsmouth: J. Griffin, 1886), p. 99. It would be inappropriate to conclude that by 1886 'adequate attention' meant that colonial affairs had advanced to the front rank in British politics. As J. C. R. Colomb put it, Britons still viewed imperial affairs through the wrong end of a telescope. See [Anon.], *Conference and Banquet of the Imperial Federation League*

(London: Cassell, 1886).
60. Brassey, *Naval Annual 1887* (Portsmouth: J. Griffin, 1888), p. 54.
61. Ibid., p. 55.
62. Ibid., p. 56.
63. Ibid., p. 57.
64. Ibid., p. 59.
65. As the Carnarvon Commission had recommended.
66. Brassey, *Naval Annual 1887*, pp. 63–7.

8

Experiment in Imperial Co-operation

The Colonial Conference of 1887 was not a spontaneous outpouring of the kinship and affection that British peoples felt for one another. It occurred specifically because a delegation of the vociferous Imperial Federation League requested that the conference experiment be carried out.[1] The league pursued two main lines of policy: *Zollverein* (customs union) and *Kriegsverein* (Imperial defence). Lord Salisbury's Conservative government acquiesced in the request, probably because it felt that concrete discussion of the *Zollverein* issue would point up practical differences and kill the idea of parliamentary federation, and certainly because it wished to use the league's advocacy of *Kriegsverein* to secure increased colonial contributions to imperial defence costs.[2] In his account of the conference's work and accomplishments, Professor Tyler has stressed the large amount of time devoted to imperial defence and the fact that this was in accordance with the will of the British hosts.[3] Yet very little time or energy was expended on the Cape of Good Hope's defences, and there was practically no discussion on Canada. The context in which the conferees considered imperial defence, therefore, seems somewhat unreal.[4]

In the main, defence discussions at the Colonial Conference revolved around attempts by the imperial government to secure a 'sharing' of the financial burden. More specifically, the Australian and New Zealand governments were pressed to contribute to the cost and maintenance of the Royal Navy's Australasian squadron and to the cost of fortifying and manning King George Sound and Thursday Island. The first of these objects was first put forward by the imperial government on 15 April 1887. The conference's president, Colonial Secretary Sir Henry Holland, read a letter from the Admiralty to the new Commander-in-Chief proceeding to the Australian station, authorizing him to continue the negotiations begun by Admiral Sir George Tryon in 1885 for Australasian contributions to the Royal Navy.[5] This missive outlined four proposals made during Tryon's negotiations:

1. The Admiralty proposed that Australasian colonies jointly undertake to pay both the cost of construction and maintenance of ships intended for the Australian squadron. In ten years' time the ships would pass to joint ownership by the Australasian colonies.
2. New South Wales, Tasmania and Queensland proposed that the colonies together should pay 5 per cent of the cost of construction, and maintain the ships, which would remain Admiralty property.
3. Victoria colony proposed that the colonies bear the annual maintenance charge only.
4. New Zealand offered simply to contribute an annual cash sum of £20,000 on the understanding that a ship should remain constantly in New Zealand waters.

Sir Henry Fairfax, the new Australian squadron commander, was authorized to state that the Admiralty was prepared to negotiate on the basis of the 5 per cent offer, and, as an added inducement to Victoria, was prepared to increase the size of the force. It was this proposal that Holland presented to the Australasian delegates.

South Australia supported Victoria's position that Australasian contributions should not exceed the squadron's annual maintenance costs. Yet Victoria colonial MP Alfred Deakin made it clear that his colony's objection to Admiralty requests was based not merely on desire to avoid expense, but on the understanding that imperial security arrangements rested on the principle that the British government provided sea defence while the colonies provided security ashore and garrisons for certain harbours.[6] Moreover, Deakin wanted to know on what principle the cost-sharing was determined. Was it on a population basis, a shipping basis, or precisely what?[7] The imperial authorities did not answer these questions. Indeed, they could not in any authoritative fashion. Even the Carnarvon Commission reports – the most exhaustive examination of the matter – provided no recommendations for apportioning shares of the imperial defence financial burden.[8] Yet it speaks volumes for the carelessness with which the British government framed its proposals that it did not produce, and probably did not consult, the findings of that Commission.

On 18 April the Admiralty again put its proposal forward on the 5 per cent basis, this time making the further concession that any additional maintenance that a war might entail would be absorbed by the British government.[9] The objections of New Zealand were countered by a guarantee that two ships would be permanently stationed in New Zealand waters in peacetime, but that in wartime their disposition would rest with the Australian squadron Commander-in-Chief.[10] This proposal was favourably considered by the delegates and was then wired to Australasia for the approval of the governments concerned. All agreed to the scheme, even Victoria. In a conciliatory speech Deakin stated that Victoria agreed, not for reasons of conviction, but for the sake of the promotion of empire unity.[11]

This agreement, and especially Victoria's acquiescence, showed clearly that the Australasians were prepared to go a long way to make the conference a success, even conceding the imperial government's terms. Yet the negotiations had been clumsily handled and it was wise that the British used the initial good feeling of the delegates at the conference's opening to secure what they regarded as their most important object. The negotiations over the proposed defence of King George Sound revealed quite a different spirit.

To understand the Colonial Conference debate on King George Sound it is necessary to emphasize that absolutely no defences existed there in 1887. The Carnarvon Commission report reflected ambivalence on the question of the Sound's strategic value, and Sir Andrew Clarke's recommendations of 1884 omitted mention of it. There had been, moreover, no sign from Australasia that the colonists intended to fill the gap. During the 1885 Russian war scare the Colonial Office, acting on the advice of the new Colonial Defence Committee, offered to supply armaments for King George Sound, if the various Australasian colonies would construct works and see that the guns were manned.[12] The Australasians did not respond eagerly, and when the British government saw that the immediate threat of war had passed the matter was not urged further. In 1886, however, the Australian Federal Council suggested a joint scheme by which the Australasians would share the cost of defending the Sound with the mother country.[13] Nothing came of the proposal, and there matters rested as of 1887.

The question of defending King George Sound was raised at the conference on 24 April by the president.[14] He claimed that the need for such defence 'has been fully recognized by the Imperial Government and the Australasian Colonies'. He also mentioned the Federal Council's proposal of 1886, and that the base's defence had been considered by Colonel Scratchley in 1881. Furthermore, the need for defences there had been recently raised and amplified by Admiral Tryon when Commander-in-Chief of the Australian squadron. The type of defence necessary to secure the base need only be modest, because of the proposed increase in size of the squadron, but Tryon urged that it be defended so that the fleet would be completely free to attend to its proper and more important duties. Holland also referred to Lord Derby's Colonial Office offer of 1885. In sum, he asked that the whole subject be reconsidered on a more permanent basis. He proposed that the Australasians provide works and troops, and the home government, although unable to furnish armaments of the most recent type in view of its many other commitments, would send some outdated guns that should be adequate for defence against the type of attack envisaged. The best solution, Holland stated, would be for the colonies themselves to provide guns of the newest type, but failing that the British government would provide, free of charge, second-class armament plus a number of submarine mines.

Before dealing with the reception that the delegates to the conference gave to these proposals, it is worth examining the reasoning on which they were based.[15] It is evident that neither Holland nor the proposal's author had any clear idea why King George Sound should be defended, or why such defence should be mainly laid to the charge of the Australasian colonies. His first sentence, stating that the need for defences there was recognized by both home and colonial governments, indicates that he considered the problem as one involving mutual interest and responsibility. He stated that the Australasian colonists had considered the problem in 1886, but also emphasized that Admiral Tryon had raised the matter, fostering the impression that the Admiralty too was interested. Further, he suggested that King George Sound needed to be defended so that the Australasian squadron would be free to act without being uneasy about the harbour falling into enemy hands. The reference to Lord Derby's proposal of 1885 further heightened the impression that the imperial government was vitally interested in securing the Sound.

Holland's proposals were vague, hasty and ill-considered. Doubtless he anticipated vague opposition on the part of the colonists but assumed that it would not be of an intelligent nature. Here, however, the president had made a grave error. Having some knowledge of the comparative values of new and old ordnance through their local harbour defence efforts, the initial colonial respondents indicated that they would contribute nothing towards the erection of outmoded defences.[16] They emphasized the imperial value of the place and furthermore chided the president for springing his paper on the delegates without allowing them time to study it.[17] At this point Secretary of State for War Edward Stanhope stated that it was desirable that King George Sound be defended as soon as possible and old guns could be quickly sent out: hence the rationale for the imperial government's offer.[18] This rather ridiculous statement was not seriously contested, for the delegates began to realize that if they did not accept the old armament the home government was not prepared to contribute a penny towards new guns. Stanhope then dilated on the large-scale commitments of the imperial government as regarded coaling station defence, and it required pressing by Sir Samuel Griffith, Premier of Queensland, to extract the concrete statement that the colonists could expect old guns or nothing from Britain.[19] Victoria politician James Service termed this a rather unhelpful attitude and pictured the delegates going home to tell their people that they had exchanged good hard cash for a few obsolete guns.[20] Stanhope expressed sympathy, but then returned to the theme of heavy British defence commitments, adding that Her

Majesty's government had never admitted the responsibility for land defence on the Australasian continent.[21]

The colonial delegates then began to realize that imperial authorities wanted the cost of defending King George Sound to be borne solely by the Australasian colonies. Sir Graham Berry, agent-general for Victoria, voiced this chilling realization: 'I always understood, and I never heard it denied until today that the Imperial Government simply required the assistance of the Australasian Colonies in that work, and not that they wanted them to do the whole of it.' It was a pity, he added, that the colonies were not told of this policy before, in which case their attitude might have been quite different. Stanhope replied that King George Sound had been recommended for abandonment by the Carnarvon Commission but that the matter was subsequently revived by the 1885 Colonial Defence Committee and upon reconsideration the British government was prepared to assist; 'but', he went on, 'I am not prepared to admit that at all times the Imperial Government has considered that they were bound to assist in contributing to the defence of King George Sound. They have been willing to do so, and they have shown themselves willing to do so, but the question rests with the Colonies.'[22] 'We cannot admit for a moment', he bluntly informed the delegates, 'the principle of sharing in the land defence of Australia.'

Hence, during the first day of discussions concerning King George Sound, the whole basis on which the colonists thought proposals for its defence rested, was discovered to be a misunderstanding, or perhaps it would be fairer to say that the home government had abruptly and without prior warning changed the rules. It was only at this stage that the imperial government sought to strengthen its case by promising to issue an edited version of the Carnarvon Commission reports to the delegates.[23] Between the first and second discussions of King George Sound the delegates from Western Australia informed Stanhope that the colonists would be prepared to share the cost of works and manpower for its defence if Her Majesty's government would provide new armaments.[24]

The discussion of 2 May was reserved for consideration of the Sound. The delegates expected some intimation from the president on the British government's reaction to Western Australia's proposal. They were disappointed. Holland informed the delegates that the War Office did not propose to defend King George Sound because of its value as a coaling station, but rather to deny it to a marauding enemy. Sir John Downer, the premier of South Australia, replied that this was the first intimation given to the delegates that the Admiralty considered the harbour unimportant.[25] Certainly Admiral Tryon had not given that impression to the colonies.[26] The Admiralty's spokesman, Captain Hall of the Intelligence Division, reiterated Holland's explanation: the navy thought the establishment of a coaling station at King George Sound unnecessary from an imperial point of view, but that the place should nonetheless be defended sufficiently to deny it as a refuge harbour to possible enemy attackers.[27] Alfred Deakin, whose opinions were consistently clear-sighted and moderate, suggested that the heart of the matter was that both home and colonial governments were interested in defending King George Sound, and that the task of the conference was simply to establish a reasonable cost division between the two.[28] The day's discussion had proceeded on the assumption that the British government might supply the desired new guns, and although it ended on an uneven and unsettled note, there was hope that on this basis colonial co-operation would follow from any reasonable proposal from Her Majesty's government, despite the fact that the colonists were restive, possibly feeling that the home authorities had not been completely open about the whole matter.

The last word on the subject at the conference came from the home government in a statement issued by the president on 6 May that effectively shelved the whole question. The main points of this paper were:[29]

1. The president was unaware that Her Majesty's government had ever considered that the cost of defending these places should be borne by it.
2. The Intercolonial Conference at Sydney in 1881 had passed a resolution to the effect that the land defence of Australasian ports should be supplied by the several colonies interested. Although the colonists had subsequently dissociated King George Sound and Torres Straits from the terms of the resolution, Her Majesty's government considered they fell under its terms.
3. That these places had no special claim to be considered separately from other Australasian ports.
4. That both ports were necessary to large Australian interests.
5. That were it not for the fact that Queensland and Western Australia could not afford to defend these places unaided the problem would probably never have arisen.
6. That Lord Derby's offer of help in 1885 was a completely altruistic emergency offer.
7. That although the scheme now put forward was more moderate than Scratchley's earlier one, opinion as to the size of possible naval attack had since changed, while the increase of the Australian squadron had lessened the danger of attack.
8. That *only* coal attracted an enemy at King George Sound, and an enemy was not likely to risk attack by the Australian squadron to secure coal.
9. That the armament offered by the British government was not perfect

but that it was considered by the War Office to be adequate under the circumstances.
10. That for these reasons Her Majesty's government was not prepared to go beyond the original offer.

The document concluded by pointing out that had the home government's generous offer been accepted, the base would have had some defence and all that would have remained to be done would be the provision of better armament when circumstances permitted. These recommendations were unacceptable to the Australasian delegates and the question of providing defence for King George Sound was dropped.

It is risky to assign praise or blame to participants in historic meetings, but it seems only reasonable to draw some conclusions in the case of the 1887 Colonial Conference, since one of the primary purposes of the meeting was to arrange a workable system of imperial defence based on co-operation between the home and colonial governments. In the case of the discussions regarding the defence of King George Sound, the responsibility for failure rests squarely on the shoulders of the home government. That is not to say that the delegates from the Australasian colonies were unreserved supporters of 'imperial' defence and found their enthusiasm blocked by the British government's attempt to make it completely 'colonial'. The situation was more complicated than that. It was also much more serious. As an experiment in inter-empire co-operation it was a disastrous venture.

Looking at the question on grounds of strategic necessity with the advantage of hindsight, if it be admitted that an attack on Australasian trade was a possibility in wartime, then the defence of King George Sound was as necessary and perhaps more necessary than the defence of Sydney, Melbourne or Adelaide.[30] It seems probable, contemporary Admiralty opinion notwithstanding, that to spurn a coaling station situated at the focal point of all Australasian trade crossing the Indian Ocean was strategic madness that can be explained only by the assumption that the Admiralty was not always an accurate judge of its own naval needs. In this case it did not want the place enough to bear the cost of its defence in the navy estimates, and thus allowed financial reasons to override strategic considerations.

Whether the Admiralty's decision was right or wrong, however, matters little in light of the fact that these decisions were nearly always adverse to the retention and consequent defence of King George Sound as a coaling station. After the exceptions of the Jervois and 5 June 1877 (the Duke of Cambridge's Defence Committee) memoranda, official decisions were invariably against the retention of King George Sound. The Admiralty, Milne's Defence Committee and the Carnarvon Commission all recommended that it not be defended. These recommendations were largely based on Admiralty opinion, the colonies concerned not being consulted, although Western Australia was informed of the decision.

Yet through all of this deliberation there had been a lingering suspicion that it was a mistake to leave the harbour completely undefended. In his report Scratchley had suggested that the place would be dangerous in the hands of an enemy, and so the Carnarvon Commission, while recommending no action by the imperial government, did suggest that King George Sound had some importance *vis-à-vis* Australasian trade and that the Australasians ought to defend it. It is clear that the Royal Commissioners found this problem so difficult that they washed their hands of it. Ever since the withdrawal of troops from the self-governing colonies the policy of the British government had been largely based on the catch-phrase 'self-government begets self-defence'. The beautiful symmetry of this convenient hypothesis was spoiled in the Sound's case by the fact that Western Australia did not have responsible government. Allied to that fact was the even more important one that the colony was poor.[31] The Colonial Office spurned the request of its poor dependent for the defence of its life-line on grounds of strategy, yet it was prepared to suggest to the Australian colonies as a group that this base within the territory of a poor dependency of the Colonial Office was their joint responsibility.

Oddly, the right of the British government to make such a request was never challenged upon these grounds. Yet it may be that the remembrance of this ungenerous – here again Carnarvon's 'churlish' would be an appropriate description – action, coupled with the realization that the Australian colonists had generally responded magnificently to British proposals by defending their own harbours, awoke some conscience. Along with the lingering suspicion that King George Sound might be after all strategically important this sentiment may have contributed to Derby's proposals of 1885. It is more likely that the Colonial Office and War Office had few doubts about the strategic importance of the base but little desire to go to the Treasury for the funds, and that Lord Derby's offer was simply an attempt to get the majority of its defence paid for by the Australians.

By 1887 memory of Australasian promptness in providing for their own defence had grown dim and Britain again determined that the colonists should defend King George Sound, for it was the president who raised the subject at the conference. Holland requested something for nothing and the method he used in attempting to secure it contained the surest recipe for its being spurned at a colonial conference: contempt for the reasoning power of the colonial delegates.[32] Had he stated baldly that the home government could not afford to pay for the defence of King George Sound he might have been successful in inducing the colonies to help, and he at least would have received a respectful hearing. Had he stated that the home government was not concerned, for strategic reasons, with the defence of King George Sound, he might yet have induced the

Australasians to agree to pay for it. What he did do, however, was to offer a few obsolete guns under the guise of a worthwhile gift and attempt, in a loosely reasoned argument, to shift the total responsibility for the defence of that harbour on to the colonials; and when his arguments were, not surprisingly, questioned, he shifted his ground disastrously and finally concluded by issuing a petulant paper.

In the same year as the Colonial Conference Sir Thomas Brassey was personally inspecting the coaling stations and naval bases in the Indian Ocean and throughout the Australasian Colonies. Writing in the *Naval Annual* the next year he deplored the home government's lack of imagination with regard to the importance of overseas bases generally and King George Sound in particular. The harbour could, he admitted, be permanently blocked by sinking ships in its entrance, but this was hardly the thing one expected from a power claiming to be mistress of the seas. His observation on the way the subject was dealt with at the Colonial Conference was trenchant: 'Having invited the representatives of our Colonies to meet in London in much pomp and circumstance, it was impolitic to allow an important decision to be postponed upon a trifling issue.'[33]

NOTES

1. On 11 August 1886 the Imperial Federation League delegation was received by Lord Salisbury, prime minister; Edward Stanhope, Colonial Secretary; and the Earl of Dunraven, Undersecretary of State for the Colonies. Included in the delegation were such defence advocates as Sir Charles Nugent, Sir Henry Barkly, Captain J. C. R. Colomb and Sir Thomas Brassey. Colomb spoke on the defence needs and it is clear that even Salisbury was impressed by this aspect of possible imperial co-operation, referring to it as a 'somewhat urgent question'. For an account of the interview, and a record of the invitations sent out see PRO: CO 323/366-15482.
2. Ibid.
3. J. E. Tyler, *The Struggle for Imperial Unity, 1868–1895* (London: Longmans, Green, 1936). For a description of events at the First Colonial Conference see also Richard Jebb, *The Imperial Conference* (London: Longmans, Green, 1911), Vol. 1.
4. Cape defences were discussed at a closed meeting when the Cape delegates agreed to meet half of the expense required for the defence of Table Bay (Cape Town Harbour). See John Ewing, 'South Africa in the World War', in A. P. Newton and E. A. Bevians with Eric A. Walker (eds), *The Cambridge History of the British Empire*, Vol. 8: *South Africa, Rhodesia, and the Protectorates* (Cambridge: Cambridge University Press, 1936), p. 737.
5. These negotiations resulted from the interest shown in 1884 by the First Naval Lord, Admiral Cooper Key, who wished to unify Australasian naval efforts. See C. C. Penrose Fitzgerald, *Life of Vice-Admiral Sir George Tryon, KCB* (3rd edn, Edinburgh: William Blackwood, 1892), p. 209. Cooper Key's interest was originally awakened because of a request that colonial naval officers be included in the *Navy List*. The official account is contained in 'Colonial Office Memorandum

on the Proposed Scheme for Increase of the Imperial Squadron in Australasian Waters', March 1887, PRO: CO 812/38-62.
6. Alfred Deakin (1856–1919): Australian politician; MP Victoria, 1880; Chief Secretary, 1886–90; delegate to Commonwealth Convention, 1900; Prime Minister of Australia. 1903–4; 1905–8; 1909–10.
7. 'Proceedings of the Colonial Conference', *Parl. Papers*, 1887, Vol. 56, p. 38.
8. Since the Commission left the matter vague.
9. 'Proceedings of the Colonial Conference', *Parl. Papers*, 1887, Vol. 56, p. 155.
10. Ibid., p. 159.
11. Meeting of 25 April 1887, ibid., p. 304.
12. Ibid., p. 245.
13. Ibid.
14. 'Paper on the Necessity for Defending King George's [*sic*] Sound', ibid., pp. 245–6.
15. See Jebb, *The Imperial Conference*, Vol. 1, pp. 34, 49, 50.
16. Especially Sir James Lorimer, Minister of Defence for Victoria who had some special knowledge of artillery, a fact referred to in the report of the *Sydney Morning Herald* on these negotiations. Quoted in Thomas Brassey, *Naval Annual*, 1888 (Portsmouth: J. Griffin, 1889), pp. 68–9.
17. Especially Sir Samuel Griffith, Premier of Queensland, whose remarks indicate that he was prepared to adopt almost any proposal Her Majesty's government thought necessary, but was alienated by the manner of presentation.
18. Edward Stanhope, cited in 'Proceedings of the Colonial Conference', *Parl. Papers*, 1887, Vol. 56, p. 253.
19. Ibid., p. 255.
20. Ibid., p. 259. James Service (1823–99): colonial politician; Premier Victoria, 1883–85; carried Bill for Federal Council of Australia, 1884.
21. Ibid., p. 260.
22. The first time at the conference that the Carnarvon Commission reports were used to buttress the British government's argument that King George Sound should be defended by Australasians.
23. Holland wrote to Carnarvon at the time, requesting permission to circulate such a version. Carnarvon did not give his permission until 16 June 1887. The conference ended in May. Yet the first and second reports and extracts from the third appear in the Appendix to the volume on the Colonial Conference as papers laid before the conferences.
24. 'Proceedings of the Colonial Conference', *Parl. Papers*, 1887, Vol. 56, p. 292.
25. Sir John Downer, South Australia Premier, quoted in ibid., p. 421.
26. A feeling that had been heightened by the fact that during the Russian scare of 1885 a corvette and a sloop were detained at King George Sound to protect the stocks of coal there. See Brassey, *Naval Annual*, 1887, p. 56.
27. Captain Hall, RN, Chief of Intelligence Division at Admiralty, quoted in 'Proceedings of the Colonial Conference', *Parl. Papers*, 1887, Vol. 56, p. 428.
28. Chief Secretary, Victoria.
29. See also Jebb, *The Imperial Conference*, Vol. 1, pp. 52, 53.
30. [Ed. note: although the Sound could not be held by a foreign ship for any length of time, and a superior British force could easily retake it. Putting guns there might have given an enemy the means to hold it. I am indebted to Dr Andrew Lambert for pointing this out.]
31. A population of some 4,000.
32. Jebb, *The Imperial Conference*, Vol. 1, p. 58.
33. Brassey, *Naval Annual*, 1888, p. 64.

Conclusion

Considerable historical attention has been given to the influences spurring the development of the new Commonwealth out of the old empire. The 1870s and 1880s have never been regarded as a particularly important period in the process, despite the agitation, almost completely unofficial, for imperial federation. In fact the imperial federation movement is mainly interesting as an example of how strong public opinion in favour of imperial unity failed to translate its aims into a politically relevant issue. A study of the emergence of the concept of imperial defence during these decades is more rewarding, since it reveals how the whole imperial 'apparatus' reacted to the only consistent problem that involved the empire as a whole during these years.

The study throws some light on official reaction at various levels to the problem involved in the defence of a vast, mutually dependent, oceanic empire during a time of extensive naval technological change and comparatively slight international tension. It gives some idea of the difficulties faced by military and naval planners under the cramping effect of a hostile political ethos when handling problems in need of sympathetic political interest and control. Finally, it describes the roots from which imperial defence, as a modern conception, sprang. In 1887 the term referred almost completely to defence of coaling stations, though involving some recognition of world-wide naval function. By 1917 it referred to the whole available machinery for land, sea and air co-operation within the empire.[1] Coaling station defence was the first problem that involved the empire as a whole in the age of the 'new' imperialism. Those concerned with it had to face nearly all the basic difficulties which confronted their successors when dealing with still broader problems of political support, interdepartmental co-operation and inter-empire co-ordination. Not all the original difficulties were resolved in this era, but attempts at their solution in the course of wrestling with coaling station defence strategy shed much light on what would ultimately be required. Moreover, growing understanding of the requisites for imperial defence

CONCLUSION

began to percolate slowly through Whitehall and even be appreciated in parliament.

The historical value of charting the development of imperial defence strategy does not depend upon pointing to what was accomplished in terms of *matériel* by 1887. Although something had been achieved toward securing Australasian government assistance – especially with regard to harbour defence – actual British government expenditure on efficient defences for bases for which it admitted prime responsibility was slight in proportion to the time spent investigating the problem. For this reason the study has evaded, as far as possible, the temptation to deal with types and quantities of material defences, and has concentrated on the development of policy and administrative machinery. If the concrete results were slight, much reason may be found in the fact that empire problems, not to say military ones, occupied an extremely small part of governmental time except when specific difficulties such as the Gold Coast, Zulu and Afghan wars forced such attention momentarily.

By 1887, what can be termed the 'Colomb–Jervois' strategic approach to imperial defence was generally accepted in War Office and Admiralty circles, and by the Conservative government, although it had not completely discredited the 'Fortress England' mentality.[2] While neither Canada nor South Africa were prepared to go very far in contributing to overall empire defence either in making contributions to the Royal Navy or in securing their own harbours, such was not true of the Australasian colonies. The fact that half of the time used for discussion at the 1887 Colonial Conference was given over to colonial defence issues demonstrates how much importance the British hosts attached to the subject. Here the Australasians not only reaffirmed their acceptance of responsibility for harbour defence but also admitted the principle of corporate imperial defence responsibility by agreeing to contribute to the cost of maintaining the Royal Navy squadron in Australian waters. The negotiations over the defence of King George Sound indicated how rudimentary was the co-operative machinery at that stage, and how important it was that such machinery be improved upon.

Finally, the establishment of the permanent Colonial Defence Committee in 1885 indicated that the British government had become aware that interdepartmental agreement at home was a necessary prerequisite to the securing of co-operation between the parts of the empire in defence matters. The appointment of the Hartington Commission in 1887 to examine the relations of the War Office and Admiralty with each other and the Treasury was a result of similar thinking.

These advances along the road of imperial defence were not, of course, entirely due to events involved in the development of coaling station strategy. It would be difficult to evaluate the extent to which events such as the failure to relieve General Gordon (1884–85), Stead's agitation for a bigger fleet in the *Pall Mall Gazette* (1884) and the activities of the Imperial Federation League influenced political leaders. Yet it is fair to say that the coaling station movement (if such a word is not too strong) provided practical experience at the official level for translating into action the fruits of various forms of external pressures on the politicians.

Any attempt to estimate the comparative value of the various impulses that lay behind imperial defence as it stood in 1887 must, because of the quiet background in which they worked, be tentative. Nevertheless, on the negative side there is clear evidence of the general Liberal attitude to imperial defence, borne out by the reaction of Gladstone's government to empire problems in the early 1870s, and by the complete antipathy of his second administration to the purpose, work and reports of the Carnarvon Commission. Allied with these attitudes was the concurrent political belief that the value of any administration could be gauged by its success in producing small budgets. Of this belief Gladstone was the prime exponent but by no means the only devotee. Apart from causing general suspicion of things connected with empire – the very word conjuring up vast expense chargeable to the British Treasury – this budgetary attitude curtailed development of inter-service co-operative planning by exploiting the confusion created by technological development as an excuse for not wasting government funds. This exploitation of confusion was not very difficult because the confusion was so widespread. It had three main facets: confusion regarding technological developments in the two separate services; confusion where these technological developments overlapped, as in the defence of home ports; and confusion caused by the reflection of both these sets of problems in the imperial field.

Another negative feature was the insular traditionalist approach of individual government departments which, though not so insurmountable an object as might at first be supposed, had nonetheless to be overcome. This obstacle in the way of the development of a unified scheme of imperial defence manifested itself chiefly in lack of co-operation between departments, specifically the War Office, Admiralty and Colonial Office. Any improvement required agreement on the basic requirements of imperial defence, machinery for working out details in concert, and sustained political interest and control to keep it operating smoothly. Here it is significant to note that the vast sprawling divided War Office showed itself more adaptable than the comparatively well-organized Board of Admiralty.

The third great difficulty, always excepting general public apathy to imperial problems, was the lack of appreciation of the new role that the self-governing colonies of the empire would play in any overall scheme for imperial defence. Here was the co-operative problem again, but in this case it was basically political, involving contacts between colonial governments, and requiring support in the way of departmental unity in

CONCLUSION

Britain with regard to actual defence requirements. Here too British imagination was little in evidence, and the colonies were never really taken into the confidence of defence-planners in London. Lack of colonial representation was the greatest defect of the Carnarvon Commission. Even at the 1887 Colonial Conference the conference table was used more by the British government in an attempt to secure monetary contributions to defence than in an attempt to achieve the co-operation based on mutual understanding of common problems that might have produced the end desired.[3] On the positive side, Gladstone and the Liberals must be given a kind of inverted credit, since the very antipathy of the 1868–74 government to the empire and the armed forces produced a reaction in favour of the former that was a basic requirement to making plans to defend it.

Among individual contributions, J. C. R. Colomb's was crucial. There were, no doubt, vast economic forces at work that made necessary an appreciation such as his of the relationship of naval function to the vulnerable nature of Britain's dependence on seaborne trade, and the value of bases providing coal and other facilities for the fleet. Yet Colomb's was the first mind to grasp the linkages in a global context. He was a 'sea-soldier' who worked entirely from a strategic premise. 'Trade follows the Flag' was not a general argument of exponents of united empire until the 1880s, and at the time he first put his arguments forward they existed in his mind alone. Moreover, it would be hard to find a rationalization of strategic and economic interdependence founded on a firm technological premise that has stood the test of time as well. Colomb was the pioneer of imperial defence. Had he been German his strategic theories might have been translated into English and reverenced in Britain, but he was not, and his thought is not generally sought after, his excellent biographical record collects dust, and his share in the victory of the Battle of the Falkland Islands (1914) remains obscure.[4]

In the same way the department of state that adopted and developed his thought, the War Office, does not constitute a field of study that nineteenth-century historians generally consider profitable. This same remark may be similarly applied to the Colonial Office, and in smaller measure to the Admiralty.[5] In the latter part of the century the empire found its military heroes in such men as Napier, Roberts, Gordon and Wolseley, who captured the public imagination. But for the steady persistent day-to-day work done by officialdom in London, little more space is given than that necessary to stress lack of imagination, conservative tendencies and torpid operation. It is one of the purposes of this study to suggest that although Victorian Whitehall could hardly be described as a school for forward-looking reformers, its tendencies were more progressive, responsible and sane than has been generally represented.

It was rather when the political element intervened that less consequential results followed, and even then progressive ideas were sometimes laid by and put forward again by Whitehall officials when times seemed more propitious. The struggle for political (and fiscal) control over entrenched government departments was undoubtedly necessary to the development of democracy in Britain, yet the results might well have been less beneficial had political control come more quickly. Such an eventuality is suggested by the case of the Boer War, the failures of which, despite professional warnings, were in large measure traceable to political control being sought at the expense of fighting efficiency.

Through Jervois and Simmons at the War Office, both of whom accepted and developed Colomb's thought, through Herbert and Meade at the Colonial Office, who recognized the need for interdepartmental co-operation, and through Milne at the Admiralty, as the first member of the board to be aware that coal would be a problem in future wars, these departments all made important contributions to the development of imperial defence strategy.

The present study is not strictly concerned with the impact of public opinion on imperial defence. Nor does there seem to be much evidence that government policy towards empire was greatly influenced by it during the major part of the period. Yet Stead's *Pall Mall Gazette* in September 1884 constituted a notable exception. The First Lord and the First Naval Lord in office in 1884 have been strenuously and competently defended by their biographers, especially in regard to Stead's charges that ship construction was not in proportion to the needs of the service and the country.[6] In view of the vast increases in naval construction which took place during the next ten years, such laborious justifications seem a trifle forced, especially considering the Gladstonian attitude towards the armed forces. First Lord Lord Northbrook is stated to have felt that the only really useful result of Stead's publicity was to force expenditure for coaling station defence.[7] This supposed solicitude accords ill with the party-political manner with which he discredited Carnarvon's honest concern when the subject was debated in the Lords.[8] Whatever may be said of the value of Stead's articles in promoting increased naval construction, it is clear that his influence compelled the government to do something for coaling station defence, and provided imperial security policy with the public support that made it weigh with politicians of both parties.

Carnarvon's share in the emergence of the concept of imperial defence can safely be termed decisive. His importance to this study has compelled attention to his defects of temperament to such an extent that they stand more clearly revealed than perhaps their importance warrants. From the moment he began to realize that Cardwell's troop withdrawals had more to do with anti-imperialism than strategy, and spoke out on the subject, until the time when imperial defence was the most important topic of

CONCLUSION

discussion, was indeed the principal *raison d'être* of the first Colonial Conference, he was its consistent supporter. The Royal Commission of which he was president constituted, despite its defects of detail and the suppression of its recommendations, the first official recognition that the empire had an essential unity, but one that demanded hitherto unheard-of efforts of co-operation and understanding even to approach the solution of any common defence problem. Due largely to Carnarvon's persistence, the Commission concluded its work. Had it not reported, an authoritative basis for the defence of empire trade might never have been issued. Further, the Australasian colonies would have come to the conference of 1887 in a much more troubled frame of mind, if indeed without the tug of imperial defence there had been a conference at all.

It is on this basis, rather than on its slight material manifestations, that imperial defence emerges as a significant historical development during the period under consideration. For the conception of the modern Commonwealth had many of its roots in the colonial conferences of which the 1887 meeting was the first. To this important imperial landmark collective defence contributed both a main topic for discussion and what background of experience there existed for dealing with it. In this way the development of the idea of imperial defence had a fairly large, not to say basic, effect on the moulding of the Commonwealth as we know it. Not only did it supply the common theme, but also the common method of going about the treatment of imperial problems having a common interest.

On the military side, the emergence of imperial defence in the years 1868–87, produced less obvious but equally important results. It might perhaps be too much to claim that the formation of the Committee of Imperial Defence in 1904, and what preparedness there was for the First World War, were direct results of what has been studied here. Factors such as the growing international tension 1890–1914, the lessons learned from the South African War, and the far-reaching contributions of particular individuals like Lord Fisher, Lord Esher, Sir Robert Borden, Joseph Chamberlain and Sir R. B. Haldane, must all be taken into account. Yet the idea that Britain's defence was inextricably bound up with empire defence as a whole was made clear during these early years, through reference to what later became only one part of the recognized requirements of a complete system of imperial defence. These beginnings were a miniature testing ground for the vast developments that followed later on, and although the number and complexity of the problems facing the Committee of Imperial Defence from 1904 onwards were greater than those facing their official predecessors, the central problems of co-operation were the same. In the event it proved that effective co-operative military planning in Great Britain required a combination of tact, frankness, patience and regular consultation. These needs were largely met by

1914, although War Office dominance of imperial defence planning had, by 1911, *overturned* the navy's primacy in imperial strategy and set the stage for Kitchener's armies.[9]

Defence planners between 1868–87 made the empire-wide, that is to say the 'imperial', nature of modern British defence clear and of immediate importance. They provided a body of doctrine for dealing with a particular problem – coaling station defence – on an imperial basis. Finally, their experience of the difficulties involved provided much guidance for those who came to wrestle with the same problems but on an increased scale, in an atmosphere more politically congenial to their vital work.

NOTES

1. The year that dominion ministers took seats on the War Cabinet. It might then be called Imperial War Cabinet. See Ivor Jennings, *Cabinet Government* (Cambridge: Cambridge University Press, 1951).
2. When Lord Randolph Churchill resigned rather than increase the military estimates in 1886, Lord Salisbury wrote, when supporting his heads of War Office and Admiralty, that 'The undefended state of many of our ports and coaling stations is notorious, and the necessity for protecting them has been urged by a strong Commission, and has been admitted on both sides in debate. To refuse to take measures for their protection would be to incur the gravest responsibility.' See Winston S. Churchill, *Lord Randolph Churchill* (London: Macmillan, 1906), Vol. 2, p. 237.
3. Writing in 1897 Sir George Sydenham Clarke was pleased that at last the colonial press showed appreciation of the fact that 'To Australasia, the Channel and Mediterranean Fleets are fully as important as the Squadron in Australasian waters.' See Clarke and James R. Thursfield, *The Navy and the Nation* (London: John Murray, 1897), pp. 26, 27. This implies – and the conference proceedings bear it out – that this fact was not appreciated in 1887.
4. [Ed. note: J. C. R. Colomb's pioneering efforts are much more widely appreciated today than when Dr Schurman wrote his thesis. W. C. B. Tunstall's chapter in the *Cambridge History of the British Empire* on imperial defence 1815–70 acknowledges Colomb's importance in initiating systematic consideration of imperial defence requirements in the age of steam. Moreover, Schurman's own *The Education of a Navy* contains an entire chapter on Colomb's work and influence.]
5. There had been much written about government policy, but not so much on the role of the permanent staff at the Colonial Office in determining that policy.
6. Philip H. Colomb, *Memoirs of the Right Honourable Sir Astley Cooper Key* (London: Methuen, 1898), pp. 410–55, and Bernard Mallet, *Thomas George Earl of Northbrook, GCSI. A Memoir* (London: Longmans, Green, 1908), pp. 199–217.
7. Mallet, *Northbrook*, p. 206.
8. It is the writer's belief that Carnarvon did not speak for party reasons.
9. A disastrous development, I think.

Appendix

This Appendix illustrates the defence history of one particular empire base, selected from the group of more than 20.

ESQUIMALT: 1868–87

Esquimalt, situated on the southern tip of Vancouver Island, British Columbia, is today the west coast headquarters of the Royal Canadian Navy. One hundred years ago it was nothing but a good harbour conveniently near the growing town of Victoria in the days when gold was British Columbia's chief attraction. In 1855 it became a base for the Royal Navy and by 1865 it had become headquarters for the North Pacific squadron.[1] Strategically, its location was not fortunate, as British trade with the west coast of North America and the main Pacific was slight, as Britain possessed no territory on the western side of the Americas and the nearest British territory was the Falkland Islands, 7,280 knots away via Cape Horn. This problem of the isolation of Esquimalt was bad enough in the era of sailing vessels that could keep at sea for long periods, but the advent of steam, when cruising came to depend upon coal, made the situation even worse. Furthermore, there was no regular contact overland between the new dominion of Canada and British Columbia, and it was widely held that British North America was indefensible against attack from the United States. In any event, the Royal Navy, believing that an unfortunate base was better that none at all, kept Esquimalt as the headquarters for the North Pacific Squadron until the turn of the century.

In 1871 British Columbia entered the Canadian Confederation, under terms that included the promised construction of a transcontinental railway within ten years. This railway, when complete, would change Esquimalt's strategic position for it would bring cable contact with England and rail connection with the imperial post at Halifax, making possible the rapid shipment of troops and supplies in the event of an emergency. Yet the route chosen for the line – running close to the US border for some 50 miles – rendered traffic disruption by hostile American overland action a likely and relatively easy military operation.

It was also proposed, soon after British Columbia joined the federation, that a dry dock be established at Esquimalt, to be financed jointly by the dominion, provincial and imperial governments. After much delay the work was taken over completely by the Canadian government and the dock was officially opened on 20 July 1887.[2] The Canadian Pacific Railway was not completed until 1885 and the Admiralty did not actively propose to enlarge the base until 1887, when its defence was tentatively apportioned between the imperial and dominion governments: the War Office assuming responsibility for the proposed armament and Canada that for the proposed works.[3]

Canadian historians generally have found little between the years 1865 and 1887 to interest them in the history of Esquimalt. For the historian of imperial defence, however, the events of the years between the establishment of North Pacific Naval Headquarters and the point at which Canadian and imperial governments agreed to share responsibility for land defences are interesting and instructive. In 1865 Esquimalt's value was naval and concerned only naval people. By 1887 it concerned not only the Admiralty, but the War Office, the Colonial Office, and the dominion government in Canada as well. Aside from the obvious fact that Esquimalt became Canadian territory in 1871 this transformation was the result of a concurrent transformation in the official perception of imperial defence. The latter shift was the direct result of the coming of steam to the navy.

The seriousness of the coal problem became apparent during the Franco-Prussian War, when the Admiralty realized that a good many coaling stations used in time of peace were in foreign hands and would be virtually useless in wartime.[4] From this realization it was only a step to awareness that the navy's traditional role as commerce protector was profoundly threatened by the defenceless condition of British bases which would supply coal to the fleet. Accordingly, at Admiralty instigation, the War Office took the problem of coaling station defence under consideration. Recommendations for their defence were drawn up by Sir William Jervois in the Office of the Inspector General of Fortifications in 1875 and were considered but not acted on by the Secretary of State for War.[5]

Although it did not stimulate government action, this initial recognition of coaling station importance illuminated the close connection between coaling stations and commerce protection, and made clear that the navy did not regard itself as responsible for the local defence of such installations. Jervois stated that the Admiralty's cardinal rule for fixed defences stressed the navy's freedom of action: 'the fleet is required for cruising [to protect seaborne commerce] and cannot be kept in harbour to guard its own supplies'.[6]

Jervois mentioned Esquimalt, along with ten other naval bases, but it was not singled out for special attention in his modest defence proposals, save that it was listed as being totally undefended. Yet whereas Esquimalt had engaged the attention of the Admiralty alone in 1865, the War Office was now also interested, as were the Canadians because of the proposed dry dock.

The coaling station subject lay dormant until 1877–78, when Anglo-Russian relations deteriorated to the brink of war. At this point the War Office Defence Committee chaired by the Duke of Cambridge rated the importance of coaling base defence almost on par with that of commercial ports in the United Kingdom, and Esquimalt was given more serious consideration.[7] The Defence Committee also listed overseas coaling stations in order of importance, excluding Gibraltar, Malta, Halifax and Bermuda, which were designated imperial fortresses. The Canadian Pacific base was eighth in priority.[8]

Order of importance was determined by utility of location with regard to protection of seaborne commerce and on naval requirements such as the quality of the harbour. If the former were the sole criterion, Esquimalt's location, far from heavily travelled trade routes, would doubtless have pushed it further down the list. At the same time, however, it was the only British naval base on the west coast of the American continents; it was easily defensible in the physical sense, and naval authorities considered its defence important. Moreover, the negotiations regarding the proposed dry dock had to be considered. Hence the War Office, which preferred to act on the basis of a simple ratio between value of passing commerce to amount of defensive armament per station, found itself brought up short by the reasonable, if not compelling, opinions held by the Admiralty.

Although many claimed that the advent of steam battleships in the 1840s had 'bridged the Channel', a few more perceptive observers endeavoured to point out that steam, while not rendering England any more accessible to an invading force, did, because of problems of coal supply in warships with inefficient engines and limited bunkerage, confound commerce protection, especially for a nation with a huge merchant marine, heavily reliant upon overseas trade.[9] Further, it was urged that national energy would be put to more efficient use by grappling with these intensified naval problems than by treating these problems, in an unenlightened manner, as insoluble.

Two schemes were thus put forward for Esquimalt's defence. The first, of a temporary nature, would have allotted the site £9,000 out of £243,000 to be devoted to the defence of 12 coaling stations. This sum would have furnished a single gunboat, six heavy, and six light artillery pieces and the ancillary works, plus a garrison of 688 men.[10] Such defence would have done little for Esquimalt's military security against anything more serious than a hit-and-run raiding expedition. A second, more permanent, scheme called for the expenditure of £120,000 at Esquimalt, out of the total sum of £2,297,412 intended for all 12 bases. The scale of fortification would have been commensurably larger: eight heavy and six light guns, £78,000 for works ashore, and £12,000 for submarine defences.[11] As in the case of the 1875 proposals, no immediate action was taken on either scheme.

By early 1878, however, as the Anglo-Russian situation became even more threatening, the coaling station problem was again thrust to the forefront of strategic consideration. Accordingly, a Colonial Defence Committee was appointed to recommend emergency measures for their defences. Although created in response to a short-term emergency, this committee continued to consider naval base defence until the spring of 1879, and, when dissolved, was replaced by a Royal Commission which sat until 1882. The fact that the Colonial Defence Committee was inter-departmental indicates the government's appreciation of the complexity of the subject. This trend toward departmental co-operation was continued by the Commission, the appointment of the latter body being further evidence of the importance of its subject. A second feature that began with the formation of the Colonial Defence Committee and continued until the Royal Commission dissolved was the emergence of the Colonial Office, not only as a participant in these inquiries, but, in both cases, as the originating and controlling body.

The Colonial Defence Committee and the Royal Commission differed in that the former was set up to deal with emergency measures in 1878 while the latter was appointed to draft broad recommendations dealing with imperial defence on a permanent basis. But they can be treated together in this context as joint contributors to the final reports of the Royal Commission, and will be referred to as the Milne Committee and the Carnarvon Commission after their respective chairmen: Admiral Sir Alexander Milne and Lord Carnarvon.

The Milne Committee at once found that the empire had far too little ordnance to arm all the coaling stations considered important.[12] With specific regard to Esquimalt, moreover, there were no regular army troops at, or available for, British Columbia. Yet even given these unpromising circumstances the emergency provoked action. The Admiralty reluctantly loaned naval guns from their Esquimalt stores for land defence and suggested that, since the Canadians were concerned with the security of Victoria, they might jointly assist in the defence of the vulnerable naval base.[13] The Milne Committee, having recommended the provision of six heavy and six light guns for Esquimalt without possessing the means to provide such armament, could hardly demur.[14] But although the Colonial

Office agreed to approach the Canadian government, it was pessimistic, pointing out that Esquimalt was, by definition, a purely imperial responsibility.[15] Surprisingly enough, the Canadian government offered to supply men and construct works at Esquimalt.[16] Lieutenant-Colonel de la Chevois T. Irwin, Canadian Assistant Inspector of Artillery, went to Victoria in May 1878 and supervised work on the earthwork batteries until their completion at the end of August.

Canadian reaction to the Colonial Office request for help certainly relieved the immediate danger somewhat, but at the same time further complicated the already complex problem involved in any attempt to provide permanent defences. The enthusiasm aroused under the threat of war soon gave way to caution on both sides of the Atlantic when the threat vanished. No provision had been made for underwriting Canadian assistance or the paying for the navy's guns, and by September 1878 Colonial Secretary Sir Michael Hicks-Beach was writing to the Governor-General for an exact report on Canadian efforts.[17] He further pressed for suspension of the work until that report could be studied in Britain. Later in the year an uneasy War Office suggested that Canadian efforts should be surveyed by an imperial officer.[18] The Colonial Office warned the War Office that Canada's prompt help in the emergency could not be lightly dismissed, and in the end Canadian and imperial officers were sent to inspect the Esquimalt defences jointly while the Canadian government made it clear that the dominion did not intend to become involved in any scheme of permanent defence.[19]

Neither of the military reports evinced coherent strategic thought. Both were agreed that Esquimalt was useful and should be fortified but the reasons given lacked strategic consensus. Canadian Royal Artillery Colonel Strange thought the base important, but his reasons were not strategic. Rather he argued that the sums proposed for the construction of the dry dock warranted guarantee by defences.[20] While acknowledging Esquimalt's poor location, British Royal Engineers Lieutenant-Colonel Lovell urged strong fortifications as it was the only northern Pacific naval station. He maintained the Milne Committee's recommendation – based on the possibility of attack by small unarmoured ships – inadequate and indicative of how little importance that Committee attached to the base. He envisaged that in wartime the North Pacific squadron would join the China squadron and be continually at sea, leaving Esquimalt open to attack by ironclads. He also pointed out that the base gave command of American naval activity in the Pacific, clearly regarding the United States as a possible foe, and that Canadian manpower assistance would be required to meet this formidable menace. In fact, Lovell, while not putting forward a weighty argument for the defence of Esquimalt, urged that were it to be fortified at all, it should be fortified strongly.[21]

On the basis of Strange's and Lovell's evidence, but not on their conclusions, the War Office issued a memorandum on Esquimalt's defences in December 1880.[22] It judged the place indefensible against a determinedly hostile United States, and suggested only that 'troops and stores' be thrown 'into Esquimalt in a comparatively short time' in the event of an emergency.[23] If the navy insisted on its land defence, the memorandum added, provision should be made, but only against possible attack by Russian cruisers. As far as the United States was concerned, it concluded pessimistically, Esquimalt's security would have to depend on peace between America and Britain. On the basis of this War Office view and his own survey, Colonel Crossman subsequently advocated spending £194,500 on works at Esquimalt, to be manned by 1,300 men.[24]

Prime Minister Sir John A. Macdonald's testimony to the Commission must have strongly influenced its views regarding Esquimalt. Certainly it vitally affected its attitude to Canadian defence generally.[25] Sir John's evidence was based on the conviction that war with the United States was so unlikely that the possibility was not a strategically realistic conception. Moreover, he maintained, any attempt to define proportional colonial and imperial defence responsibility in peacetime was only likely to cause colonial opposition to any commitment – on financial grounds – and that such unfavourable peacetime publicity would in turn probably diminish what otherwise might be generous colonial response to empire defence requirements in an emergency. Throughout his testimony Macdonald refrained from discussing Canadian coast defence, except to suggest that the Canadians would render a good deal of assistance in an emergency. From a Canadian point of view Macdonald valued Esquimalt as a point from which Canadian grain could be dispatched when the Canadian Pacific Railroad was completed. When asked why the place should be defended, however, he gave the navy answer: 'it is supposed that Esquimalt is the proper place for a rendezvous for the North Pacific Squadron. It is a good harbor, and defensible, and it is in immediate proximity to the coal-fields of the island.'[26] When questioned further whether it would be worthwhile defending Esquimalt if Canadian produce did not ship from British Columbia in quantity, he properly refused to comment on what was clearly a more general imperial strategic problem. General Sir John Lintorn Simmons, a member of the Commission, devoted some effort to attempting to persuade Macdonald to agree with the premise that if another port in British Columbia carried the bulk of Canadian commerce it would be wise to defend that port instead of Esquimalt. But Macdonald was consistently the politician rather than the strategist, and his answers were noncommittal.[27] In short, the prime minister made it clear that Esquimalt was an imperial and not a Canadian concern, and having refused to discuss strategic details and degrees of responsibility, he confined himself to presenting non-military factual evidence and speculating realistically upon political possibilities, concluding that

APPENDIX

Esquimalt was, though a useful outlet for Canadian commodities, a British problem.

The last source of evidence for the Commission's recommendations on Esquimalt was the testimony of First Naval Lord Admiral Sir Astley Cooper Key, given almost two years after that of Macdonald.[28] His views were blunt and unequivocal. A second naval base was needed in that area of the Pacific, but at that time only Esquimalt was available. Therefore it should be heavily defended: strongly enough, that is, to resist a United States attack. That was all.

The commissioners disagreed on their final recommendations regarding Esquimalt. The majority report, signed by all but two of the commissioners, concluded that, on strategic grounds, Esquimalt was indefensible and almost valueless.[29] It therefore recommended that the base be abandoned and that the warships stationed there be sent to join the China squadron at Hong Kong. This conclusion was justified on the basis of the vast distance separating Esquimalt from main British trade routes; the conviction that the base could not be defended against the United States; and the opinion that British Columbia offered too little financial attraction to tempt a Russian attack. These facts hardly warranted the £194,500 and 1,300 men Crossman had estimated requisite for its proper defence.

The commissioners did not, however, ignore the delicate question of British–Canadian relations, nor the expense and the time already spent on defending and surveying the base. They acknowledged Canada's confederation pledge to construct the Canadian Pacific Railroad, and its pledge to the British Columbians that Canadian influence would be used towards retaining Esquimalt as a naval base. The latter promise was, of course, bolstered by the Admiralty's avowed intention to construct a dry dock there. Bearing in mind these non-military considerations, the majority report stated that if the Canadians would construct permanent defensive works and provide a garrison, the commissioners were prepared to recommend that the British government should supply ordnance and professional assistance.

This compromise proposal, however, was rejected by former First Naval Lord and chairman of the preceding Colonial Defence Committee, Sir Alexander Milne in a dissenting report.[30] Milne maintained that the proposal to remove the squadron to the western Pacific exceeded the compass of the Commission and was 'an interference with the Executive Departments of State'. He argued that Esquimalt should be defended as per his committee's recommendations of April 1878. The reasons given – which constituted the first semi-official Admiralty attempt to justify its position – included Esquimalt's usefulness in peacetime as a base from which to show the flag and ferry diplomatic representatives. In wartime, he reasoned, the fleet would proceed to join the main Pacific squadron, thereby conceding the main contention of the majority report.[31] Milne's stated rationale, therefore, was flimsy. His real motives were illuminated in a letter to Sir Henry Barkly. He did not desire, he told his colleague, to disrupt the unanimity of the report but army views had, thanks to the influence that General Simmons exercised on the Commission, prevailed over navy opinions in a matter which was the latter's bailiwick: 'it is Simmons versus the Navy that I won't stand'.[32] Ironically, departmentalism prevailed in a commission set up precisely because departmental treatment of defence problems made their resolution so difficult.

What was Esquimalt's real significance, in view of the fact that the efforts of defence planners between 1875 and 1882 produced little in the way of concrete results at the base? For contemporaries, perhaps the lessons were slight, but for the historian the subject adumbrates two larger topics. First it highlights the problem of British–Colonial relations. Both the Canadian government's statements disclaiming financial responsibility for Esquimalt's permanent defences after the crisis of 1878 had passed, and the testimony of Sir John Macdonald underlined the deep-seated aversion of colonial governments to any binding permanent responsibility with regard to empire defence. At the same time, Canada's action during the 1878 crisis and Macdonald's remarks both pointed to the substantial reserves of imperial feeling in Canada that could be tapped in an emergency, providing that rigid delineation of colonial responsibility was not attempted beforehand or heavy-handedly.

From the standpoint of imperial defence considered globally, this paradox meant that Canada was vulnerable unless the home government undertook entire responsibility (and cost) for defence, since no long-term plans could rely on Canadian contributions except in so far as they allowed for what might be done in time of crisis. Indeed, in the British government's handling of the Canadian defence problem, political considerations took precedence over military ones, the emphasis being the maintenance of political goodwill at the expense of immediate military efficiency, as the section of the Commission's majority report concerning Esquimalt illustrates. This policy – more implied than explicitly stated – boded well for the future home–colonial relations, and doubtless helped nurture Canadian willingness to contribute to imperial defence – as the First World War would demonstrate – but in the short term it did nothing to relieve the anxiety of British defence planners.

Second, the deliberations surrounding Esquimalt starkly reveal the lack of sympathy – to say nothing of co-operation – between the concerned departments at Whitehall. The Milne Committee took the form that it did because it was realized that regular interdepartmental communication did not exist. Yet neither that committee nor the more imposing Royal Commission possessed the means of completely resolving conflicts that a century of civil service retrenchment had produced.

APPENDIX

Recommendations might be worked out in some harmony (although even that hope was barren in Esquimalt's case), but recommendations were useless as long as the power to give them effect was lacking. This critique is not to suggest that the technical advice of the departments was not necessary, but, rather, that it required the presence of a dominating politician to make the technicians work with an eye toward the common good rather than toward protecting their own turf. The Admiralty was particularly culpable in this respect. It had its own criteria for what constituted naval necessities, and whatever one may suspect, it is impossible to determine whether those standards were arrived at by inductive or deductive reasoning. The War Office, on the other hand, sprawling and divided as it was, attempted to deal with problems handed it by the Admiralty in a constructive and co-operative manner. What was needed was a politician to control and direct such efforts, but, Carnarvon apart, so long as defence of colonial ports meant expenditure and no money was forthcoming from the Treasury little could be expected. Esquimalt made this difficulty particularly clear.

NOTES

1. G. P. de T. Glazebrook, *A History of Canadian External Relations* (Toronto: Oxford University Press, 1942), p. 56; Gerald S. Graham, *Empire of the North Atlantic* (Toronto: University of Toronto Press, 1950), p. 283.
2. F. V. Longstaff, *Esquimalt* (Victoria, BC, Canada: The Victoria Book and Stationery Co., 1941), p. 39.
3. Graham, *Empire of the North Atlantic*, p. 284n.
4. Granville to Admiralty, 12 July 1870, NMM: MLN/166/4.
5. William F. D. Jervois, 'Memorandum by Colonel Sir W. F. D. Jervois, KCMG, CB, RE, with Reference to the Defenceless Condition of our Coaling Stations and Naval Establishments Abroad', 7 January 1875, Carnarvon Papers, PRO 30/6-122. Jervois' memorandum was passed on to Secretary of State for War Gathorne-Hardy on 9 January 1875, and by him to the Cabinet on 12 January.
6. The Commander-in-Chief of the army, Prince George, Duke of Cambridge, supported Jervois' findings and recommendations.
7. 'Memorandum by the Defence Committee at their Meeting of the 5th of June 1877 with reference to the Defence of Commercial Harbours at Homes, and of Coaling Stations Abroad', 5 June 1877 (hereafter referred to as memorandum, 5 June 1877), PRO 30/6-122.
8. Behind Simons Bay (Cape of Good Hope), Hong Kong, Singapore, Jamaica, King George Sound (Western Australia), Trincomalee (Ceylon) and Mauritius, and ahead of St Lucia (British West Indies), the Falkland Islands, Ascension and Fiji.
9. Notably Lord Palmerston. For scholarly treatment of the commerce protection problem, see W. C. B. Tunstall's essay on imperial defence, 1815–70 in *The Cambridge History of the British Empire* (Cambridge: Cambridge University Press, 1940), Vol. 2, pp. 807–41 and Howard D'Egville, *Imperial Defence and Closer Union* (London: P. S. King, 1913).
10. See the table attached to the memorandum drawn up by the Inspector-General of Fortifications, approved by the War Office (Duke of Cambridge) Defence

Committee in May 1877, PRO 30/6-122.
11. See Appendix B attached to the 5 June 1877 memorandum, PRO 30/6-122.
12. Milne to CO, 12 March 1878, PRO 30/6-124, no. 9.
13. Admiralty to CO, 15 May 1878, PRO 30/6-124, no. 101; CO to Admiralty, 10 April 1878, PRO 30/6-124, no. 65. The guns were evidently old worn naval pieces whose return to Britain (for condemnation) had been delayed on the advice of Major-General Sir Edward Selby Smyth, Canadian militia commander.
14. 'Report of a Colonial Defence Committee on the Defence of Esquimalt', April 1878, PRO 30/6-124. The Milne Committee further suggested that the garrison consist of local volunteers.
15. CO to WO, 18 May 1878, PRO 30/6-124, no. 109; Hicks-Beach to Dufferin (Colonial Secretary to Canada), 15 May 1878, PRO 30/6-124, no. 100.
16. Dufferin to Hicks-Beach, 11 May 1878, PRO 30/6-124, no. 88a; see also Dufferin to Hicks-Beach, 19 June 1878, PRO 30/6-124, no. 124.
17. CO to WO, 13 June 1878, PRO 30/6-124, no. 171; Hicks Beach to Dufferin, 6 September 1878, PRO 30/6-124, no. 325.
18. WO to CO, 10 December 1878, PRO 30/6-124, no. 357.
19. CO to WO, 19 December 1878, PRO 30/6-124, no. 359; Lord Lorne (Canadian Governor-General) to Hicks-Beach, 19 May 1879, PRO: CO 812-14, no. 33. The officers – Lieutenant-Colonel Strange, RA for Canada and Lieutenant-Colonel Lovell, CRE for Britain – were dispatched in the summer of 1879.
20. Carnarvon Commission Third Report, Appendix 4, no. 124, enclosure 4.
21. Ibid., Appendix 4, no. 124, enclosure 2. See also PRO: CO 812-16, no. 177. Lovell's report is a cardinal example of the muddle-headedness which often passed for strategic thought. If the squadron based at Esquimalt was to join the China squadron in wartime, it is difficult to understand of what importance Esquimalt itself would be to naval operations or how its destruction would benefit an enemy.
22. Ibid., Appendix 4, no. 130.
23. This recommendation looked ahead to the completion of the Canadian Pacific Railroad.
24. Carnarvon Commission Third Report, p. 24.
25. See Alice R. Stewart, 'Sir John A. Macdonald and the Imperial Defence Commission of 1879', *Canadian Historical Review*, 35, 2 (June 1954): pp. 121–39.
26. Ibid., p. 126.
27. Ibid.
28. Carnarvon Commission Third Report, p. 608. Cooper Key served as First Naval Lord from 1879 to 1886.
29. Ibid., pp. 23–5.
30. Ibid., pp. 31–3. Commission member Sir Henry Barkly also signed the minority report.
31. Because of prevailing winds and paucity of coaling stations, Milne argued that this journey would be made by sailing south to southern latitudes and then proceeding to Hong Kong, completely under sail.
32. Milne to Barkly (copy), NMM: MLN/163/2.

Bibliography

NOTE ON SOURCES

During the period there was a good deal of agitation for a comprehensive imperial defence system, but this agitation was largely confined to members of the Royal Empire Society, the Royal United Services Institution and the Imperial Federation League. Of those, Sir J. C. R. Colomb was the leading figure. The actual pamphlet literature dealing with defence concerns *vis-à-vis* the empire grew steadily between the 1860s and late 1880s and had reached huge proportions by 1887. With the exception of the special instances included here, however, such literature dealt more with details, technical development in defence matters, or with vague aspirations for an empire parliament at Westminster. Since this study is not directly concerned with public opinion, only that literature which seemed to have a direct bearing on the subject has been included.

With a few notable exceptions, standard 'tombstone' biographies of nineteenth-century politicians, soldiers and sailors are unrewarding for the student of imperial defence. To cite but one example, the biography of Sir Michael Hicks Beach, who instigated the Carnarvon Commission, has only a few lines that mention the bare fact. The same caveat applies to special studies of the period.

In the main, this work is based on two types of unpublished sources; public records and the manuscripts of certain key individuals. In some cases the two types overlap.

The most valuable of these sources were the Carnarvon Papers in the Public Record Office. This extensive collection in itself furnished the general outline of study and provided the bulk of the evidence presented. It was especially valuable for tracking the origins of imperial defence thought in official circles during the 1874–77 period and, of course, for the Carnarvon Commission's unofficial correspondence. It also contains one of the few readily available unexpurgated copies of the third report of that commission.

The Kimberley Papers form a useful counterpart to those of Carnarvon, giving as they do a clear picture of Liberal ministerial attitudes to empire and defence, and particularly of the 1880–85 Gladstone administration's attitude to the work of the Carnarvon Commission. They also form a valuable source of information for Kimberley's period at the Foreign Office (1894–95).

The papers consulted at the Royal Archives, Windsor – both those of Queen Victoria and the Duke of Cambridge – provide valuable evidence at crucial points in the development of the history. Since the Duke of Cambridge held such a unique position as Commander-in-Chief of the army, an appreciation of his judgement and methods is necessary and relevant to the subject.

The papers of Sir Alexander Milne contain the particular Admiralty memoranda and correspondence (1868–74) which made the future developments of coaling station defence intelligible in official terms. They also hold valuable correspondence and memoranda concerning the Carnarvon Commission, of which Milne was a member, and a wealth of information on all manner of British naval administration as well as detailed material relating to Milne's service afloat. The papers are now much better catalogued than when Dr Schurman used them in the 1950s.

The Disraeli Papers, then at Hughenden Manor and now at the Bodleian Library, Oxford, called for much more research time than the extent of their use indicates. They demonstrated, as far as such papers can prove, that Disraeli was not consistently interested in empire in the sense indicated by the Crystal Palace speech. Extensive search suggested that what Monypenny and Buckle did not write about Disraeli's political career is not worth stating. The papers are admirably indexed and annotated.

Finally, the Colonial Office, War Office and Admiralty records preserved in the Public Record Office were used to provide continuity to this history between 1879 and 1885. The Colonial Office correspondence with the two military departments was covered in detail. Admiralty and War Office correspondence with the Colonial Office was used for the purpose of cross-checking and also for obtaining the opinion of certain naval and army officers whose official appointments made them influential in shaping policy.

PRIMARY SOURCES

Archival materials

Colonial Office Records, Public Record Office (PRO)
    CO 323, 339–69: Correspondence between the Colonial Office and Admiralty and the Colonial and War Offices; general correspondence on colonial defences, 1879–87.

CO 808-65: dispatches to colonial governors, 1885.
CO 812-14, 816, 821, 824, 930, 838: confidential prints, 1878–87.

Admiralty Papers (PRO)
ADM 1/6509, 65410, 6511, 6541, 6566, 6604, 6644, 6682, 6683, 6721, 6722, 6784, 6785, 6786: secretary 'in-letters' from the Colonial Office, 1879–85.

War Office Records (PRO)
WO 32/88, 118, 120, 121, 131, 138, 147, 148, 153, 192, 206, 219, 236, 261, 262, 265: Correspondence between the War and Colonial Offices, 1879–85.
WO 33/22, 31, 42, 46, 47, 261: War Office memoranda, 1879–85.

Papers of Henry Howard Molyneux Herbert, 4th Earl of Carnarvon (PRO)
PRO 30/6-5, 6-8, 6-11, 6-12: Correspondence with Cabinet ministers, 1874–78.
PRO 30/6-14: Correspondence with the Commander-in-Chief of the army, 1874-78.
PRO 30/6-25, 6-26, 6-32, 6-33: Correspondence with colonial governors, 1874–78.
PRO 30/6-51: Miscellaneous memoranda, 1874–78.
PRO 30/6-52: Correspondence relative to the Royal Commission on Colonial Defence, 1879–82.
PRO 30/6-115: Confidential defence memoranda, 1875–77.
PRO 30/6-122: Confidential War Office Defence Committee acts and memoranda, 1875–77.
PRO 30/6-124: Correspondence of the Colonial Office (Milne) Defence Committee, 1878 (this correspondence continues in PRO: CO 812-14.
PRO 30/6-125: Confidential War Office defence memoranda, 1880–81.
PRO 30/6-126: Third and Final Report of the Royal Commission appointed to enquire into the Defence of British Possessions and Commerce Abroad, with Appendix and Minutes of Evidence (confidential), 1882.
PRO 30/6-131: Confidential prints and memoranda on defence matters with reference to the Royal Commission on Colonial Defence and the first imperial conference, 1880–87.

Kimberley Hall, Norfolk
Kimberley Papers: the political correspondence of the 1st Earl of Kimberley (traced and catalogued by the Historical Manuscripts Commission, National Register of Archives):

PC/A/2, 6, 8, 14, 19, 41: Correspondence with Cabinet members, 1870–74.

PC/A/24: Correspondence with the Permanent Undersecretary of State for the Colonies.

PC/16a,b,c, 21, 25, 39: Correspondence with colonial governors, 1870–74.

PC/A/7: Correspondence with the Commander-in-Chief of the army, 1873–74.

PC/A/42: Journal of events under the Gladstone ministry, 1868–74.

PC/B/8, 17, 21, 23, 28a,b,c: Correspondence with Cabinet members, 1880–82.

PC/B/6, 10, 12, 14, 15, 18, 22, 25, 27: Correspondence with colonial governors, 1880–82.

PC/B/24: Correspondence and Cabinet memoranda concerning the Royal Commission on Colonial Defence, 1880.

National Maritime Museum (NMM), Greenwich
Milne Papers: the papers of Admiral of the Fleet Sir Alexander Milne, Bart.
MLN/143/1-4, MLN/144/1-5, MLN/145/2-5, MLN/146/2,4, MLN/147/3-5, MLN/148/1-3, MLN/163/12, MLN/165/1,3,5,7,10,11,12, MLN/166/3,4, MLN/169/9,13,18.

Windsor Castle: Royal Archives
Papers of Queen Victoria and Prince George, Duke of Cambridge
RA ADD.MSS: Cambridge Papers; the military and political correspondence of the Duke of Cambridge, 1868–85. At the time Dr Schurman utilized this collection it had not been integrated into the filing and cataloguing system used in the Royal Archives. The papers were grouped in bundles by dates (yearly, half-yearly and quarterly). RA A-38, 40, 42, 60, 66, 78; B-29, 35; D-29; E-16; 26, 37, 54, 55, 58, 59, 61; I-63; O-22, 25, 39; P-24, 25, 26; R-53; W-10: Royal Collection; Correspondence to and from Queen Victoria concerning colonial defence, 1868–85.

Hughenden Manor, Buckinghamshire (administered by the National Trust)
Hughenden Papers: the correspondence of Benjamin Disraeli, 1st Earl of Beaconsfield (now in the Bodleian Library, Oxford University).

These papers did not, with a solitary exception, contribute to Dr Schurman's research in any but a negative way. After extensive consultation he concluded that all material relating both to Disraeli's interest in the colonies and his interest in imperial defence was made public by his biographers, W. F. Monypenny and George Earl Buckle. [Ed. note: copies of several of the Admiralty memoranda by Alexander Milne, George Ward

Hunt and others can be found in the Hughenden Papers as well as the Carnarvon Papers. The relevant citations for those mentioned in the text are B/XX/Hu, B/XXI/C, B/XXI/H.]

Newspapers and periodicals

Blackwood's Edinburgh Magazine.
Journal of the Royal United Services Institution.
Naval Science: A Quarterly Magazine for Promoting the Improvement of Naval Architecture, Marine Engineering, Steam Navigation, and Seamanship, ed. Edward J. Reed (London: Lockwood, 1872–75).
The Nineteenth Century.
Pall Mall Gazette (London), Vol. 60 (August–November 1884), especially nos 6092, 6096, 6112, 6116.
Proceedings of the Royal Colonial Institute.
Royal Engineer Institute Papers.
The Times (London), 1884–87.
Transactions of the Institute of Naval Architects.

Parliamentary papers, official reports, etc.

Army List
British Parliamentary Papers (generally known as *Parliamentary Papers*) (London: HMSO).
Carnarvon Commission, *Report of the Royal Commission Appointed to Make Enquiry into the Condition and Sufficiency of the Means of the Naval and Military Forces Provided for the Defence of the More Important Sea-ports within our Colonial Possessions and Dependencies* (London: HMSO, 1881) (confidential).
Hansard, *Parliamentary Debates*, 3rd series (London).
Hartington Commission, *Report of the Royal Commission Appointed to Inquire into the Civil and Professional Administration of the Naval and Military Departments and the Relationship of those Departments to each other and to the Treasury* (London: HMSO, 1890) (strictly confidential).
Hartington Commission, 'Further Report of Royal Commissioners Appointed to Inquire into the Civil and Professional Administration of the Naval and Military Departments and the Relation of those Departments to each other and to the Treasury', *Parliamentary Papers* (1890), Vol. 19, pp. 1–143.
Navy List
'Report of a Royal Commission on the Defences of the United Kingdom', *Parliamentary Papers* (1860), Vol. 23, pp. 431–606.
'Report of the Royal Commission Appointed to Inquire into Several

matters relating to Coal in the United Kingdom 1871', *Parliamentary Papers* (1871), Vol. 18, pp. 1–1322.

'Report of the Select Committee on Coal together with Minutes of Evidence', *Parliamentary Papers* (1873), Vol. 10, pp. 1–43.

'Return for Six Months Ending 30 June 1869 Showing the Description and Quality of Coal Consumed on Board each Ship of the Navy', *Parliamentary Papers* (1868–69), Vol. 38, pp. 449–77.

War Office List

Books and pamphlets

Adderley, C. B., *Letter to the Rt Hon. Benjamin Disraeli, MP on the Present Relations of England with the Colonies* (London: Parker, Son & Bourn, 1861).

Anon., *Imperial Federation: Report of the Conference* (London: Cassell, 1884).

Anon., 'Imperial Federation' in *Report of the Conference, July 29, 1884* (London: Cassell, 1884).

Anon., *Conference and Banquet of the Imperial Federation League* (London: Cassell, 1886).

Arthur, George (ed.), *The Letters of Lord and Lady Wellesley* (London: William Heinemann, 1922).

Baker, Harold, *The Territorial Forces* (London: John Murray, 1909).

Bestable, C. F., *The Commerce of Nations* (London: Methuen, 1892).

Bowden-Smith, N., *Naval Recollections, 1852–1914* (London: Army & Navy Co-operative Society, 1914).

Bowen, G. F., *Thirty Years of Colonial Government*, ed. F. Lane-Poole (London: Longmans, Green, 1889).

——, *The Federation of the British Empire* (London: Kegan Paul, Trench, 1889).

Brassey, Thomas, *A Colonial Naval Volunteer Force* (London: Longmans, Green, 1878).

——, *The British Navy: Its Strengths, Resources, and Administration*, 6 vols (London: Longmans & Green, 1882).

——, *The Naval Annual 1886* (Portsmouth: J. Griffin, 1886).

——, *The Naval Annual 1887* (Portsmouth: J. Griffin, 1888).

——, *The Naval Annual 1888* (Portsmouth: J. Griffin, 1889).

——, *The Royal Naval Reserve, the Mercantile Marine, and the Colonies* (London: Edward Stanford, 1898).

Campbell, John Douglas Sutherland, Lord Lorne, 9th Duke of Argyll, *Imperial Federation* (London: Swan Sonnenschein, 1885).

Childers, Hugh C. E., *Army Organization* (London: Longmans, Green, 1881).

Clarke, George Sydenham, *Fortifications* (London: John Murray, 1890).
——, *My Working Life* (London: John Murray, 1927).
Colomb, J. C. R., *The Defence of Great and Greater Britain* (London: Edward Stanford, 1880).
Cunningham, G. C., *A Scheme for Imperial Federation* (London: Longmans, Green, 1895).
Dilke, Charles, *Problems of Greater Britain* (London: Macmillan, 1895).
Disraeli, Benjamin, 1st Earl of Beaconsfield, *The Letters of Disraeli to Lady Bradford and Lady Chesterfield*, 2 vols, ed. Lawrence J. L. Dundas, 2nd Marquis of Zetland (London: Ernest Benn, 1929).
Elliot, George, *A Treatise on Future Naval Battles and How to Fight Them and on Other Naval Tactical Subjects* (London: Sampson Low, Marston, Searle & Rivington, 1885).
Esher, Reginald, *Journals and Letters of Reginald, Viscount Esher*, 4 vols, ed. Oliver Esher (London: Ivor Nicholson & Watson, 1938).
Gathorne-Hardy, Gathorne, *The Diary of Gathorne Hardy, Later Lord Cranbrook, 1866–1892: Political Selections*, ed. Nancy Johnson (Oxford: Clarendon Press, 1981).
Gregory, William, *An Autobiography* (London: John Murray, 1894).
Grey, Earl, *The Commercial Policy of the British Colonies and the McKinley Tariff* (London: Macmillan, 1892).
Haldane, Richard B., *An Autobiography* (London: Hodder & Stoughton, 1929).
Harvey, M. H., *The Trade Policy of Imperial Federation* (London: Swan Sonnenschein, 1892).
Herbert, Henry Howard Molyneux, 4th Earl of Carnarvon, *The Defence of the Empire*, ed. G. S. Clarke (London: John Murray, 1897).
Howe, Joseph, *A Letter to C. B. Adderley on the Relations of England with her Colonies* (London: Edward Stanford, 1863).
Hunt, George Ward, *Speech of the Right Hon. George Ward Hunt, MP (First Lord of the Admiralty) on Moving the Navy Estimates in the House of Commons, Monday, April 20, 1874* (London: Cornelius Buck, 1874).
Jenkins, Edward (ed.), *Discussions on Colonial Questions* (London: Strahan, 1872).
Jervois, William F. D., *Defence of New Zealand* (Wellington, n.p., 1884).
Labilliere, F. P., *The Future Relations of England with her Colonies* (London: W. W. Head, 1869).
——, *The Permanent Unity of the Empire* (London: Unwin, 1875).
——, *The Political Organization of the Empire* (London: Edward Stanford, 1881).
——, *Federal Britain* (London: Marston, 1894).
Matthews, Jehu, *A Colonist on the Colonial Question* (London: Longmans, Green, 1872).

McFie, R. A., *Colonial Questions* (London: Longmans, Green, Reader & Dyer, 1871).
Mackintosh, C. H., *The Canadian Parliamentary Companion and Annual Register* (Ottawa: Citizen, 1878).
Palmer's Index to the Times (London: Samuel Palmer, 1867–86).
Parkin, George R., *Imperial Federation* (London: Macmillan, 1852).
Ramm, Agatha (ed.), *The Political Correspondence of Mr Gladstone and Lord Granville*, 2 vols (London: Royal Historical Society, Camden 3rd Series, Vol. 81, 1952).
Rogers, Frederic, *Letters of Frederic Lord Blachford*, ed. George E. Marindin (London: John Murray, 1896).
Ross, P. H. W., *Federation and the British Colonies* (London: Sampson, Low, Marston, Searle & Rivington, 1887).
Rowe, C. J., *Bonds of Disunion* (London: Longmans, Green, 1883).
Scott, Percy, *Fifty Years in the Royal Navy* (London: John Murray, 1919).
Traill, H. D., *Central Government* (London: Macmillan, 1886).
Victoria, RI, *Speeches from the Throne and Messages from the Crown, 1843–1869* (privately printed at the Foreign Office, 1870).
Wodehouse, John, 1st Earl of Kimberley, *Journal of Events during the Gladstone Ministry 1868–73, by John, First Earl of Kimberley*, ed. E. Drus (London: Royal Historical Society, 1958).
Wolseley, Garnet, *The Story of a Soldier's Life*, 2 vols (London: Constable, 1903).
Young, Frederick, *An Address on Imperial Federation* (London: Edward Stanford, 1885).

Articles and essays

Barnaby, Nathaniel, 'On the Fighting Power of the Merchant Ship in Naval Warfare', *Transactions of the Institute of Naval Architects*, 18 (1877): 1–23.
Colomb, J. C. R., 'Colonial Defence and Colonial Opinion', *Proceedings of the Royal Colonial Institute*, 1873 (published separately: London: Simpkin Marshall, 1877).
——, 'Russian Development and our Naval and Military Position in the North Pacific', *Royal United Services Institution Journal*, 21 (1878): 659–707.
Currie, Donald, 'Maritime Warfare', *Royal United Services Institution Journal*, 21 (1878): 228–47.
Key, Astley Cooper, 'Naval Defence of the Colonies', *Nineteenth Century*, 20 (1886): 284–93.
Nugent, C. H., 'Imperial Defence: Abroad', *Royal United Services Institution Journal*, 28 (1884): 464–85.

BIBLIOGRAPHY

Stewart, Alice R. 'Sir John A. Macdonald and the Imperial Defence Commission of 1879', *Canadian Historical Review*, 35, 2 (June 1954): 121–39.

SECONDARY SOURCES

Periodicals

Canadian Historical Review.
Journal of the Society for Army Historical Research.
Political Science Quarterly.

Books and pamphlets

Asquith, H. H., *Fifty Years of Parliament*, 2 vols (London: Cassell, 1926).
Aydelotte, William G., *Bismarck and British Colonial Policy* (Philadelphia: University of Pennsylvania Press, 1937).
Ballard, George, *The Black Battlefleet*, ed. N. A. M. Rodger (Annapolis, Maryland: Naval Institute Press, 1980).
Barnett, Corelli, *Britain and her Army 1509–1970: A Military, Political and Social Survey* (London: Penguin, 1970).
Baxter, James Phinney, *The Introduction of the Ironclad Warship* (Cambridge, MA: Harvard University Press, 1933).
Beeler, John, *British Naval Policy in the Gladstone–Disraeli Era, 1866–1880* (Stanford, CA: Stanford University Press, 1997).
Biddulph, Robert, *Lord Cardwell at the War Office* (London: John Murray, 1904).
Blake, Robert, *Disraeli* (New York: St Martin's Press, 1967).
Bodelsen, C. A., *Studies in Mid-Victorian Imperialism* (Copenhagen: Gyldendalske Boghandel, 1924).
Bourne, Kenneth, *The Foreign Policy of Victorian England, 1830–1902* (Oxford: Clarendon Press, 1967).
Brewer, A. J., *Protection in South Africa* (Stellenbosch: Pro Ecclesia, 1903).
Brown, Benjamin, *The Tariff Reform Movement in Great Britain, 1881–1895* (New York: Columbia University Press, 1943).
Chalmers, Robert T., *A History of Currency in the British Colonies* (London: Eyre & Spottiswoode for HMSO, 1893).
Chesnau, Roger and Eugene Kolesnik (eds), *Conway's All the World's Fighting Ships, 1860–1905* (London: Conway Maritime Press, 1979).
Childers, Spencer, *Life and Correspondence of Hugh C. E. Childers*, 2 vols (London: Longmans, Green, 1901).
Churchill, Winston S., *Lord Randolph Churchill*, 2 vols (London: Macmillan, 1906).

Clapham, John H., *An Economic History of Modern Britain*, 3 vols (Cambridge: Cambridge University Press, 1926).

Clarke, George S. and James Thursfield, *The Navy and the Nation* (London: John Murray, 1897).

Clausewitz, Carl von, *On War*, trans. J. J. Graham, 3 vols (London: Routledge & Kegan Paul, 1949).

Clowes, William L. with Clements Markham, Alfred Thayer Mahan, H. W. Wilson and Theodore Roosevelt, *The Royal Navy: A History from the Earliest Times to the Death of Queen Victoria*, 7 vols (London: Sampson, Low, 1897–1903).

Cole, D. H., *Imperial Military Geography* (8th edn, London: Sifton Preed, 1935).

Colomb, Philip H., *Memoirs of the Right Honourable Sir Astley Cooper Key* (London: Methuen, 1898).

Corbett, Julian S., *Some Principles of Maritime Strategy* (London: Longmans, Green, 1930).

Corbett, Julian S. and Henry Newbolt, *Official History of the War: Naval Operations*, 5 vols (London: Longmans, Green, 1920–31).

Crewe-Milnes, Robert Offley Ashburton, 1st Marquis of Crewe, *Lord Rosebery*, 2 vols (London: John Murray, 1931).

Dawson, William Harbutt, *Richard Cobden and Foreign Policy* (London: George Allen & Unwin, 1926).

D'Egville, Howard, *Imperial Defence and Closer Union* (London: P. S. King, 1913).

Dennison, George T., *The Struggle for Imperial Unity* (London: Macmillan, 1909).

Dictionary of National Biography, 1911–21, Supplement (Oxford: Oxford University Press).

Dunlop, John K., *The Development of the British Army 1899–1914* (London: Methuen, 1938).

Earle, Edward Mead (ed.), *Makers of Modern Strategy* (1st edn., Princeton, NJ: Princeton University Press, 1943).

Egerton, Hugh, *A Short History of British Colonial Policy* (London: Methuen, 1908).

Eldridge, C. C., *England's Mission: The Imperial Idea in the Age of Gladstone and Disraeli* (London: Macmillan, 1973).

——, *Victorian Imperialism* (Atlantic Highlands, NJ: Humanities Press, 1978).

Ewart, John S., *The Kingdom of Canada, Imperial Federation and the Colonial Conferences, the Alaska Boundary, and Imperial Defence* (Toronto: Moran, 1908).

Fitzgerald, C. C., *Penrose Life of Vice-Admiral Sir George Tryon, KCB* (3rd edn, Edinburgh: William Blackwood, 1892).

Fitzmaurice, Edmund, *The Life of Lord Granville*, 2 vols (London:

Longmans, Green, 1905).
Folsom, A., *The Royal Empire Society* (London: George Allen & Unwin, 1933).
Forrest, George, *The Life of Lord Roberts, VC* (London: Cassell, 1914).
Fortesque, John, *History of the British Army*, 13 vols (London: Macmillan, 1930).
Gardiner, A. G., *The Life of Sir William Harcourt*, 2 vols (London: Constable, 1923).
Gardiner, Robert (ed.), *Steam, Steel and Shellfire: The Steam Warship 1815–1914* (London: Conway Maritime Press, 1992).
Gastrell, William, *Our Trade in the World, 1885–1895* (London: Chapman & Hall, 1897).
Glazebrook, G. P. de T., *A History of Canadian External Relations* (Toronto: Oxford University Press, 1942).
Goerlitz, Walter, *The German General Staff* (London: Hollis & Carter, 1953).
Goodenough, W. H. and J. G. Dalton, *The Army and the British Empire* (London: HMSO, 1895).
Gordon, D. C., *The Dominion Partnership in Imperial Defence, 1870–1914* (Baltimore, MD: Johns Hopkins University Press, 1965).
Graham, Gerald S., *Empire of the North Atlantic* (Toronto: University of Toronto Press, 1950).
——, *The Politics of Naval Supremacy* (Cambridge: Cambridge University Press, 1965).
Gull, E. M., *British Economic Interests in the Far East* (London: Oxford University Press, 1943).
Hamilton, C. I., *Anglo-French Naval Rivalry, 1840–1870* (London: Oxford University Press, 1994).
Hardinge, Arthur, *The Life of Henry Howard Molyneux Herbert, Fourth Earl of Carnarvon*, 3 vols (London: Oxford University Press, 1925).
Hardy, Alfred E., *Gathorne Hardy, First Earl of Cranbrook. A Memoir. With Extracts from his Diary and Correspondence*, 2 vols (London: Longmans, Green, 1910).
Harrop, A. J., *England and the Maori Wars* (London: New Zealand News, 1937).
Headrick, Daniel, *Tools of Empire* (New York: Oxford University Press, 1981).
Hicks Beach, Victoria, *Life of Sir Michael Hicks Beach*, 2 vols (London: Macmillan, 1932).
Hill, J. R. (ed.), *The Oxford Illustrated History of the Royal Navy* (New York: Oxford University Press, 1995).
History of the Times, 2 vols (London: The Times, 1939).
Holland, Bernard, *The Life of Spencer Compton Cavendish, Eighth Duke of Devonshire*, 2 vols (London: Longmans, Green, 1911).

James, David, *The Life of Lord Roberts* (London: Hollis & Carter, 1954).
Jane, Fred T., *The British Battlefleet*, 2 vols (London: The Library Press, 1915).
Jebb, Richard, *The Imperial Conference*, 2 vols (London: Longmans, Green, 1911).
Jennings, Ivor, *Cabinet Government* (Cambridge: Cambridge University Press, 1951).
Johnson, S. C., *British Emigration to North America* (London: Routledge, 1913).
Keith, A. B., *Responsible Government in the Dominions*, 2 vols (Oxford: Clarendon Press, 1928).
Kennedy, Greg and Keith Neilson (eds), *Far-Flung Lines: Essays in Honour of Donald Mackenzie Schurman* (London: Frank Cass, 1997).
Kennedy, Paul M., *The Rise and Fall of British Naval Mastery* (Malabar, FL: Robert Krieger, 1976).
Kiewiet, C. W. de, *The Imperial Factor in South Africa* (London: Oxford University Press, 1937).
Knaplund, Paul, *Gladstone and Britain's Imperial Policy* (London: George Allen & Unwin, 1927).
Knowles, L. C. A., *The Economic Development of the British Overseas Empire* (London: George Routledge, 1924).
Lambert, Andrew, *Battleships in Transition: The Creation of the Steam Battlefleet 1815–1860* (London: Conway Maritime Press, 1984).
Langer, William L., *The Diplomacy of Imperialism, 1890–1902* (New York: A. A. Knopf, 1952).
Leathes, Stanley (ed.), *Cambridge Modern History* (Cambridge: Cambridge University Press, 1910).
Lewis, Michael, *The Navy of Britain* (London: George Allen & Unwin, 1949).
Longstaff, F. V., *Esquimalt* (Victoria, BC, Canada: Victoria Book & Stationery, 1941).
Lowe, C. J., *The Reluctant Imperialists: British Foreign Policy, 1878–1902*, 2 vols (New York: Macmillan, 1969).
Lucas, Charles, *The Empire at War* (London: Oxford University Press, 1921).
Luvaas, Jay, *The Education of an Army: British Military Thought, 1815–1940* (Chicago, IL: University of Chicago Press, 1964).
McCarthy, Justin, *A History of our Own Times* (London: Chatto & Windus, 1907).
Mackay, Ruddock, *Fisher of Kilverstone* (Oxford: Clarendon Press, 1973).
Magnus, Philip, *Gladstone* (New York: E. P. Dutton, 1964).
Mallet, Bernard, *Thomas George Earl of Northbrook, GCSI. A Memoir* (London: Longmans, Green, 1908).

Marder, Arthur J. (ed.), *Fear God and Dread Nought: The Correspondence of Admiral of the Fleet Lord Fisher of Kilverstone. Volume I: The Making of an Admiral 1854–1904* (London: Jonathan Cape, 1952).

——, *From The Dreadnought to Scapa Flow: The Royal Navy in the Fisher Era, 1904–1919*, 5 vols (New York: Oxford University Press, 1961–70).

——, *The Anatomy of British Sea Power: A History of British Naval Policy in the Pre-Dreadnought Era, 1880–1905* (repr. edn., New York: Pantheon Books, 1976).

Martineau, John, *The Life and Correspondence of Sir Bartle Frere*, 2 vols (London: John Murray, 1895).

Monypenny, William F. and George Earl Buckle, *The Life of Benjamin Disraeli, Earl of Beaconsfield*, 6 vols (New York: Macmillan, 1910–20).

Morley, John, *The Life of Richard Cobden*, 2 vols (London: T. Fisher Unwin, 1903).

——, *Life of William Ewart Gladstone*, 3 vols (London: Macmillan, 1903).

Morrell, W. P., *New Zealand* (London: Ernest Benn, 1935).

Northcote, Parkinson C., *War in the Eastern Seas, 1793–1815* (London: George Allen & Unwin, 1954).

Parkes, Oscar, *British Battleships, 1860–1950* (London: Seeley Service, 1957).

Partridge, Michael, *Military Planning for the Defence of the United Kingdom, 1814–1870* (Westport, CT: Greenwood, 1989).

Pelling, Henry, *The Origins of the Labour Party* (London: Macmillan, 1954).

Ponsonby, Arthur, *Henry Ponsonby* (London: Macmillan, 1942).

Preston, Anthony and John Major, *Send a Gunboat!* (London: Longmans, Green, 1967).

Rasor, Eugene, *British Naval History since 1815: A Guide to the Literature* (New York: Garland, 1990).

Richmond, Herbert, *Imperial Defence and Capture at Sea in War* (London: Hutchinson, 1932).

Robinson, Ronald, John Gallager and Alice Denny, *Africa and the Victorians* (New York: St Martin's Press, 1961).

Rodger, Nicholas A. M., *The Admiralty* (Lavenham, Suffolk: Terence Dalton, 1979).

Ropp, Theodore, *The Development of a Modern Navy: French Naval Policy, 1871–1914*, ed. Stephen Roberts (Annapolis, MD: Naval Institute Press, 1987).

Roskill, Stephen, *The War at Sea, 1939–1945* (London: HMSO, 1954).

Rostow, W. W., *The British Economy of the Nineteenth Century* (Oxford: Clarendon Press, 1949).

Sandler, Stanley, *The Emergence of the Modern Capital Ship* (Newark: University of Delaware Press, 1979).
Schurman, Donald M., *The Education of a Navy: The Evolution of British Naval Strategic Thought, 1867–1914* (London: Cassell, 1965).
——, *Julian S. Corbett, 1854–1922* (London: Royal Historical Society, 1981).
Seeley, J. R., *The Expansion of England* (London: Macmillan, 1904).
Semmel, Bernard, *Liberalism and Naval Strategy: Ideology, Interest and Sea Power during the Pax Britannica* (Boston: Unwin Hyman, 1986).
Shannon, Richard, *The Crisis of Imperialism* (London: Hart-Davis Macgibbon, 1974).
——, *Gladstone* (London: Hamish Hamilton, 1982).
Sheppard, Edgar (ed.), *The Private Life of the Duke of Cambridge* (London: Longmans, Green, 1907).
Skelton, O. D., *The Life and Times of Sir Alexander T. Galt* (Toronto: Oxford University Press, 1920).
Smellie, K. B., *A Hundred Years of Government* (London: Duckworth, 1937).
Smith, Goldwin, *The Empire* (London: John Henry & James Parker, 1863).
Spender, J. A., *Life of Sir Henry Campbell-Bannerman*, 2 vols (London: Hodder & Stoughton, 1925).
Stacey, C. P., *Canada and the British Army 1846–71* (London: Longmans, Green, 1936).
Strachan, Hew, *The Politics of the British Army* (Oxford: Clarendon Press, 1997).
Sumida, Jon T., *In Defence of Naval Supremacy: Finance, Technology and British Naval Policy, 1889–1914* (Boston, MA: Unwin Hyman, 1989).
Thompson, George C., *Public Opinion and Lord Beaconsfield, 1875–1880*, 2 vols (London: Macmillan, 1886).
Thornton, A. P., *The Imperial Idea and its Enemies* (London: Macmillan, 1959).
Tyler, J. E., *The Struggle for Imperial Unity, 1868–1895* (London: Longmans, Green, 1936).
Verner, Willoughby, *The Military Life of HRH George, Duke of Cambridge*, 2 vols (London: John Murray, 1905).
Vetch, R. H., *Life of Lt-General Sir Andrew Clarke* (London: John Murray, 1905).
Walker, Eric A, *The British Empire* (London: Oxford University Press, 1924).
——, *A History of South Africa* (London: Longmans, Green, 1947).
Wallace, Frederick William, *Wooden Ships and Iron Men* (London: Hodder & Stoughton, 1925).

BIBLIOGRAPHY

Ward, John, *British Policy in the South Pacific* (Sydney: Australasian Publishing Co., 1948).
Weintraub, Stanley Disraeli, *A Biography* (New York: Truman Talley/Dutton, 1993).
Whyte, Frederic, *The Life of W. T. Stead*, 2 vols (New York: Houghton Mifflin, 1925).
Young, G. M., *Victorian England: Portrait of an Age* (London: Oxford University Press, 1936).

Articles and essays

Bartlett, C. J. 'The Mid-Victorian Reappraisal of Naval Policy', in Kenneth Bourne and D. C. Watts (eds), *Studies in International History* (London: Longman, 1967), pp. 189–208.
Beeler, John, '"A One Power Standard?": Great Britain and the Balance of Naval Power, 1860–1880', *Journal of Strategic Studies*, 15 (1992): 548–75.
——, '"Fit for Service Abroad": Promotion, Retirement, and Royal Navy Officers, 1830–1890', *Mariner's Mirror*, 81 (1995): 300–12.
——, 'Steam, Strategy, and Schurman: Imperial Defence in the Post-Crimean Era, 1856–1905', in Greg Kennedy and Keith Neilson (eds), *Far-Flung Lines: Essays in Honour of Donald Mackenzie Schurman* (London: Frank Cass, 1997).
Bond, Brian, 'The Effect of the Cardwell Reforms, 1874–1904', *Journal of the Royal United Services Institution*, 106 (1961): 229–36.
Erickson, Arvel B., 'Edward T. Cardwell, Peelite', *American Philosophical Society* (1959): 1–107.
Ewing, John, 'South Africa in the World War', in A. P. Newton and E. A. Bevians (eds) with Eric Walker, *The Cambridge History of the British Empire*, Vol. 8: *South Africa, Rhodesia, and the Protectorates* (Cambridge: Cambridge University Press, 1936).
Harcourt, Freda. 'Disraeli's Imperialism 1866–1868: A Question of Timing', *The Historical Journal*, 23, 1 (1980): 87–109.
Kennedy, Paul M., 'Imperial Cable Communications and Strategy, 1870–1914', in idem (ed.), *The War Plans of the Great Powers, 1880–1914* (London: George Allen & Unwin, 1979). (Originally published in the *English Historical Review*, 86, 341 (1971): 728–52.)
Lambert, Andrew 'The Royal Navy 1856–1914: Deterrence and the Strategy of World Power', in Keith Neilson and Elizabeth J. Errington (eds), *Navies and Global Defense: Theories and Strategy* (Westport, CT: Greenwood Press, 1995).
Neilson, Keith '"Greatly Exaggerated": The Myth of the Decline of Britain before 1914', *International History Review*, 13 (1991): 695–725.

Ranft, Bryan 'The Protection of British Seaborne Trade and the Development of Systematic Planning for War, 1860–1906', in Ranft (ed.), *Technical Change and British Naval Policy, 1860–1939* (London: Hodder & Stoughton, 1977).

Rodger, Nicholas A. M., 'The Design of the Inconstant', *Mariner's Mirror*, 61, 1 (1975): 9–22.

———, 'The Dark Ages of the Admiralty, 1869–1885', *Mariner's Mirror*, 61, 4 (1975): 331–42; 62, 1 (1976): 33–46; 2 (1976): 121–8.

———, 'British Belted Cruisers', *Mariner's Mirror*, 64, 1 (1978): 23–35.

———, 'The First Light Cruisers', *Mariner's Mirror*, 65, 3 (1979): 209–30.

———, 'British Naval Thought and Naval Policy, 1820–1890: Strategic Thought in an Era of Technological Change', in Craig L. Symonds (ed.), *New Aspects of Naval History* (Annapolis, MD: Naval Institute Press, 1981).

Schuyler, R., 'The Recall of the Legions', *American Historical Review*, 26, 1 (1920): 18–36.

———, 'The Climax of Anti-Imperialism in England', *Political Science Quarterly*, 36, 4 (December 1921): 537–60.

Tucker, Albert, 'Army and Society in England 1870–1900: A Reassessment of the Cardwell Reforms', *Journal of British Studies*, 2 (1961): 110–41.

Tunstall, W. C. B., 'Imperial Defence, 1815–1870', in *Cambridge History of the British Empire* (Cambridge: Cambridge University Press, 1940), Vol. 2, pp. 807–41.

———, 'Imperial Defence, 1870–1897', in *Cambridge History of the British Empire* (Cambridge: Cambridge University Press, 1959), Vol. 3, pp. 230–54.

Unpublished works

Blumenthal, Harvey, 'W. T. Stead's Role in Shaping Official Policy: The Navy Campaign of 1884', PhD dissertation, George Washington University, 1984.

Index

Adelaide, 67, 71, 148
Aden, 28, 40n37, 65, 97n59, 110, 122n52, 127, 129, 131, 136
Admiralty, 4, 6, 10, 23, 24, 25, 28, 29, 30, 31, 32, 33, 34, 38n11, 42n64, 49, 51, 61, 62, 63, 65, 78n19, 80n60, 83, 85, 124n88, 130, 132, 134–5, 137–8n15, 140n50, 142–3, 146, 148–9, 150–1n5, 153, 154, 155, 156, 160–1, 165, 167; and naval bases, 52–3, 54, 55, 66, 67, 68, 69, 70, 72, 73, 158n2; and the Carnarvon Commission, 86, 89, 102, 103, 104, 107, 108, 109, 111, 113, 114–15, 116, 117, 120n26, 121n43, 122n46, n52, 123n67, 124n93, 125n96, n98, n101, 127; *see also*: British navy, inter-departmental relations
Africa, 1, 2, 23, 28, 109, 127; *see also*: South Africa, Egypt, Cape Colony
Airey, G. J., 120n28
Alabama C. S. S., 11, 13, 18n33, 33, 48
Alexandria, 37n11, 122n56
Antigua, 28, 33, 38n11, 52, 54, 97n59
army: *see* British army
Ascension Island, 28, 33, 34, 38n11, 51, 52, 55, 60n64, 65, 97n59, 109, 110, 122n48, 167n8
Asquith, Herbert, 8
Atlantic Ocean, 28, 52, 109
Australasia, 26, 47, 49, 50, 54, 59n44, n45, 65, 71, 73–4, 76, 86, 87, 88, 91, 93, 96n29, 142–4, 145–6, 147, 148, 149, 150, 150–1n5, 151n22, 153, 157, 158n3; Carnarvon

Commission recommendations for defence of, 104–7
Australia, 2, 3, 12, 13, 19n37, 26, 28, 29, 30, 31, 32, 33, 45, 52, 53, 61, 66, 67, 71, 78n25, 78n34, 87, 109, 120n26, n28, n29, n20, 120–1n36, 127, 129, 142–4, 146; *see also*: Australasia, New South Wales, Northern Australia, Queensland, South Australia, Victoria, Western Australia
Australian Squadron, 105, 142–4, 145, 158n3
Ayde, John, 22–3, 36n3

Bahamas, 28, 73, 74, 97n59, 123n67, 135
Barbados, 38n11, 65, 73, 97n59, 112, 135
Barkly, Henry, 63, 77n11, 84, 93, 112, 115, 150n1, 166, 168n30
Barnaby, Nathaniel, 49, 83, 94n4, 103
Beach, Michael Hicks, 62, 64, 70, 72, 75–6, 77n8, 78n34, 84, 85, 87, 96n29, 118, 122n53, 163
Beaconsfield, Lord: *see* Disraeli, Benjamin
Bermuda, 14, 15, 16, 28, 33, 51, 66, 81n83, 111, 123n68, 161
Berry, Graham, 146
Blachford, Lord, 13, 20n52
Blake, Robert, 96n45, 127
Blyth, Henry, 120n28
Bombay, 28, 113
Bowen, George, 91

185

Brassey, Thomas, 85, 88, 94n9, 95n16, 130, 132, 136–7, 150, 150n1
Bright, Charles, 98n81
Bright, John, 6–7, 16n4, 25, 89
British army, 23; and reform, 7, 12, 16n5, 19n42, 22, 35n1, 135; *see also*: War Office
British Empire, 1, 118, 152; extent of pro-Empire sentiment, 26–7; 56n1, 59n44, 154; Conservative Party attitudes toward, 43–4, 45–6; defencelessness of, 1878, 73; plans for defence of, 1880–87, 129–30; *see also*: imperial defence, imperial policy
British Columbia, 66, 114, 124n88, 159, 160, 164, 165
British Commonwealth, 1, 152, 157
British Honduras, 101, 102, 126, 135
British Merchant Marine, 101–2
British navy, 2, 159, 164; and coal, 23–4, 29–30, 37–8n11, 135; and technological change, 5, 22, 23–4, 28–31, 36n6, 36–7n9, 38n13, 38–9n19, 41n55, 41–2n57, 42n64, 83, 102–3, 117, 125n97, 154, 161; and imperial defence, 22–4, 26–8, 30–2, 33–4, 35–6n2, 38n14, n16, 46, 48–9, 105, 124n88, 152, 153, 156; overseas bases, 52–3, 55, 76, 100–1, 142–3; Carnarvon Commission report on, 102–4, 108, 119n17, 120n26, 121n43; *see also*: Admiralty
Buller, Charles, 3
Byng, Admiral, 3

Cadogan, Lord, 84
Campbell-Bannerman, Henry, 8–10, 17n17
Cambridge, George, Duke of, 20n54, 58n28, n30, 90–1, 98n66, 133, 135, 137n1, 161; and imperial defence, 13–16, 20n56, 22–3, 32, 36n3, 46, 48–9, 50, 51, 53, 60n61, 94n3, 97n63, 111–12, 129, 167n6; *see also*: Duke of Cambridge's defence committee
Camperdown, Lord, 90, 132
Canada, 1, 2, 3, 11–12, 13, 14, 15, 26, 32, 42n60, 44, 55, 61, 65, 73–4, 79n42, n44, n47, n49, n53, 85, 88, 124n88, 135, 153; Milne committee's recommended defences for, 68–71, 72, 78n23; and the Carnarvon Commission, 91, 93, 98–9n86, 111, 114–15, 118, 123–4n83; and Esquimalt, 159–67; *see also*: Esquimalt
Canadian Pacific Railroad, 159, 160, 164, 165, 168n23
Cape Colony, 15, 28, 33, 38n11, 51, 63, 64, 136, 142; Milne committee's recommendations for, 71–2, 80n75; Carnarvon Commission's recommendations for, 100–2, 109, 127; *see also*: Cape of Good Hope, South Africa
Cape Comerin (India), 28
Cape Horn, 55, 114, 159
Cape of Good Hope, 14, 15, 21n66, 50, 51, 52, 54, 55, 64, 75, 84, 87, 88, 93, 97n59, 109–10, 118–19n3, 119n5, n6, 126, 129, 131, 133, 137, 139n40, 142, 150n4, 167n8; *see also*: Cape Colony, Simons Bay, South Africa, Table Bay
Cape Town, 2, 61, 71–2, 100; *see also*: Cape Colony, Simons Bay, South Africa, Table Bay
Cape Verde Islands, 65
Cape York (Australia), 32, 33, 53
Captain, HMS, 25, 38n18, 38–9n19
Cardwell, Edward, 7, 12, 13, 14–16, 19n41, 22, 33, 35n1, 41n47, 44, 45, 47, 61, 73, 83, 133, 156
Carnarvon, Lord, 13, 20n53, 31, 56n5, 128, 131–4, 135, 138n18, 139n40, 149, 151n23, 156–7, 158n8, 167; as Colonial Secretary, 43–7, 56n4, 57n22, 58n28, 59n50, 61, 62, 77n7, 95n13; and coaling station defence, 49–50, 59n47, 81n101; and the Carnarvon Commission, 84, 85–6, 87–90, 91, 92–3, 94, 96n43, 97n56, 98n81, 100, 105, 112–13, 115, 116, 117, 118, 118–19n3
Carnarvon Commission, 7, 77, 130, 131–2, 133, 135, 136, 137, 140n49, n57, 141n65, 143, 144, 146, 148, 151n8, n22, n23, 157, 162, 164–7; appointment of, 83–4; composition of, 85–6, 95n21; work of, 86–8, 90–4, 96n29, n31, n39, 97n54, n56,

INDEX

n59, n61, n63, 98n64, n81, 98–9n86, 99n88, 138n24, 155; and the Gladstone government, 1880–85, 88–90, 96n43; Reports by: 1st, 93, 100–2, 119n9; 2nd, 93, 102–7, 119n14; 3rd, 93, 107–16, 119n9, 120n28, 121n42, n43, 122n51, 123n68, n75, 123–4n83, 124n88, 125n105, 135; secrecy of Reports, 90, 102, 107, 121–2n45, 137n1, 139n39, n40; assessment of, 116–18; response to, 126–9, 135–6, 154

Ceylon, 33, 54, 64, 92, 93, 97n59, 112, 113–14, 117, 123n79, 135, 136–7, 167n8

Channel, English, 27, 28, 30, 42n64, 158n3

Charlottetown (Prince Edward Island), 69

Chelmsford, Lord, 72, 80n78

Childers, Hugh C. E., 25; and the Carnarvon Commission, 85, 86–7, 88, 92, 93, 95n16, 97n54, 99n88, 101, 116, 126, 127, 128, 138n16, 139n39

China, 23, 28, 54, 97n63, 127

China Squadron, 111, 114, 128, 163, 165, 168n21

Clarke, Andrew, 127–9, 136, 138n16, n18, n21, n24, 140n48, n57, 144

Clarke, George S., 134, 138n16, 140n48

coal, 24, 25, 29–30, 31–3, 37–8n11, 40n40, 55, 64–5, 78n34, 80n60, 86, 100, 102, 103–4, 107, 108, 110, 114, 115, 119n21, 122n51, n53, 147, 160

coaling stations, 28, 32, 33–4, 48–50, 51, 52–6, 59n47, 64, 86–7, 91, 92, 97n59, 152, 158n2, 168n31; Carnarvon Commission and, 104, 108, 109–12, 114, 117, 118, 118–19n3, 122n46; plans for defence of 1880–87, 127–9, 130–1, 132, 133–4, 136–7, 138n24, 139n29, n44, 140n58, 140–1n59, 150, 156

Cobden, Richard, 6–7, 10

Cocos Islands, 97n59, 110, 122n50

Code, John, 113

Colomb, John C. R., 40n28, 84, 94n9, 95n11, 130, 133, 138–9n26, 140–1n50, 150n1; and imperial defence strategy, 26–9, 32, 33, 34, 40n36, 46, 49, 50, 51, 59n54, 61, 63, 102, 153, 155, 156, 158n4; and the Carnarvon Commission, 85–6, 103, 118

Colombo (Ceylon), 74, 92, 97n59, 113–14, 136–7

Colonial Conference (1887), 134, 138–9n26, 150n3, n4, 153, 155, 157; and Australian defence, 142–4; debates on King George Sound, 144–50

colonial defence, 5, 15, 16, 22–3, 27, 32, 42n60, 45, 62, 64, 66, 81–2n110, 94n1, 109, 140n48, n49, n50; *see also*: imperial defence

Colonial Defence Committee (1885), 134–5, 136, 140n48, n49, n50, n52, 144, 146, 153

Colonial Naval Defence Act (1865), 106, 120–1n36

Colonial Office, 10, 13, 31, 32, 42n60, 47, 49, 50, 66, 95n13, 129, 134, 140n48, 154, 155, 156, 160, 163; and Milne's defence committee, 61, 62–3, 67–8, 70, 72, 73, 74–6; and the Carnarvon Commission, 84, 85, 88, 91, 92, 93, 94n9, 96n31, n39, 97n61, 98–9n86, 102, 105, 108–9, 113, 116, 117–18, 123n67, 125n98, n103, 126–7, 137n1; and Colonial Conference (1887), 144, 149; *see also*: inter-departmental relations

Colonial Office colonial defence committee: *see* Milne's defence committee

colonial policy, 12–16, 109; and 'separation' issue, 10–12, 18n27, 19n40, 25, 43; *see also*: colonial defence, colonial self-government; imperial defence; imperial federation; imperial policy

colonial self-government, 5; and imperial defence policy, 66–70, 87, 99n88, 131, 154–5

Committee of Imperial Defence (1904), 157–8

Conservative Party, 5, 6, 10, 43, 44, 45, 46; and empire, 56n2, n3

Constantinople, 62

187

Cooper, Daniel, 120n28
Crossman, Colonel, 164, 165
Currie, Donald, 50, 59n47, 61, 98n81, 118–19n3
Cyprus, 97n59, 110, 122n56

Dakar (West Africa), 109
Deakin, Alfred, 143, 144, 147, 151n6
Delahay St, 87, 88, 91, 94, 96n30, 118
Derby, Lord (Edward Henry Stanley), 127, 137n9, 144, 145, 146, 149
Devastation, HMS, 25, 30, 36–7n9, 39n22, 41–2n57, 42n64, 120–1n36
Diego Garcia (Chagos Archipelago), 97n59, 110, 121n44
Disraeli, Benjamin, 3, 7, 17n16, 26, 27, 28, 31, 38n16, 39n25, 56n5, 62, 84, 95n13; and empire, 43–5, 49, 56n2
Disraeli government, 1874–80, 39n22, 84, 88; and the empire, 43–4, 56n3, 95n18, 122n56
Downer, John, 146
Drury, E. R., 98n81, 120n28
Dufferin, Lord, 42n60, 44, 57n10, 70, 79n44
Duke of Cambridge's defence committee, 32, 48, 50, 51, 53, 129, 132–4; and coaling station defence, 55–6, 58n34, 65, 69, 71, 72, 148, 161
Dunraven, Lord, 150n1

East India Squadron, 54, 128
Egypt, 2, 28, 32, 122n56, 124n93
Esquimalt (Vancouver Island), 33, 51, 55, 65, 79n50, 80n60, n68, 88, 128, 135; Milne committee recommendations for, 68, 69–71; Carnarvon Commission recommendations for, 93, 97n59, 112, 113, 114–15, 118, 123–4n83; development of plans for defence of, 159–67, 167n8, 168n13, n19, n21, n23
Europe, 9, 30, 68, 129
Exchequer, 5, 31, 83; *see also*: Treasury, inter-departmental relations

Fairfax, Henry, 143
Falkland Islands, 28, 32, 33, 34, 51, 52, 53, 55, 60n67, 66, 97n59, 114, 155, 159, 167n8

Far East, 100, 110–11, 127
Fiji, 28, 50, 51, 54, 55, 66, 97n59, 167n8
Fisher, John A., 130, 135, 139n28, 140n53, 157
Foreign Office, 8, 25, 73, 87, 96n31, 115
'Fortress England', 22–3, 25, 26, 27, 33, 36n3, 48, 51, 140n58, 153
France, 24, 25, 36n3, 122n54
Franco-Prussian War, 8, 25, 38n17, 160
Frere, Bartle, 71, 80n74, 81n101, 87, 88, 96n39, 98n81, 108

Gallagher, Jack, 2
Galle (Ceylon), 54, 60n72, 64–5, 92, 97n59, 113, 117
Galt, Alexander, 85
Gambia, 97n59, 109
Gathorne-Hardy, Gathorne, 34, 45, 47, 48, 49, 51, 57n22, 61, 62, 77n3, 167n5
Gibraltar, 14, 15, 16, 28, 33, 37n11, 66, 100, 109, 110, 161
Gilford, Lord, 30, 31, 41n55, 62, 77n5, 85
Gladstone, William, 3, 6–8, 9, 10, 12, 14, 17n14, n16, 19n37, n39, 25, 26, 30, 31, 33, 38n17, 40n47, 43, 47, 88, 90, 121n43, 126, 128, 129–30, 131, 132, 154, 155, 156
Gladstone governments:
  1868–74, 22, 25, 29, 30, 39n22, 85; and colonial policy, 10–16, 26, 27, 44, 154
  1880–85, 88, 136; and the Carnarvon Commission, 88–90, 101, 107, 121n43, 154; subsequent imperial defence policy, 126–9, 131–2, 139n40, n4
  1886, 136
  1892–94, 140n50
Gordon, Charles, 93, 97n63, 129, 153, 155
Goschen, George J., 25
Graham, Gerald S., 3
Granville, Lord, 11, 13, 18n30, 90
Grey, George, 14
Griffith, Samuel, 145, 151n17

Halifax, 2, 14, 16, 28, 33, 44, 51, 66, 111, 123n68, 159–60, 161

INDEX

Hall, William H., 146
Hamilton, Robert C. G., 85, 95n18
Harrop, A. J., 12
Hartington, Lord, 127, 137n13
Hartington Commission, 8–9, 153
Hawaiian Islands, 51, 55, 59n56
Heligoland, 65
Herbert, Robert W. G., 13, 20n52, 59n50, 62, 64, 102, 126–7, 140n48, 156
Hicks Beach, Michael: see Beach, Michael Hicks
Holland, Henry, 85, 95n17, 142, 143, 144–5, 146, 149–50, 151n23
home defence, 9, 22–3, 27, 35–6n2, 51, 57n22, 76, 83, 129, 140n58, 154, 161; see also: 'Fortress England'
Hong Kong, 28, 29, 33, 38n11, 51, 52, 54, 58n28, 64, 72, 73, 75, 91, 97n59, 110–11, 113, 114, 115, 129, 131, 136, 165, 167n8, 168n31
Hornby, Geoffrey Phipps, 30, 31, 139n28
Hunt, George Ward, 25, 30, 31, 46, 50

imperial defence, 5, 9, 10, 12, 14–15, 16, 22–3, 26–9, 30–5, 37–8n11, 42n65, 51 64, 84; and coaling stations, 52–6, 62, 63; Milne committee recommendations for, 63–76; shortcomings of, 1878, 73; and the Carnarvon Commission, 86–7, 93, 102–4, 117–18; plans for, 1880–87, 127–9, 131, 132, 136–7, 142–50; assessment of 1868–87, 152–8; see also: colonial defence
imperial federation, 2, 152
Imperial Federation League, 130, 138–9n26, 142, 150n1, 154
imperial fortresses, 14–15; see also: Bermuda, Gibraltar, Halifax, Malta
imperial policy, 43–4, 66, 72, 108–9, 120n26, 142–4; see also: colonial policy
India, 8, 14, 23, 28, 40n37, 53, 54, 56n2, 65, 83, 86, 100, 110, 131, 136
India Office, 62, 127, 129
Indian Ocean, 14, 28, 55, 148
inter-departmental relations, 62, 66, 67–8, 69–71, 72–3, 74–7, 81n101, 93, 108–9, 116–18, 124n93, 130,
134–6, 137–8n15, 140n51, 149, 153, 154, 155, 166
Irwin, Chevois T., 163

Jamaica, 28, 33, 38n11, 48, 51, 52, 54, 55, 65, 73, 97n59, 111–12, 128, 136, 167n8
Jekyll, H., 63, 85, 90, 91, 92, 94, 112, 127
Jervois, William Francis Drummond, 32, 42n60, n61, 46, 47, 49, 50, 59n45, 61, 63, 65, 72, 78n25, 87, 88, 96n29, 104, 105, 118, 153, 160–1; memorandum on imperial defence, 32–5, 42n65, 48, 49, 50, 52, 53, 54, 74, 148, 167n5, n6

Kennedy, Arthur, 120n28
Key, Astley Cooper, 109, 111, 112, 113, 114, 117, 122n47, n48, 125n101, 150–1n5, 156, 165, 168n28
Kimberley, Lord, 11–12, 13, 17n16, 18n32, 20n53, 61, 133; and the Carnarvon Commission, 88, 89, 90, 92, 93, 94, 116, 125n103, 126–7
King George Sound (Western Australia), 28, 30, 32, 33, 51, 52–3, 54, 65, 66, 67–8, 74, 76, 97n59, 105, 137, 167n8; Carnarvon Commission and, 106–7; Colonial Conference (1887) and, 142, 144–50, 151n22, n26, n30, 153
Kingston (Ontario), 14, 15, 16
Knaplund, Paul, 7

Labuan (Borneo), 73, 97n59, 112, 113, 123n75, 135
Liberal Party, 5, 6–8, 25, 45, 46, 56n2, 89, 128, 133, 139n39, 155
Liberalism: and defence policy, 6–10, 13, 15, 23, 38n:17, 44, 96n43, 154
London, 1, 32, 66, 67, 68, 87, 150, 155
Lorimer, James, 151n16
Lorne, Lord, 93, 118, 125n104
Lovell, J. E., 46, 80n68, 163–4, 168n19, n21
Lowe, Robert, 12

Macdonald, John A., 42n60, 91, 93, 97n56, 98–9n86, 114, 118, 123–4n83, 164–5, 166
Mahan, Alfred T., 135

189

Malta, 14, 15, 16, 28, 33, 37n11, 66, 110, 122n56, 161
Mauritius, 14, 16, 28, 29, 33, 51, 52, 53, 54–5, 64, 72, 91, 93, 97n59, 98n64, 110, 113, 122n52, n53, n54, 128, 136, 137, 167n8
Malaysia, 28, 34; *see also*: Penang, Singapore
Meade, Robert, 127, 140n48, 156
Mediterranean Sea, 28, 31, 37n11, 110, 121n43, 122n56
Mediterranean Squadron, 62, 158n3
Melbourne, 54, 71, 111, 148
Milne, Alexander, 4, 23–4, 25, 30–2, 33, 34, 36n7, 37–8n11, 39n22, 41n55, 46, 49, 53, 55, 63, 65, 67, 84, 85, 124–5n95, 128, 156; as member of Carnarvon Commission, 87–8, 92, 96n43, 124–5n95; dissents from majority, 93, 112–17, 123n75, 165–6, 168n31
Milne's defence committee (1878–79), 83–4, 85, 112, 115, 118, 122n48, 163–4, 165, 166–7, 168n14; appointment of, 61–3, 77n4; composition of, 63–4; initial reports of, 64–6; and King George Sound, 67–8, 107, 148; and Canada, 68–71, 72, 78n23; and Cape Colony, 71–2, 80n75, n76; and the Far East, 73; and inter-departmental relations, 74–7
Morley, John, 7
Morley Committee (1882), 129

Nanaimo (Vancouver Island), 70
New South Wales, 28, 29, 44, 105, 120n26, 143
New Zealand, 11, 12, 13, 26, 28, 44, 46, 49, 59n45, 65, 68, 78n19, 91, 105, 142, 143
Newfoundland, 65, 97n59
North America, 66, 102, 111, 127, 159; *see also*: United States
North Borneo, 110–11
Northbrook, Lord, 88, 89, 96n43, 98n81, 117, 127, 131–4, 139n44, 156
Northcote, Stafford, 31
Northern Australia, 97n59
Nugent, C. H., 51, 53, 59n55, 60n71, 130, 138n24, 150n1; memorandum on coaling station defence, 50–1, 54–6, 60n61, 65, 69, 79n53, 119n4

Ord, Harry St George, 67, 78n35
ordnance: for coaling station defence, 64, 65, 66, 69, 71, 72, 73, 78n30, 79n47, n49, 80n74, n76, 101, 104, 111, 131, 136–7, 140n58, 144–5, 147–8, 161–2, 168n13
Ottawa, 68, 70
Ottoman Empire, 50, 51, 94n3, 122n56

Pacific Ocean, 28, 40n36, 50, 55, 59n54, 101–2, 115, 159, 163, 165
Pacific squadron, 49, 52, 54, 72, 159, 160, 163, 164, 165–6
Pall Mall Gazette, 50, 59n53, 130, 153–4, 156
Penang (Malaysia), 97n59, 110–11, 123n58
Parkes, Henry, 44, 57n9
Pearsall, Alan, 3
Perim (Yemen), 97n59, 110
Perth, 67
Port Castries (St Lucia), 111–12
Port Elizabeth (Cape Colony), 109
Port Hamilton (Korea), 110–11, 122n57
Port Louis (Mauritius), 33, 64, 97n59
Port Royal (Jamaica), 33, 48, 52, 73, 97n59, 112
Port Said (Egypt), 32, 33, 53

Quebec, 13, 14, 15, 16
Queensland (Australia), 13, 105, 143, 145, 147

Réunion (Indian Ocean), 110, 122n54
Rhodes, Cecil, 3
Robinson, Hercules, 44, 57n9
Robinson, Ronald, 2, 3
Rosario, HMS, 46, 57n26
Rosebery, Lord, 1
Royal Colonial Institute, 26, 39n24, 40n32, 49, 51, 94n9, 95n11
Royal Commission on Army and Navy Administration: *see* Hartington Commission
Royal Commission on Colonial Defence: *see* Carnarvon Commission
Royal Commission on the Defences of the United Kingdom, 22, 27, 32

INDEX

Royal Commission on matters relating to Coal, 29
Royal Navy: *see* British navy
Royal United Services Institution, 50, 59n47, n54, 138n24
Russia, 2, 54, 65, 111, 114, 164, 165; war scares with:
   1877–78, 49, 50, 51, 62–3, 66, 73, 76, 83, 94n3, 95n13, 122n52, n56, 123n63, 161, 162, 166
   1885, 122n57, 134, 140n48, 144, 151n26
Russo-Turkish War, 50–1, 62–3

St Helena, 28, 32, 33, 53, 65, 97n59, 109, 110, 125n98, 137, 141n65
Saint John (New Brunswick), 69
St John's (Newfoundland), 65, 72, 74, 76, 81n83, 97n59
St Lucia (Windward Islands), 51, 54, 55, 97n59, 111–12, 128, 135, 136, 167n8
Salisbury, Lord, 3, 56n5, 150n1, 158n2
Salisbury government, 1886–92, 136, 142, 153; proposals for King George Sound, 144–8
Sargood, P. T., 120n28
Scratchley, Peter, 105, 120n27, 144, 147, 149
Select Committee on Colonial Defence, 22
Service, James, 145
Seychelles Islands, 97n59, 110
Shanghai, 29
Sierra Leone, 28, 65, 97n59, 109, 137
Simmons, John Lintorn, 51, 59–60n57, 62, 63, 76–7, 83, 84, 85, 156; as member of Carnarvon Commission, 87, 90, 112, 116, 118–19n3, 123n75, 164, 166
Simons Bay (Cape Colony), 28, 33, 51, 52, 52, 64, 71, 75, 97n59, 100–1, 108, 109, 129, 131, 133, 137, 167n8
Singapore, 20n56, 28, 29, 33, 34, 51, 52, 53, 54, 64, 72, 73, 75, 97n59, 111, 113, 123n57, n64, 128, 129, 131, 136, 137, 167n8
Smith, W. H., 134
Smyth, Edward Selby, 69, 70, 79n44, 168n13
South Africa, 2, 3, 40n32, 57n6, 94n3, 100, 118–19n3, 153; *see also*: Cape Colony, Cape of Good Hope
South African squadron, 52, 54
South America, 53
South Australia, 87, 106–7, 120–1n36, 143, 146
Stacey, C. P., 12, 13
Stanhope, Edward, 145–6, 150n1
Stanley, Frederick, 58, 79n43, 84
Stead, W. T., 130, 136, 139n29, n44, 153–4, 156
Stirling, H. O., 30, 52
Strange, T. Bland, 80n68, 163–4, 168n19
Suez Canal, 21n66, 28, 50, 54, 100, 110, 121n43
Sydney (Australia), 28, 40n36, 71, 105, 147, 148
Sydney (Cape Breton Island), 69

Table Bay (Cape Colony), 64, 71, 74, 75, 80n76, 97n59, 100–1, 129, 131, 133, 137, 150n4
Tarleton, John Walter, 30
Tasmania, 66, 67, 143
telegraphs, 51, 59n47, 91, 110, 122n52, 123n58, n68, 137, 137–8n15
Thomson, David, 3
Thursday Island (Queensland), 97n59, 105, 110–11, 137, 142
The Times (London), 130–1
Treasury, 6, 10, 62, 69, 72; and imperial defence expenditure, 74–6, 81n101, 84, 85, 88, 93, 97n54, 109, 130, 132, 134, 136, 140n51, 140n58, 149, 153, 154, 167; *see also*: Exchequer, inter-departmental relations
Treaty of Berlin, 64, 68, 122n56
Trincomalee (Ceylon), 28, 33, 38n11, 51, 52, 60n72, 64, 72, 75, 97n59, 110, 113–14, 117, 125n101, 128, 135, 136–7, 167n8
troops: withdrawal of from the colonies, 11–13, 20n43, 26, 27, 33, 44, 50, 61, 105; proposed restoration of, 44–6, 57n22, 59n50, 77n3; for garrisoning coaling stations, 91, 97n54, 99n88, 101, 108, 109, 111, 135, 168n14
Tryon, George, 142–3, 144, 145, 146

191

Tunstall, W. C. B., 3, 121n42, 158n4, 167n9
Turkey: *see* Ottoman Empire
Tyler, J. E., 142

United States, 2, 3, 11–12, 54, 59n56, 114, 123–4n83, 159, 163–4, 165; *see also*: North America

Vancouver Island, 28, 33, 40n36, 51, 55, 65, 68, 69–71, 112, 114, 159; *see also*: Esquimalt
Victoria, Queen, 13, 14, 15, 22, 32, 38n17, 42n61, 90, 93, 107, 127, 128, 129–30, 131, 137n1, 138n18
Victoria (Australia), 44–5, 105, 106, 120n30, 120–1n26, 143–4, 145, 146
Victoria (British Columbia), 159, 162, 163
Vogel, Julius, 68, 79n39, 85

Walker, Eric, 2, 3
War Office, 8, 10, 12, 24, 26, 32, 33, 34, 35, 46–7, 61, 83, 84, 91, 96n39, 125n97, 133, 135, 136, 140n50, n54, 153, 154, 158n2, 160, 161, 163, 164, 167; and imperial defence policy, 47–9, 51–6, 62–3, 69, 70, 71, 72, 73, 74, 76–7, 134, 155–6; and Carnarvon Commission, 86, 89, 91, 92, 93, 94n3, 98–9n86, 101, 105, 106, 108, 109, 110, 111, 112, 113, 114, 115, 116, 117–18, 119n4, 123n67, 124n88; plans for coaling station defence, 1880–87, 127–9, 130, 138n24, 139n44, 140n48, 146, 149, 153; *see also*: British army, inter-departmental relations
War Office Defence Committee: *see* Duke of Cambridge's defence committee
Wellington, Arthur, Duke of, 51
West Indies, 14, 28, 65, 66, 73, 111–12, 123n66, n67, n68, 127, 135, 167n8
Western Australia, 28, 30, 33, 51, 52, 67–8, 69, 78n31, 91, 97n59, 107, 146, 147, 149, 151n31, 167n8
Whitbread, Samuel, 90, 97n56
Wodehouse, John, Earl of Kimberley: *see* Kimberley, Lord
Wolseley, Garnet, 14, 80n74, 88, 96n39, 98n66, 124n93, 128, 155

Zanzibar, 100